# Hangeu

| Simple Vowels | | | |
|---|---|---|---|
| 아 [a] (father) | 애 [ae] (hat) | | |
| 야 [ya] (yard) | 얘 [yae] (yam) | | |
| 어 [eo] (hut) | 에 [e] (met) | | |
| 여 [yeo] (yearn) | 예 [ye] (yes) | | |
| 오 [o] (home) | 외 [oe] (köln) | 와 [wa] (wan) | 왜 [wae] (wag) |
| 요 [yo] (yoke) | | | |
| 우 [u] (do) | 위 [wi] (wind) | 워 [wo] (won) | 웨 [we] (wet) |
| 유 [yu] (you) | | | |
| 으 [eu] (taken) | 의 [ui] (taken+we) | | |
| 이 [i] (ink) | | | |

The "ㅇ" written with each vowel is an unvoiced consonant which functions to indicate where an initial consonant may be affixed to the vowel when writing a syllable. See the inside back cover for information on forming syllables.

# KOREAN
## PHRASE BOOK
### FOR TRAVELERS

# KOREAN
## PHRASE BOOK
### FOR TRAVELERS

 Hollym

**KOREAN PHRASE BOOK**
**FOR TRAVELERS**

Copyright © 1987, 2012
Kim Jung-sup, Cho Hyun-yong & Lee Jung-hee

First published in 1987
Revised edition, 2012
Fourth printing, 2016
by Hollym International Corp., USA
**Phone** 908 353 1655
http://www.hollym.com          e-Mail contact@hollym.com

 Hollym

Published simultaneously in Korea
by Hollym Corp., Publishers, Seoul, Korea
**Phone** +82 2 734 5087          **Fax** +82 2 730 5149
http://www.hollym.co.kr          **e-Mail** info@hollym.co.kr

ISBN: 978-1-56591-404-9
Library of Congress Control Number: 87-82975

*Printed in Korea*

# Preface

This phrase book is designed to help foreign travelers in Korea directly communicate with Koreans while traveling. The book contains essential Korean expressions for thosè who want to make most of the Korean language for the various situations that you might encounter during a trip. For this, we suggest topics and situations in the same sequence as in a trip so that you can easily look for the expressions you need. We also have basic expressions and vocabulary for emergencies such as getting sick, losing your luggage, having a car accident, or getting lost, etc. to help you solve the problems.

In this book, reflecting the Korean colloquial form, the base ending form is "-아/어요" [-a/eoyo] which is currently often used in daily conversations. But for expressions used for asking for favors or requests, we use a more formal form. Also, the book carries some of the expected questions and answers that you might have in daily conversations so that you have a better understanding of interactive conversations. If a pattern drill is possible with different words, we put substitute words and pronunciations below the sentence and a reference section at the back of this book which will extend your application.

Along with situational Korean expressions, we included a pronunciation and a grammar section to help you understand basic Korean sentence structure and grammar at the beginning of the book. Supportive pronunciation and reference guides, practical tips on Korean culture and etiquette which comes with each expression will also be a great help to the travelers. At the back of the book, you will be able to refer to the variety of Korean vocabulary. Even more, all the Korean expressions in the book are spelled in the Roman alphabet to best guide you to correct reading and pronunciation.

We hope that all the foreign travelers in Korea could better communicate with the aid of this book to best enjoy the beautiful country.

Kim Jung-sup, Cho Hyun-yong
& Lee Jung-hee

# Contents

## SIGHTSEEING

## EATING & DRINKING OUT

## SHOPPING

## ENTERTAINMENT

## HEALTH

# EMERGENCY

# RETURNING

# Introduction to Korean

Hangeul, the Korean alphabet, was invented by scholars commissioned by King Sejong the Great of the Joseon Dynasty, and was promulgated in 1446 as an easier way for the common people to be able to read and write. Before that Koreans used Chinese characters, and the study of the characters was limited to the upper class. The great advantage of hangeul is that it is one of the most scientific phonetic alphabets made easy anyone can learn.

Hangeul is so simple that its twenty-four letters can be learned in minutes with the aid of the hangeul-in-a-hurry charts at the inside front cover of this book. The charts at the inside back cover illustrate how to write each letter and how to combine the letters into syllables. In Korean, there are not as many tenses, nor as many particles. However, Korean grammar is potentially confusing at first for English speakers because the verb occurs at the end of the sentence.

Korean consonants are pronounced much as they are in English, though they assume different shades of sound when they appear as initials, medials, or finals. The five stressed consonants are pronounced with the greatest possible stress but with no expulsion of air. For example, "ㄸ" [tt] is pronounced much like the [t] in "stay." They are pronounced with a heavy expulsion of air. The "ㅋ" [k] is similar, for example, to the [k] in "kill." Vowels are pronounced essentially as noted on the inside front cover.

## KOREAN ALPHABET, HANGEUL

|  | ㄱ g | ㄴ n | ㄷ d | ㄹ r | ㅁ m | ㅂ b | ㅅ s |
|---|---|---|---|---|---|---|---|
| ㅏ a | 가 ga | 나 na | 다 da | 라 ra | 마 ma | 바 ba | 사 sa |
| ㅑ ya | 갸 gya | 냐 nya | 댜 dya | 랴 rya | 먀 mya | 뱌 bya | 샤 sya |
| ㅓ eo | 거 geo | 너 neo | 더 deo | 러 reo | 머 meo | 버 beo | 서 seo |
| ㅕ yeo | 겨 gyeo | 녀 nyeo | 뎌 dyeo | 려 ryeo | 며 myeo | 벼 byeo | 셔 syeo |
| ㅗ o | 고 go | 노 no | 도 do | 로 ro | 모 mo | 보 bo | 소 so |
| ㅛ yo | 교 gyo | 뇨 nyo | 됴 dyo | 료 ryo | 묘 myo | 뵤 byo | 쇼 syo |
| ㅜ u | 구 gu | 누 nu | 두 du | 루 ru | 무 mu | 부 bu | 수 su |
| ㅠ yu | 규 gyu | 뉴 nyu | 듀 dyu | 류 ryu | 뮤 myu | 뷰 byu | 슈 syu |
| ㅡ eu | 그 geu | 느 neu | 드 deu | 르 reu | 므 meu | 브 beu | 스 seu |
| ㅣ i | 기 gi | 니 ni | 디 di | 리 ri | 미 mi | 비 bi | 시 si |

| ㅇ - | ㅈ j | ㅊ ch | ㅋ k | ㅌ t | ㅍ p | ㅎ h |
|---|---|---|---|---|---|---|
| 아 a | 자 ja | 차 cha | 카 ka | 타 ta | 파 pa | 하 ha |
| 야 ya | 쟈 jya | 챠 chya | 캬 kya | 탸 tya | 퍄 pya | 햐 hya |
| 어 eo | 저 jeo | 처 cheo | 커 keo | 터 teo | 퍼 peo | 허 heo |
| 여 yeo | 져 jyeo | 쳐 chyeo | 켜 kyeo | 텨 tyeo | 펴 pyeo | 혀 hyeo |
| 오 o | 조 jo | 초 cho | 코 ko | 토 to | 포 po | 호 ho |
| 요 yo | 죠 jyo | 쵸 chyo | 쿄 kyo | 툐 tyo | 표 pyo | 효 hyo |
| 우 u | 주 ju | 추 chu | 쿠 ku | 투 tu | 푸 pu | 후 hu |
| 유 yu | 쥬 jyu | 츄 chyu | 큐 kyu | 튜 tyu | 퓨 pyu | 휴 hyu |
| 으 eu | 즈 jeu | 츠 cheu | 크 keu | 트 teu | 프 peu | 흐 heu |
| 이 i | 지 ji | 치 chi | 키 ki | 티 ti | 피 pi | 히 hi |

# Pronunciation Guide

## THE KOREAN LETTERS AND THEIR SOUNDS

### 1. Vowels

#### 1) Simple Vowels

| Korean Letter | Romanization | English Sound |
|:---:|:---:|:---|
| ㅏ | a | as *a* of father |
| ㅑ | ya | as *ya* of yard |
| ㅓ | eo | as *u* of hut |
| ㅕ | yeo | as *you* of young |
| ㅗ | o | as *o* of home |
| ㅛ | yo | as *yo* of yoke |
| ㅜ | u | as *o* of do |
| ㅠ | yu | as *you* of you |
| ㅡ | eu | as *e* of taken |
| ㅣ | i | as *i* of ink |

#### 2) Diphthongs

| Korean Letter | Romanization | English Sound |
|:---:|:---:|:---|
| ㅐ | ae | as *a* of hat |
| ㅒ | yae | as *ya* of yam |
| ㅔ | e | as *e* of met |
| ㅖ | ye | as *ye* of yes |
| ㅚ | oe | as *o* of Köln |
| ㅟ | wi | as *wi* of wind |
| ㅢ | ui | approximately the sound of *e* of taken followed by *e* of we |

| ㅘ | wa | as *wa* of wan |
|---|---|---|
| ㅝ | wo | as *wo* of wonder |
| ㅙ | wae | as *wa* of wag |
| ㅞ | we | as *we* of wet |

## 2. Consonants

### 1) Simple Consonants

| Korean Letter | Romanization | | | Examples | English Sound |
|---|---|---|---|---|---|
| | Initial | Medial | Final | | |
| ㄱ | g | g/k | k | gagu(가구), guk(국) | as grocery |
| ㄴ | n | n | n | nun(눈), eonni(언니) | as name |
| ㄷ | d | d/t | t | datda(닫다) | as depend |
| ㄹ | r | r/l | l | radio(라디오), ori(오리), dal(달) | as rain or lily |
| ㅁ | m | m | m | ma-eum(마음), mom(몸) | as mother |
| ㅂ | b | b/p | p | bibimbap(비빔밥) | as book |
| ㅅ | s | s | t | siso(시소), ot(옷) | as spring |
| ㅇ | - | - | ng | ai(아이), gong(공) | as king |
| ㅈ | j | j | t | juso(주소), baji(바지), nat(낮) | as John |
| ㅊ | ch | ch | t | chaek(책), gicha(기차), bit(빛) | as church |
| ㅋ | k | k | k | ko(코), seuki(스키), bueok(부엌) | as kiss |
| ㅌ | t | t | t | tomato(토마토), mit(밑) | as tank |
| ㅍ | p | p | p | podo(포도), upyo(우표), ip(입) | as pump |
| ㅎ | h | h | t | hayata(하얗다), giho(기호) | as high |

## 2) Double Consonants

| Korean Letter | Romanization | | | Examples | English Sound |
|---|---|---|---|---|---|
| | Initial | Medial | Final | | |
| ㄲ | kk | kk | k | kkakda(깎다), tokki(토끼) | as Jack |
| ㄸ | tt | tt | – | ttada(따다), mettugi(메뚜기) | as stay |
| ㅃ | pp | pp | – | ppuri(뿌리), oppa(오빠) | as spy |
| ㅆ | ss | ss | t | ssada(싸다), ajeossi(아저씨) | as essence |
| ㅉ | jj | jj | – | jjigae(찌개), jjapjjalhan(짭짤한) | as pizza |
| ㄳ | | ks | k | neok(넋), neoksi(넋이) | |
| ㄵ | | nj | n | antta(앉다), anjeun(앉은) | |
| ㄶ | | n | n | manta(많다), maneun(많은) | |
| ㄺ | | k/lg | k | ikda(읽다), ilgeun(읽은), dak(닭) | |
| ㄻ | does not apear as initial | m/lm | m | samda(삶다), salmeun(삶은), sam(삶) | |
| ㄼ | | p/lb | p | yapda(얇다), yalbeun(얇은) | |
| ㄾ | | lt | l | hulta(훑다), hulteun(훑은) | |
| ㄿ | | lp | p | eupda(읊다), eulpeun(읊은) | |
| ㅀ | | l | l | silta(싫다), silko(싫고) | |
| ㅄ | | ps | p | gap(값), gapsi(값이) | |

18

# SOUND CHANGES AND TRANSCRIPTION

1. Basic Principles for Transcription

- Romanizaion is based on the standard Korean pronunciation.
- All the Roman letters are written in lowercase and no symbols or punctuation marks are used.
- Romanization follows the principle of "one letter (or set of letters) per phoneme."
- A hyphen is used optionally when it is necessary to remove ambiguity from syllables: *ga-eul* (가을, fall) versus *gae-ul* (개울, stream).

2. Summary of the Transcription System

1) Vowels are transcribed as follows:

(1) Simple Vowels:

| Korean Letter | Romanization |
|:---:|:---:|
| ㅏ | a |
| ㅑ | ya |
| ㅓ | eo |
| ㅕ | yeo |
| ㅗ | o |
| ㅛ | yo |
| ㅜ | u |
| ㅠ | yu |
| ㅡ | eu |
| ㅣ | i |

## (2) Diphthongs

| Korean Letter | Romanization |
|---|---|
| ㅐ | ae |
| ㅒ | yae |
| ㅔ | e |
| ㅖ | ye |
| ㅚ | oe |
| ㅟ | wi |
| ㅢ | ui |
| ㅘ | wa |
| ㅝ | wo |
| ㅙ | wae |
| ㅞ | we |

\* NOTE:
  i) Long vowels are not marked in transcription.
  ii) "ㅢ" is transcribed as [ui], even when it is pronounced as [i].


## 2) Consonants are transcribed as follows:

### (1) Plosives (Stops)

| | | |
|---|---|---|
| ㄱ g / k | ㄲ kk | ㅋ k |
| ㄷ d / t | ㄸ tt | ㅌ t |
| ㅂ b / p | ㅃ pp | ㅍ p |

### (2) Affricates

ㅈ j     ㅉ jj     ㅊ ch

### (3) Fricatives

ㅅ s     ㅆ ss     ㅎ h

### (4) Nasals

ㅁ m     ㄴ n / ng

(5) Liquids

ㄹ l / r

## 3. Special Provisions for Transcription

Changes to certain sounds are necessary for linking words without a pause.

1) ㄱ, ㄷ, and ㅂ are transcribed respectively as *g*, *d*, and *b* when they appear before a vowel, but are transcribed as *k*, *t*, and *p* before consonants or at the end of a word.

가구 gagu furniture
갈비 galbi rib
벚꽃 beotkkot cherry blossom
밥 bap cooked rice
바둑 baduk go
숟가락 sutgarak spoon

2) ㄹ is transcribed as *r* before a vowel, and as *l* before a consonant or at the end of a word, ㄹㄹ is transcribed as *ll*.

사랑 sarang love
발 bal foot
물건 mulgeon thing
진달래 jindallae azalea

3) When Korean sound values change as in the following cases, the results of those changes are transcribed as follows:

(1) The case of assimilation of adjacent consonants

냇물 naenmul stream
부엌문 bueongmun kitchen door

심리 simni psychology
압력 amnyeok pressure
종로 jongno Jongno
독립 dongnip independence
진리 jilli truth
백마 baengma white horse
신라 silla Silla

(2) The case of the epenthetic ㄹ and ㄹ
가랑잎 garangnip fallen leaves
담요 damnyo blanket
홑이불 honnibul sheet
물약 mullyak liquid medicine
풀잎 pullip grass leaf

(3) The case of palatalization
굳이 guji obstinately
같이 gachi together
해돋이 haedoji sunrise

(4) The case when ㄱ, ㄷ, ㅂ, and ㅈ are adjacent to ㅎ
국화 gukwa chrysanthemum
낳다 nata to bear
밟히다 balpida to be stamped
맞히다 machida to hit

* NOTE:
i) In the Romanization system, aspirated sounds are not
reflected in cases of nouns where ㅎ follows ㄱ, ㄷ, and ㅂ:
국회 (gukhoe). However, in this book, aspirated sounds are
transcribed to avoid confusion in pronunciation: 국회 (gukoe).

    ii) Tense (or glottalized) sounds are not reflected in cases when morphemes are compounded, as in the examples below.

        *e.g.* 압구정 Apgujeong

4) When there is a possibility of confusion in pronunciation, or a need for segmentation, a hyphen(-) may be used.

    연구 yeon-gu research
    종로에 jongno-e in Jongno
    물가에 mulga-e ashore

5) The first letter is capitalized in proper names.

    인천 Incheon
    세종 Sejong
    대구 Daegu

6) Personal names are presented family name first, followed by a space and then the given name. A hyphen will separate given names except that non-Sino-Korean given names may be joined without a hyphen.

    김수미 Kim Su-mi
    정 마리아 Jeong Maria
    남궁 동자 Namgung Dong-ja

    \* NOTE:
    In the transcription of personal names and names of administrative units, assimilated sound changes before or after a hyphen are not transcribed.

7) Administrative units such as 도, 시, 군, 구, 읍, 면, 리, 동, and 가 are transcribed respectively as *do, si, gun, gu, eup, myeon, ri, dong,* and *ga,* and are preceded by a hyphen.

    강원도 Gangwon-do

인사동 Insa-dong
신창읍 Sinchang-eup
교산리 Gyosan-ri
종로3가 Jongnosam-ga
청주시 Cheongju-si
강남구 Gangnam-gu

* NOTE:
Terms for administrative units such as 특별시, 광역시, 시, 군, 읍, and so on may be omitted.

8) Names of geographic features, cultural properties, and man-made structures may be written without hyphens.

해운대 Haeundae
불국사 Bulguksa
금강 Geumgang
경복궁 Gyeongbokgung
속리산 Songnisan
독립문 Dongnimmun

* NOTE:
Hyphens may be inserted in words of five syllables or more.
*e.g.* 금동 미륵 보살 반가사유상 *Geumdong-mireuk-bosal-banga-sayusang*

9) Some proper names which cannot be abruptly changed in view of international practices and common longstanding transcriptions.

이순신 Yi Sun-shin
이화 Ewha
연세 Yonsei
이승만 Syngman Rhee

## PHONETIC PATTERNS

The formation of the Korean letters and words will help to follow the foregoing compact charts of the elements of the basic Korean characters and their phonemic rules. The reader will find the spelling rules.

1. The Korean alphabet consists of 24 letters: 10 vowels and 14 consonants. Each individual letter has a phonetic value and independent form; two or more letters are written together as syllables as in Latin. These represent the phonemes of the Korean language.

   The vowels are used only as medial sounds. They are: ㅏ, ㅑ, ㅓ, ㅕ, ㅗ, ㅛ, ㅜ, ㅠ, ㅡ, and ㅣ (among these ㅏ, ㅓ, and ㅣ are used for modifying or compounding medial sound; ㅐ, ㅒ, ㅔ, ㅖ, ㅚ, ㅟ, ㅢ (modified by the ㅏ, ㅓ, and ㅣ in compound).

   The 14 consonants are ㄱ, ㄴ, ㄷ, ㄹ, ㅁ, ㅂ, ㅅ, ㅇ, ㅈ, ㅊ, ㅋ, ㅌ, ㅍ, and ㅎ. The name of each consonant contains two syllables; starting with the letter itself of the first syllable and ending with the same letter of the second syllable. Thus, when decoding the name of the consonant into sound, one can start sounding with that letter and also end with that letter. The 14 consonants also have both a beginning and ending position. The consonants, except for ㅇ, ㅊ, and ㅋ are combined to make double consonants. Usually double consonants are in the ending position, except for ㄲ, ㄸ, ㅃ, ㅆ, and ㅉ. But ㄲ and ㅆ come in either position, beginning or ending.

To form a syllable or a word, a combination of consonants and vowels should be written either left-to-right or top-to-bottom.

*e.g.*
1) 가, 개, 꽤: simple consonants with various vowels
2) 까, 따, 빠, 싸, 깨, 꾀: double consonants with various vowels
3) 박(consonant+vowel+consonant), 백(consonant+double vowel+ consonant)

2. The meaning of a simple and double consonant is different.

*e.g.*
1) 개다(to fold) and 깨다(to break)
2) 지다(to lose) and 찌다(to steam)
3) 방(room) and 빵(bread)

3. In the Korean language, accent is not articulated on syllables as it is in English, thus the intonation in Korean speech is rather even and smooth.

# Grammar Guide

A few notes on grammatical details are provided for those who wish to grasp and understand the structure of the Korean language.

## ARTICLES

The Korean language does not have articles like the "a" or "the" of English. Also, the single and plural forms are not as clearly expressed in Korean as they are in English. Thus, 개 (dog) may mean *the dog, a dog, dogs* or *the dogs*, depending on the context.

## TABLE OF PRONOUNS

| English | Korean | English | Korean |
|---|---|---|---|
| I | naneun, naega | he | geuneun, geuga |
| we | urineun, uriga | his | geuui |
| my | naui | him | geureul, geuege |
| our | uriui | she | geunyeoga, geunyeoneun |
| me | na-ege, nareul | her | geunyeoui |
| us | uriege, urireul | her | geunyeo-ege, geunyeoreul |
| you | dangsineun, dangsini | they | geudeureun, geudeuri |
| your | dangsinui | their | geudeurui |
| you | dangsinege, dangsineul | them | geudeurege, geudeureul |

## ADJECTIVES

The position of the adjective in Korean language is before the noun. For example, *jaemiinneun chaek* (재미있는 책, interesting book), *yeppeun yeoja* (예쁜 여자, pretty woman), *ppalgan jangmi* (빨간 장미, red rose), etc.

I have an interesting book.

나는 재미있는 책을 가지고 있습니다.

naneun jaemiinneun chaegeul gajigo isseumnida

Another function of the adjective, like in English, is to describe the subject: *jaemiisseumnida* (재미있습니다, to be interesting), *yeppeumnida* (예쁩니다, to be pretty). Notice that these Korean words do not mean white or pretty but to be white and to be pretty.

This book is interesting.

이 책은 재미있습니다.

i chaegeun jaemiisseumnida

My friend is pretty.

제 친구는 예쁩니다.

je chinguneun yeppeumnida

## VERBS

A characteristic of the Korean sentence is the verb's position at the end. The verb in Korean functions as either something happens, someone does something or something is in a certain manner.

## 1. Position of Verb

Note that the Korean verb is placed at the end of the sentence.

- English structure: I read a book.
- Korean structure: *Na* (I) *neun chaek* (a book) *eul ikseumnida* (read).

## 2. Verb Stems and Suffixes

The verb in Korean consists of one verb stem plus one or more suffixes. For instance, the verb *oda* (오다, to come) takes suffixes in the following manner:

| Korean | Stem-Suffix | Stem-Suffix | Meaning |
|--------|-------------|-------------|---------|
| 오다 | 오– | o- | to come |
| 옵니다 | 오–ㅂ니다 | o-mnida | come |
| 옵시다 | 오–ㅂ시다 | o-psida | come |
| 옵니까 | 오–ㅂ니까 | o-mnikka | do (you) come |

## 3. Conjugations

In the Korean dictionary, verbs are shown in present tense ending with "다"[da].

> 가다 **gada** I, you, we, they go (or to go)
> 오다 **oda** I, you, we, they come (or to come)

However, in ordinary conversation the above form of the present tense is rarely heard. Instead, the suffixes such as *-mnida* (−ㅂ니다, after a vowel) or *-seumnida* (−습니다, after a consonant) are very common.

The following charts show changes to the verb according to its tense. Please note that there are certain patterns (or rules) one can make from the examples which can be applied to making various verb forms.

### 1) Present Tense

| After | Suffix | Example | Meaning |
|---|---|---|---|
| Vowel | -mnida | 사다 sada → samnida | to buy |
| Consonant | -seumnida | 참다 chamda → chamseumnida | to endure |

## 2) Past Tense

| | After | Suffix | Example | Meaning |
|---|---|---|---|---|
| V o w e l | a | -sseumnida | 사다 sada → satseumnida | bought |
| | o | -atseumnida | 보다 boda → bwatseumnida | saw |
| | e | -eotseumnida | 베다 beda → be-eotseumnida | cut |
| | i | | 기다 gida → gieotseumnida | crept |
| | u | | 주다 juda → jueotseumnida | gave |
| | hada | -yeotseumnida | 하다 hada → hayeotseumnida | did |
| | oda | -watseumnida | 오다 oda → watseumnida | came |
| C o n s o n a n t | a+c | -atseumnida | 참다 chamda → chamatseumnida | endured |
| | o+c | | 녹다 nokda → nogatseumnida | melted |
| | other vowel + con- sonant | -eotseumnida | 접다 jeopda → jeobeotseumnida | folded |
| | | | 입다 ipda → ibeotseumnida | wore |
| | | | 묻다 mutda → mureotseumnida | asked |

### 3) Future Tense

| After | Suffix | Example | Meaning |
|---|---|---|---|
| Vowel | -gesseumnida | 사다 sada → sagesseumnida | will buy |
| | | 하다 hada → hagesseumnida | will do |
| Consonant | | 입다 ipda → ipgesseumnida | will wear |
| | | 묻다 mutda → mutgesseumnida | will ask |

## OMISSION OF SUBJECT

As in other languages, it is not unusual in Korean to drop the subject of a sentence, particularly when the meaning is obvious without mentioning the details. So, *gamnida* (go) may mean I/you/he/she/they/we am/is/are going. And *gamnikka* (go) may mean Is/Are you/he/she/they going?

갑니다.

gamnida

(I'm) going.

go

서울에 갑니다.

seoure gamnida

(I'm) going to Seoul.

Seoul to go

내일 서울에 갑니다.

naeil seoure gamnida

(I'm) going to Seoul tomorrow.

tomorrow Seoul to go

나는 내일 서울에 갑니다.

naneun naeil seoure gamnida

I'm going to Seoul tomorrow.

I tomorrow Seoul to go

## DECLARATIVE & INTERROGATIVE

Unlike English, Korean has different suffixes for declarative and interrogative sentences.

학생이 갑니다.

haksaeng-i gamnida

The student is going.

학생이 갑니까?

haksaeng-i gamnikka

Is the student going?

In the above example, the suffix *da* (다) is used for a declarative and *kka* (까) for an interrogative sentence.

## NEGATIVE SENTENCES

Negatives of Korean verbs may be formed in several ways but the easiest is simply to add the negative word "안" [an], meaning *not,* before the verb.

갑니다 gamnida — going
안 갑니다 an gamnida — not going

갑니까 gamnikka — going?
안 갑니까 an gamnikka — not going?

Another negative word that comes in handy is "못" [mot], which means *can't/unable to.*

갑니다 gamnida — going
못 갑니다 mot gamnida — can't go

갑니까 gamnikka — going?
못 갑니까 mot gamnikka — can't going?

## YES & NO

When Korean speakers answer yes/no questions, they agree or disagree with the question as in, "Yes, we have no apples." This differs from English usage when the question is in the negative.

A: 내일 갑니까?
   naeil gamnikka
   Are you going tomorrow?

B: 네.

   ne

   Yes. (That's right, I'm going.)

C: 아니요.

   aniyo

   No. (That's not right, I'm not going.)


A: 안 갑니까?

   an gamnikka

   Aren't you going?

B: 네.

   ne

   Yes. (That's right, I'm not going.)

C: 아니요.

   aniyo

   No. (That's not right, I'm going.)

# BASIC EXPRESSIONS

## GREETINGS

| | |
|---|---|
| Hello. /<br>How are you? | 안녕하세요?<br>annyeonghaseyo |
| My name is _____. | 저는 _____ 라고 합니다.<br>jeoneun _____ rago hamnida |
| Nice to meet you. | 만나서 반갑습니다.<br>mannaseo bangapsseumnida |
| Where are you from? | 어디에서 왔어요?<br>eodieseo wasseoyo |
| I'm from the <u>USA</u>. | 미국에서 왔어요.<br>migukeseo wasseoyo<br><sub></sub>* Refer to page 362 for countries. |
| How have you been? | 잘 지냈어요?<br>jal jinaesseoyo |
| Long time no see. | 오랜만이에요.<br>oraenmanieyo |
| Good-bye. | 안녕히 가세요.<br>(to the person who is leaving the place)<br>annyeonghi gaseyo |
| | 안녕히 계세요.<br>(to the person who is remaining)<br>annyeonghi gyeseyo |

| | |
|---|---|
| Good night. | 안녕히 주무세요. |
| | annyeonghi jumuseyo |
| Have a good weekend. | 주말 잘 보내세요. |
| | jumal jal bonaeseyo |
| See you again. | 또 뵙겠습니다. / 또 만나요. |
| | tto boepgesseumnida / tto mannayo |

## Greetings

In Korea, the basic form of greetings is bowing (either nod or bend forward from the waist). People bow when they meet someone for the first time or when there are many people around them, or when they meet a person who is older than they are. Also, Korea is a country where greeting someone is done in many ways. When meeting someone older than yourself, you must use a more formal style of speech, and must bow courteously. You would say "안녕하세요" *annyeonghaseyo* or "안녕하십니까" *annyeonghasimnikka*, whereas among friends you would say, "안녕" *annyeong*.

## Types of Greetings

It depends on the situation. When you meet a younger person, you can just nod. When you meet someone close to you, you can just wave or shake hands. These days, many people shake hands. Also, if you meet your close friend you haven't seen in a long time, hugging is fine.

## ANSWERING

Yes. / No.
네. / 아니요.
ne / aniyo

It's good.
좋아요.
joayo

It's not good.
별로예요.
byeolloyeyo

That's alright.
괜찮아요.
gwaenchanayo

I understand.
알겠어요.
algesseoyo

I don't understand.
잘 모르겠어요.
jal moreugesseoyo

Yes, it is.
네, 그래요.
ne geuraeyo

No, it's not.
아니요, 그렇지 않아요.
aniyo geureochi anayo

## ASKING FOR FAVORS

Can I ask you a favor?
부탁 하나 해도 될까요?
butak hana haedo doelkkayo

| | |
|---|---|
| Could you lend me a pen? | 펜 좀 빌려 주시겠어요?<br>pen jom billyeo jusigesseoyo |
| Could you hold my bag for me for a moment? | 제 가방 좀 잠깐 들어 주시겠어요?<br>je gabang jom jamkkan deureo jusigesseoyo |
| Could you please explain it one more time? | 한 번 더 설명해 주시겠어요?<br>han beon deo seolmyeonghae jusigesseoyo |
| Could you speak more slowly? | 천천히 말씀해 주시겠어요?<br>cheoncheonhi malsseumhae jusigesseoyo |
| Could you help me, please? | 좀 도와주시겠어요?<br>jom dowajusigesseoyo |
| Could you be more specific? | 좀 더 구체적으로 말씀해 주시겠어요?<br>jom deo guchejeogeuro malsseumhae jusigesseoyo |
| Would you bring me some more tissue? | 휴지 좀 더 갖다 주시겠어요?<br>hyuji jom deo gatda jusigesseoyo |
| Could you spare a moment? | 잠시만 시간 좀 내 주시겠어요?<br>jamsiman sigan jom nae jusigesseoyo |
| Can you answer the phone for me? | 전화 좀 받아 주시겠어요?<br>jeonhwa jom bada jusigesseoyo |
| Would you mind if I came along? | 저도 함께 참여해도 될까요?<br>jeodo hamkke chamyeohaedo doelkkayo |

| Could you save my seat? | 제 자리 좀 맡아 주시겠어요? |
| | je jari jom mata jusigesseoyo |
| | |
| Can you give me a ride? | 차 좀 얻어 탈 수 있을까요? |
| | cha jom eodeo tal su isseulkkayo |
| | |
| It's expensive. Can you lower the price? | 값이 비싼데 조금 깎아 주시겠어요? |
| | gapsi bissande jogeum kkakka jusigesseoyo |
| | |
| Would it be OK if I asked some questions? | 궁금한 게 있는데 좀 여쭤 봐도 될까요? |
| | gunggeumhan ge inneunde jom yeojjwo bwado doelkkayo |
| | |
| Can I have a moment of your time? | 잠깐 시간 괜찮으세요? |
| | jamkkan sigan gwaenchaneuseyo |
| | |
| May I sit here? | 제가 여기에 앉아도 될까요? |
| | jega yeogie anjado doelkkayo |
| | |
| Can I go first? | 제가 먼저 가도 될까요? |
| | jega meonjeo gado doelkkayo |
| | |
| Could you get the stuff instead of me? | 제 대신 물건 좀 받아 주시겠어요? |
| | je daesin mulgeon jom bada jusigesseoyo |

## SHOWING APPRECIATION

| Thank you very much. | 정말 고마워요. |
| | jeongmal gomawoyo |

| | |
|---|---|
| Thank you so much for your kindness. | 친절하게 대해 주셔서 고마워요.<br>chinjeolhage daehae jusyeoseo gomawoyo |
| Thank you very much for helping me. | 도와주셔서 정말 고마워요.<br>dowajusyeoseo jeongmal gomawoyo |
| Thank you for everything. | 여러 가지로 고마워요.<br>yeoreo gajiro gomawoyo |
| Thank you for the birthday present. | 생일 선물 고마워요.<br>saengil seonmul gomawoyo |
| Thank you for your concern. | 염려해 주셔서 고마워요.<br>yeomnyeohae jusyeoseo gomawoyo |
| I don't know how to thank you enough. | 어떻게 감사 드려야 할지 모르겠어요.<br>eotteoke gamsa deuryeoya halji moreugesseoyo |
| I owe you a lot. Thank you so much. | 여러모로 신세를 많이 졌네요. 감사합니다.<br>yeoreomoro sinsereul mani jyeonneyo gamsahamnida |
| Thank you for encouraging whenever I have problems. | 힘들 때마다 격려해 주셔서 감사합니다.<br>himdeul ttaemada gyeongnyeohae jusyeoseo gamsahamnida |
| Thank you for inviting me to your house. | 집에 초대해 주셔서 감사합니다.<br>jibe chodaehae jusyeoseo gamsahamnida |
| Thank you for visiting even though you're very busy. | 어려운 시간 내어 방문해 주셔서 감사합니다.<br>eoryeoun sigan naeeo bangmunhae jusyeoseo gamsahamnida |

41

| Thank you for always being by my side. | 항상 옆에서 챙겨 주셔서 감사합니다.<br>hangsang yeopeseo chaenggyeo jusyeoseo gamsahamnida |
|---|---|

## APOLIGIZING

| I'm very sorry. | 정말 죄송해요.<br>jeongmal joesonghaeyo |
|---|---|
| I apologize to you from the bottom of my heart. | 진심으로 사과드려요.<br>jinsimeuro sagwadeuryeoyo |
| I'm sorry for everything. | 여러 가지로 죄송해요.<br>yeoreo gajiro joesonghaeyo |
| I'm sorry for being late. | 늦어서 죄송해요.<br>neujeoseo joesonghaeyo |
| I'm sorry to make you wait. | 오래 기다리게 해서 죄송해요.<br>orae gidarige haeseo joesonghaeyo |
| I'm sorry if I offended you. | 기분을 상하게 했다면 죄송해요.<br>gibuneul sanghage haetdamyeon joesonghaeyo |
| I want to apologize for my mistake. | 제 실수에 대해 사과드려요.<br>je silsue daehae sagwadeuryeoyo |
| Please accept my apology. | 제 사과를 받아 주세요.<br>je sagwareul bada juseyo |

I'm sorry to bother you.

귀찮게 해서 죄송합니다.
gwichanke haeseo joesonghamnida

I'm sorry about not taking care of my responsibilities in the correct order.

일 처리를 제대로 하지 못해 죄송해요.
il cheorireul jedaero haji motae joesonghaeyo

I apologize for having not been careful.

제가 좀 더 주의했어야 하는데, 죄송합니다.
jega jom deo juuihaesseoya haneunde joesonghamnida

I'm sorry to trouble you.

폐를 끼쳐 죄송합니다.
pyereul kkichyeo joesonghamnida

I'm sorry for breaking my promise.

약속을 지키지 못해서 미안해요.
yaksogeul jikiji motaeseo mianhaeyo

I'll be more careful in the future.

앞으로는 좀 더 주의하겠습니다.
apeuroneun jom deo juuihagesseumnida

I'm sorry for not working harder.

더 열심히 하지 못해서 죄송합니다.
deo yeolsimhi haji motaeseo joesonghamnida

## ASKING A QUESTION

What's this called in Korean?

이것을 한국어로 뭐라고 해요?
igeoseul hangugeoro mworago haeyo

| | |
|---|---|
| Do you understand? | 이해하시겠어요?<br>ihaehasigesseoyo |
| What's this? | 이건 뭐예요?<br>igeon mwoyeyo |
| How do you<br>pronounce this word? | 이 단어를 어떻게 발음해요?<br>i daneoreul eotteoke bareumhaeyo |
| Could you show me<br>the way <u>to the police<br>station</u>? | <u>경찰서로</u> 가는 길 좀 알려 주시겠어요?<br><u>gyeongchalseoro</u> ganeun gil jom<br>allyeo jusigesseoyo |

| | |
|---|---|
| to the police station | 경찰서로 gyeongchalseoro |
| to the embassy | 대사관으로 daesagwaneuro |
| to the hospital | 병원으로 byeongwoneuro |
| to the pharmacy | 약국으로 yakgugeuro |
| to the restroom | 화장실로 hwajangsillo |

| | |
|---|---|
| Could you tell me where<br><u>the museum</u> is? | <u>박물관이</u> 어디에 있는지 가르쳐 주시겠어요?<br><u>bangmulgwani</u> eodie inneunji<br>gareuchyeo jusigesseoyo |

| | |
|---|---|
| the museum | 박물관이 bangmulgwani |
| the broadcasting station | 방송국이 bangsonggugi |
| the subway station | 지하철역이 jihacheollyeogi |
| the school | 학교가 hakgyoga |

| | |
|---|---|
| May I ask you<br>a question? | 질문 하나 해도 될까요?<br>jilmun hana haedo doelkkayo |

| | |
|---|---|
| What does this mean? | 이것의 의미는 뭐예요?<br>igeosui uimineun mwoyeyo |
| What do you think about this? | 이것에 대해서 어떻게 생각하세요?<br>igeose daehaeseo eotteoke saenggakaseyo |
| What's this made of? | 이것은 무엇으로 만들어졌어요?<br>igeoseun mueoseuro mandeureojyeosseoyo |
| Do you have any questions about this? | 여기에 대해서 질문 있어요?<br>yeogie daehaeseo jilmun isseoyo |
| Could you give me some examples? | 예를 들어 주시겠어요?<br>yereul deureo jusigesseoyo |
| Could you explain this <u>in detail</u>? | 좀 더 <u>자세하게</u> 설명해 주시겠어요?<br>jom deo <u>jasehage</u> seolmyeonghae jusigesseoyo |

| | |
|---|---|
| in detail | 자세하게 jasehage |
| correctly | 정확하게 jeonghwakage |
| briefly | 간결하게 gangyeolhage |
| shortly | 짧게 jjalge |

| | |
|---|---|
| What is the difference in meaning between this word and that word? | 이 단어와 저 단어의 의미 차이는 뭐예요?<br>i daneowa jeo daneoui uimi chaineun mwoyeyo |

| Excuse me, could you tell me that again? | 죄송한데 다시 한 번 말씀해 주시겠어요? |
| | joesonghande dasi han beon malsseumhae jusigesseoyo |
| How do you spell this word? | 이 단어의 철자가 어떻게 되나요? |
| | i daneoui cheoljaga eotteoke doenayo |
| Feel free to ask any questions you may have. | 궁금한 것이 있으면 질문하세요. |
| | gunggeumhan geosi isseumyeon jilmunhaseyo |

## COMPLIMENTING

| It's very kind of you. | 정말 친절하시네요. |
| | jeongmal chinjeolhasineyo |
| You look great today. | 오늘 아주 멋져 보여요. |
| | oneul aju meotjyeo boyeoyo |
| The dress looks good on you. | 그 옷이 잘 어울려요. |
| | geu osi jal eoullyeoyo |
| You have beautiful eyes. | 눈이 예쁘세요. |
| | nuni yeppeuseyo |
| You're quite good with your hands. | 손재주가 정말 좋으세요. |
| | sonjaejuga jeongmal jo-euseyo |
| You did a good job. | 정말 잘 했어요. |
| | jeongmal jal haesseoyo |

| You're an excellent cook! | 요리를 정말 잘 하시는군요!<br>yorireul jeongmal jal hasineungunnyo |
| It's very nice of you to say so. | 그렇게 말씀해 주시니 고마워요.<br>geureoke malsseumhae jusini gomawoyo |
| There is nothing you can't do. | 못하는 게 없군요.<br>motaneun ge eopgunnyo |
| You have a nice car! | 멋진 차를 가지고 있군요!<br>meotjin chareul gajigo itgunnyo |
| You are really coming along. | 아주 잘 하고 있군요.<br>aju jal hago itgunnyo |
| I like your new hairstyle. | 새 헤어스타일이 잘 어울려요.<br>sae heeoseutairi jal eoullyeoyo |
| I like that idea.<br>I agree with you. | 좋은 생각이네요. 저도 동감해요.<br>jo-eun saenggagineyo jeodo donggamhaeyo |
| That was very good for your first time. | 처음인데 정말 잘 했어요.<br>cheo-euminde jeongmal jal haesseoyo |
| You have a nice personality. | 성격이 정말 좋으시군요.<br>seonggyeogi jeongmal jo-eusigunnyo |

47

## EXPRESSING EMOTION

### Happy

| | |
|---|---|
| I was so glad to hear the news. | 그 소식을 듣고 정말 기뻤어요.<br>geu sosigeul deutgo jeongmal gippeosseoyo |
| I'm so glad to hear that. | 그 소식을 들으니 무척 기뻐요.<br>geu sosigeul deureuni mucheok gippeoyo |
| That was a touching performance. | 그건 정말 감동적인 공연이었어요.<br>geugeon jeongmal gamdongjeogin gongyeonieosseoyo |
| It's been good talking with you. | 오늘 만나서 즐거웠어요.<br>oneul mannaseo jeulgeowosseoyo |
| I feel like I'm on cloud nine. | 하늘을 날듯이 기뻐요.<br>haneureul naldeusi gippeoyo |
| I feel so great today. | 오늘 기분이 정말 최고예요.<br>oneul gibuni jeongmal choegoyeyo |
| Today is the best day of my life. | 제 생애 오늘만큼 기쁜 날은 없었어요.<br>je saengae oneulmankeum gippeun nareun eopseosseoyo |
| I feel as if I'm dreaming. | 마치 꿈을 꾸고 있는 것 같아요.<br>machi kkumeul kkugo inneun geot gatayo |

It was the biggest
moment of my life.

내 생애 가장 기쁜 순간이었어요.
nae saengae gajang gippeun
sunganieosseoyo

I was happy to see
you after so long.

오랜만에 만나서 정말 기뻤어요.
oraenmane mannaseo jeongmal
gippeosseoyo

It's enjoyable and
I feel great.

정말 즐겁고 행복하군요.
jeongmal jeulgeopgo
haengbokagunnyo

I'm glad that the
outcome matched all
my hard work.

노력한 만큼 좋은 결과가 나와서
기뻐요.
noryeokan mankeum jo-eun
gyeolgwaga nawaseo gippeoyo

## Angry

I can't stand it
anymore.

정말 더 이상은 못 참겠어요.
jeongmal deo isangeun mot
chamgesseoyo

That burns me up.

정말 열 받아요.
jeongmal yeol badayo

I am so upset.

엄청 기분이 상하네요.
eomcheong gibuni sanghaneyo

I can't understand
how he / she can say
that to me.

어떻게 그렇게 말할 수 있는지 이해가
안 돼요.
eotteoke geureoke malhal su
inneunji ihaega an dwaeyo

| I am so upset that I could just explode. | 너무 화나서 폭발 직전이에요. |
| | neomu hwanaseo pokbal jikjeonieyo |

| I'm angry about him / her being so rude. | 그 사람이 너무 무례해서 화가 나요. |
| | geu sarami neomu muryehaeseo hwaga nayo |

| I'm so angry I can't speak. | 너무 화가 나서 말도 안 나와요. |
| | neomu hwaga naseo maldo an nawayo |

| I have tolerated it for a while. | 저도 그동안 많이 참았어요. |
| | jeodo geudongan mani chamasseoyo |

| I'm losing my temper. | 머리끝까지 화가 나요. |
| | meorikkeutkkaji hwaga nayo |

| I am so angry I just can't stand it anymore. | 화가 나서 견딜 수가 없어요. |
| | hwaga naseo gyeondil suga eopseoyo |

## Sad

| The movie was very sad. | 그 영화는 정말 슬펐어요. |
| | geu yeonghwaneun jeongmal seulpeosseoyo |

| I feel blue when the weather is bad. | 날씨가 나쁘면 우울해요. |
| | nalssiga nappeumyeon uulhaeyo |

| I feel really sad. | 지금 너무 슬퍼요. |
| | jigeum neomu seulpeoyo |

| | |
|---|---|
| I'm broken-hearted, I almost cried. | 눈물이 날 만큼 마음이 아파요.<br>nunmuri nal mankeum ma-eumi apayo |
| I'm so sad I don't feel like doing anything at all. | 슬퍼서 아무 것도 하고 싶지 않아요.<br>seulpeoseo amu geotdo hago sipji anayo |
| I had a heavy heart listening to the story. | 그 이야기를 듣고 마음이 많이 무거웠어요.<br>geu iyagireul deutgo ma-eumi mani mugeowosseoyo |
| I cried my eyes out with grief. | 너무 슬퍼서 눈이 붓도록 울었어요.<br>neomu seulpeoseo nuni butdorok ureosseoyo |
| Will it get better over time? | 시간이 지나면 괜찮아지겠죠?<br>sigani jinamyeon gwaenchanajigetjyo |
| What's wrong?<br>You look sad today. | 무슨 일 있어요? 오늘따라 왠지 슬퍼 보이네요.<br>museun il isseoyo oneulttara waenji seulpeo boineyo |
| I was sad after talking with him / her. | 그 사람 이야기를 듣고 슬퍼졌어요.<br>geu saram iyagireul deutgo seulpeojyeosseoyo |
| I feel bad because I failed the test. | 시험에 떨어져서 마음이 무거워요.<br>siheome tteoreojyeoseo ma-eumi mugeowoyo |

## Surprised & Scared

I was very surprised by the news.

그 소식을 듣고 매우 놀랐어요.

geu sosigeul deutgo mae-u nollasseoyo

Really? I can't believe it!

정말이에요? 믿을 수가 없어요!

jeongmarieyo mideul suga eopseoyo

It's surprising to run into you here.

여기서 당신을 만나서 깜짝 놀랐어요.

yeogiseo dangsineul mannaseo kkamjjak nollasseoyo

It never crossed my mind.

생각도 못한 일이네요.

saenggakdo motan irineyo

The story is very shocking.

그 이야기는 정말 충격적이었어요.

geu iyagineun jeongmal chunggyeokjeogieosseoyo

I was so surprised I almost shouted.

저는 놀라서 소리를 지를 뻔 했어요.

jeoneun nollaseo sorireul jireul ppeon haesseoyo

It scared me out of my wits.

십 년 감수했네요.

sip nyeon gamsuhaenneyo

I was so surprised, I'm speechless.

너무 놀라서 말이 다 안 나오네요.

neomu nollaseo mari da an naoneyo

The story was very scary.

그 이야기는 정말 무서웠어요.

geu iyagineun jeongmal museowosseoyo

It's horrifying just thinking of it.

생각만 해도 소름 끼치는 일이에요.

saenggangman haedo soreum kkichineun irieyo

I was so scared, I couldn't move.

너무 무서워서 움직일 수가 없었어요.

neomu museowoseo umjigil suga eopseosseoyo

## Worried & Concerned

I'm not sure what to do.

어떻게 해야 할지 모르겠어요.

eotteoke haeya halji moreugesseoyo

I'm worried that he has not arrived yet.

그 사람이 아직 도착하지 않아서 걱정이에요.

geu sarami ajik dochakaji anaseo geokjeongieyo

I have a big problem.

저에게 큰 문제가 생겼어요.

jeo-ege keun munjega saenggyeosseoyo

I am so worried I can't sleep.

너무 걱정이 되어서 잠도 오지 않아요.

neomu geokjeongi doe-eoseo jamdo oji anayo

Is anything the matter?

무슨 걱정거리라도 있으세요?

museun geokjeonggeorirado isseuseyo

You don't look good. What happened?

얼굴 표정이 안 좋아요. 무슨 일이 있어요?

eolgul pyojeong-i an joayo museun iri isseoyo

| I don't know what I should do. | 어떻게 하면 좋을지 잘 모르겠어요.<br>eotteoke hamyeon jo-eulji jal moreugesseoyo |
| There are so many things that my head is spinning. | 여러 가지 일로 머리가 복잡해요.<br>yeoreo gaji illo meoriga bokjapaeyo |
| It confused me. | 그 일로 고민에 빠졌어요.<br>geu illo gomine ppajyeosseoyo |
| Isn't there any way to solve this problem? | 이 문제를 해결할 방법이 없을까요?<br>i munjereul haegyeolhal bangbeobi eopseulkkayo |

## Complain

| He drives me angry. | 그 사람 때문에 화가 나요.<br>geu saram ttaemune hwaga nayo |
| It weighs heavily on me. | 그 일은 제게 너무 버거워요.<br>geu ireun jege neomu beogeowoyo |
| Why is it so boring today? | 오늘따라 왜 이렇게 따분하죠?<br>oneulttara wae ireoke ttabunhajyo |
| These days I am stressed out because of all this work. | 요즘 업무가 많아 스트레스를 받아요.<br>yojeum eommuga mana seuteureseureul badayo |
| It's tiring and not fun. | 지루하고 재미없어요.<br>jiruhago jaemieopseoyo |

These days everything bothers me.

요새 모든 일이 귀찮아요.

yosae modeun iri gwichanayo

Nothing's going to change even if you complain.

불평해도 달라질 건 없어요.

bulpyeonghaedo dallajil geon eopseoyo

Stop complaining.

불평 그만 하세요.

bulpyeong geuman haseyo

Let me know if you have any complaints.

저에게 불만이 있으면 얘기해 주세요.

jeo-ege bulmani isseumyeon yaegihae juseyo

## Disappointed & Regretful

I'm disappointed in him / her.

그 사람한테 실망했어요.

geu saramhante silmanghaesseoyo

I was very disappointed at the news.

그 소식을 듣고 저는 정말 실망했어요.

geu sosigeul deutgo jeoneun jeongmal silmanghaesseoyo

I was disappointed because he / she broke his / her promise.

그 사람이 약속을 지키지 않아서 실망했어요.

geu sarami yaksogeul jikiji anaseo silmanghaesseoyo

It is disappointing because the outcome was bad despite my best efforts.

열심히 했는데 결과가 좋지 못해서 실망이에요.

yeolsimhi haenneunde gyeolgwaga jochi motaeseo silmangieyo

| I shouldn't have done it. I regret. | 그러지 말았어야 했는데 후회가 되네요.<br>geureoji marasseoya haenneunde huhoega doeneyo |
|---|---|
| I regret having not said anything after I had second thoughts. | 좀 더 생각을 하고 말할 걸 후회가 돼요.<br>jom deo saenggageul hago malhal geol huhoega dwaeyo |
| I seem to have done stupid things. | 제가 바보 같은 짓을 한 것 같아요.<br>jega babo gateun jiseul han geot gatayo |
| There's nothing more I can do. | 이제 더 이상 어쩔 도리가 없네요.<br>ije deo isang eojjeol doriga eomneyo |
| From the bottom of my heart I regret what I did. | 제가 한 일에 대해서 진심으로 반성하고 있어요.<br>jega han ire daehaeseo jinsimeuro banseonghago isseoyo |

## Formal and Informal Forms

The use of the honorific in a Korean sentence is determined by the relationship between the speaker and the listener. "–습니다" is the ending for the polite formal style. "–아/어 요" is also polite, but to a lesser degree than "–습니다." Even if the listener is older or higher in social status than the speaker, the speaker may nonetheless use the informal style if the relationship between them is sufficiently intimate. Usually it is used in familiar relationships, such as with one's parents or elder brothers and sisters, etc.

# ENTRY INTO A COUNTRY

## WHEN BOARDING

May I see your <u>ticket</u>?
표 좀 보여 주시겠어요?
<u>pyo</u> jom boyeo jusigesseoyo

ticket
표 pyo
passport
여권 yeogwon

Where is my seat?
제 좌석은 어디예요?
je jwaseogeun eodiyeyo

Where is seat <u>12A</u>?
<u>12A</u> 자리가 어디예요?
<u>sibi</u>-ei jariga eodiyeyo
* Refer to page 345 for numerals.

Your seat is over there
by on the aisle.
손님 좌석은 저기 통로 쪽이에요.
sonnim jwaseogeun jeogi tongno
jjogieyo

I think this is my seat.
여기는 제 자리인데요.
yeogineun je jariindeyo

Our seats are not
together.
우리 자리가 떨어져 있는데요.
uri jariga tteoreojyeo inneundeyo

I'd like to sit together
with my friend.
친구와 같이 앉고 싶은데요.
chinguwa gachi ango sipeundeyo

57

| Would you mind changing your seat with me? | 자리를 바꿔 주실 수 있어요? |
| | jarireul bakkwo jusil su isseoyo |
| Could I move to the empty seat over there? | 저 쪽 빈자리에 앉아도 돼요? |
| | jeo jjok binjarie anjado dwaeyo |

| empty seat | 빈자리 binjari |
| window seat | 창가 자리 changga jari |
| aisle seat | 통로 자리 tongno jari |

| Can you help me with my baggage? | 제 짐 좀 올려 주시겠어요? |
| | je jim jom ollyeo jusigesseoyo |

| baggage | 짐 jim |
| bag | 가방 gabang |
| clothes | 옷 ot |

| Please let me through. | 좀 지나갈게요. |
| | jom jinagalgeyo |

## ON THE PLANE

| May I go to the lavatory? | 화장실에 가도 돼요? |
| | hwajangsire gado dwaeyo |
| Where is the lavatory? | 화장실이 어디에 있어요? |
| | hwajangsiri eodie isseoyo |

| | |
|---|---|
| Would you pull your chair a little forward? | 의자를 조금만 앞으로 당겨 주시겠어요?<br>uijareul jogeumman apeuro danggyeo jusigesseoyo |
| Would you mind putting your seat upright? | 의자를 똑바로 세워 주시겠어요?<br>uijareul ttokbaro sewo jusigesseoyo |
| May I put my seat back? | 의자를 뒤로 젖혀도 될까요?<br>uijareul dwiro jeochyeodo doelkkayo |
| Could you tell me how to fasten my seat belt? | 안전벨트는 어떻게 매요?<br>anjeonbelteuneun eotteoke maeyo |
| Please fasten your seat belt. | 벨트를 매 주세요.<br>belteureul mae juseyo |
| When are we going to arrive? | 언제 도착해요?<br>eonje dochakaeyo |
| How long is the flying time? | 비행시간이 얼마나 돼요?<br>bihaengsigani eolmana dwaeyo |
| Fill out this form, please. | 이 양식을 작성해 주세요.<br>i yangsigeul jakseonghae juseyo |
| Can you help me with this form? | 신고서 쓰는 거 좀 도와주시겠어요?<br>singoseo sseuneun geo jom dowajusigesseoyo |
| Can I get another one? | 하나 더 주시겠어요?<br>hana deo jusigesseoyo |
| Can I borrow a pen? | 펜 좀 빌려 주시겠어요?<br>pen jom billyeo jusigesseoyo |

| What should I write here? | 여기에 뭘 써야 돼요?<br>yeogie mwol sseoya dwaeyo |
| --- | --- |
| Is it okay? | 이거 괜찮아요?<br>igeo gwaenchanayo |

## How to Prepare Arrival Card

- Fill in all the entries in the bold line of the arrival card.
- Accompanying minors must also fill out an arrival card.

| Arrival Card | 입국신고서 | ipguksingoseo |
| --- | --- | --- |
| Surname | 성 | seong |
| Given Names | 이름 | ireum |
| Date of Birth | 생년월일 | saengnyeonworil |
| Male | 남 | nam |
| Female | 여 | yeo |
| Nationality | 국적 | gukjeok |
| Passport No. | 여권번호 | yeogwonbeonho |
| Address in Korea | 한국 내 주소 | hanguk nae juso |
| Occupation | 직업 | jigeop |
| Purpose of Visit | 여행 목적 | yeohaeng mokjeok |
| Last City / Port of Boarding | 출발지 | chulbalji |
| Flight No. | 입국편명 | ipgukpyeonmyeong |
| Vessel on Arrival | 선명 | seonmyeong |
| Signature | 서명 | seomyeong |

# FLIGHT SERVICE

| | |
|---|---|
| Is this free? | 이거 무료예요?<br>igeo muryoyeyo |
| Is there any charge for this? | 이거 유료예요?<br>igeo yuryoyeyo |
| Do you have any <u>eye drops</u>? | <u>안약</u> 있어요?<br><u>anyak</u> isseoyo |
| May I have a <u>blanket</u>? | <u>담요</u> 좀 주시겠어요?<br><u>damnyo</u> jom jusigesseoyo |

. . . . . . . . . . . . . . . . . . . . . . . . . . . . . . . . . . . . . . . . . . . . . . . . . . . . . . . . . .

| | |
|---|---|
| eye drops | 안약 anyak |
| eye patch | 안대 andae |
| English newspaper | 영자 신문 yeongja sinmun |
| magazine | 잡지 japji |
| blanket | 담요 damnyo |

. . . . . . . . . . . . . . . . . . . . . . . . . . . . . . . . . . . . . . . . . . . . . . . . . . . . . . . . . .

| | |
|---|---|
| Could you show me how to use this <u>headset</u>? | 이 <u>헤드폰</u>은 어떻게 사용해요?<br>i <u>hedeuponeun</u> eotteoke sayonghaeyo |

. . . . . . . . . . . . . . . . . . . . . . . . . . . . . . . . . . . . . . . . . . . . . . . . . . . . . . . . . .

| | |
|---|---|
| headset | 헤드폰 hedeupon |
| reading light | 독서등 dokseodeung |
| air conditioner | 에어컨 e-eokeon |
| earphones | 이어폰 ieopon |

. . . . . . . . . . . . . . . . . . . . . . . . . . . . . . . . . . . . . . . . . . . . . . . . . . . . . . . . . .

| | |
|---|---|
| This headset is broken. | 이 헤드폰은 고장났어요.<br>i hedeuponeun gojangnasseoyo |

| My seat doesn't work. | 좌석이 움직이지 않아요.<br>jwaseogi umjigiji anayo |
| Please wake me up<br>for the meal. | 식사 때 깨워 주세요.<br>siksa ttae kkaewo juseyo |
| Please don't wake me<br>up for the meals. | 식사 때 깨우지 마세요.<br>siksa ttae kkaeuji maseyo |
| I'd like <u>something to</u><br><u>drink</u>, please. | 저, 마실 거 좀 주세요.<br>jeo <u>masil geo</u> jom juseyo |

| something to drink | 마실 거 masil geo |
| something to read | 읽을 거 ilgeul geo |

| A What would you like<br>to drink? | 음료는 뭘 드릴까요?<br>eumnyoneun mwol deurilkkayo |
| B <u>Orange juice</u>,<br>please. | <u>오렌지 주스</u> 주세요.<br><u>orenji juseu</u> juseyo |

| orange juice | 오렌지 주스 orenji juseu |
| Coke | 콜라 kolla |
| Sprite | 사이다 saida |
| water | 물 mul |
| cold water | 차가운 물 chagaun mul |
| coffee | 커피 keopi |

| What do you have? | 어떤 것이 있나요?<br>eotteon geosi innayo |

| Would you like some more water? | 물 좀 더 드릴까요?<br>mul jom deo deurilkkayo |
| Would you like your coffee with <u>cream</u>? | 커피에 크림을 넣어 드릴까요?<br>keopie <u>keurim</u>eul neoeo deurilkkayo |

| cream | 크림 keurim |
| sugar | 설탕 seoltang |

| What time can I have the meal? | 식사는 언제 하죠?<br>siksaneun eonje hajyo |
| What's for <u>dinner</u>? | <u>저녁 식사</u>는 뭐예요?<br><u>jeonyeok siksa</u>neun mwoyeyo |

| dinner | 저녁 식사 jeonyeok siksa |
| lunch | 점심 식사 jeomsim siksa |
| breakfast | 아침 식사 achim siksa |

| A Would you like beef or chicken? | 소고기와 닭고기가 있는데, 어느 것으로 하시겠어요?<br>sogogiwa dakgogiga inneunde eoneu geoseuro hasigesseoyo |
| B <u>Beef</u>, please. | <u>소고기</u>로 주세요.<br><u>sogogi</u>ro juseyo |

| | |
|---|---|
| beef | 소고기로 sogogiro |
| pork | 돼지고기로 dwaejigogiro |
| fish | 생선으로 saengseoneuro |
| bibimbap | 비빔밥으로 bibimbabeuro |

I can't eat meat.
Fish, please.

저는 고기 못 먹어요. 생선으로 주세요.
jeoneun gogi mot meogeoyo
saengseoneuro juseyo

I don't feel like eating
now.

지금 먹고 싶지 않아요.
jigeum meokgo sipji anayo

Can I have it later?

나중에 먹어도 될까요?
najung-e meogeodo doelkkayo

A Are you done with
your meal?

식사 다 하셨어요?
siksa da hasyeosseoyo

B Yes, I enjoyed it.

네, 잘 먹었어요.
ne jal meogeosseoyo

B No, not yet.

아니요, 아직.
aniyo ajik

Could I have some
napkins, please?

냅킨 좀 주세요.
naepkin jom juseyo

Can I buy duty-free
items now?

지금 면세품 살 수 있어요?
jigeum myeonsepum sal su isseoyo

Can I see this one?

이것 좀 보여 주세요.
igeot jom boyeo juseyo

| How much is the discount? | 얼마나 할인됐어요?<br>eolmana harindwaesseoyo |
| I would like to have this one. | 이거 주세요.<br>igeo juseyo |
| Which cigarettes do you have? | 어떤 담배 있어요?<br>eotteon dambae isseoyo |

| cigarettes | 담배 dambae |
| cosmetics | 화장품 hwajangpum |

| Do you accept credit cards? | 신용카드도 돼요?<br>sinyongkadeudo dwaeyo |

| USD | 미국 달러 miguk dalleo |
| AUD | 호주 달러 hoju dalleo |
| CAD | 캐나다 달러 kaenada dalleo |
| HKD | 홍콩 달러 hongkong dalleo |
| EUR | 유로화 yurohwa |

## IN-FLIGHT PROBLEMS

| I'm chilly. | 추워요.<br>chuwoyo |
| I feel sick. | 몸이 불편해요.<br>momi bulpyeonhaeyo |

| | |
|---|---|
| I don't feel well. | 컨디션이 안 좋아요.<br>keondisyeoni an joayo |
| I have a <u>fever</u>. | <u>열이</u> 나요.<br><u>yeori</u> nayo |

| | |
|---|---|
| fever | 열이 yeori |
| nosebleed | 코피가 kopiga |
| cough | 기침이 gichimi |

| | |
|---|---|
| I have a <u>stomachache</u>. | 배가 아파요.<br><u>baega</u> apayo |

| | |
|---|---|
| stomachache | 배가 baega |
| chest pain | 가슴이 gaseumi |
| headache | 머리가 meoriga |

| | |
|---|---|
| I'm having trouble breathing. | 숨쉬기가 곤란해요.<br>sumswigiga gollanhaeyo |
| My stomach doesn't feel good. | 속이 좀 안 좋아요.<br>sogi jom an joayo |
| I'm dizzy. | 좀 어지러워요.<br>jom eojireowoyo |
| I feel nauseated. | 구역질이 나요.<br>guyeokjiri nayo |

| I feel like I'm going to throw up. | 토할 것 같아요.<br>tohal geot gatayo |
| Should I bring you some medicine? | 약을 가져다 드릴까요?<br>yageul gajyeoda deurilkkayo |
| Can you give me some <u>pills</u>? | <u>약</u> 좀 주시겠어요?<br><u>yak</u> jom jusigesseoyo |

| pills | 약 yak |
| airsickness pills | 멀미약 meolmiyak |
| painkiller | 진통제 jintongje |
| airsickness bag | 위생 봉투 wisaeng bongtu |

| Some water for my medicine, please. | 약 먹을 물 좀 주세요.<br>yak meogeul mul jom juseyo |
| Excuse me, could you keep it down? | 죄송한데, 좀 조용히 해 주세요.<br>joesonghande jom joyonghi hae juseyo |

## TRANSFER

| Where is the <u>Korean Air</u> transit counter? | <u>대한항공</u> 환승 카운터는 어디예요?<br><u>daehanhanggong</u> hwanseung kaunteoneun eodiyeyo |

| Korean Air | 대한항공 daehanhanggong |
| Asiana | 아시아나항공 asianahanggong |

67

| Which gate should I go to? | 몇 번 게이트로 가야 해요? |
| | myeot beon geiteuro gaya haeyo |
| When is the boarding time? | 탑승 시간은 언제예요? |
| | tapseung siganeun eonjeyeyo |
| How long is the layover? | 얼마나 대기해야 돼요? |
| | eolmana daegihaeya dwaeyo |
| I need a transit pass, please. | 통행증을 주세요. |
| | tonghaengjeungeul juseyo |
| I have to take this flight. | 이 비행기를 타야 해요. |
| | i bihaenggireul taya haeyo |
| I have to transfer here. | 여기서 갈아타야 돼요. |
| | yeogiseo garataya dwaeyo |
| Where's the transit point? | 갈아타는 곳이 어디예요? |
| | garataneun gosi eodiyeyo |
| We missed our connecting flight. | 환승 편을 놓쳤어요. |
| | hwanseung pyeoneul nochyeosseoyo |

## IMMIGRATION

| A May I see your passport? | 여권 좀 보여 주시겠어요? |
| | yeogwon jom boyeo jusigesseoyo |
| B Here's my passport. | 제 여권이에요. |
| | je yeogwonieyo |

| A Can I see your arrival card, please? | 입국신고서 좀 보여 주세요.<br>ipguksingoseo jom boyeo juseyo |
|---|---|
| B Here you are. | 여기 있어요.<br>yeogi isseoyo |
| A What is the purpose of your visit? | 방문 목적은 무엇인가요?<br>bangmun mokjeogeun mueosingayo |
| B Just traveling. | 여행이요.<br>yeohaengiyo |
| Study. | 공부요.<br>gongbuyo |
| Sightseeing. | 관광이요.<br>gwangwangiyo |
| I'm here on <u>business</u>. | <u>사업</u>차 왔어요.<br>sa-eopcha wasseoyo |

| business | 사업 sa-eop |
|---|---|
| vacation | 휴가 hyuga |

| I'm here to visit my <u>friend</u>. | <u>친구</u>를 방문하러 왔어요.<br><u>chingureul</u> bangmunhareo wasseoyo |
|---|---|

| friend | 친구를 chingureul |
|---|---|
| relatives | 친척을 chincheogeul |
| family | 가족을 gajogeul |

| A Where are you staying? | 어디에서 지낼 거예요?<br>eodieseo jinael geoyeyo |
| B I'm staying at <u>the Seoul Hotel</u>. | <u>서울 호텔</u>에서 머물 거예요.<br><u>seoul hotel</u>eseo meomul geoyeyo |

| the Seoul Hotel | 서울 호텔 seoul hotel |
| a youth hostel | 유스호스텔 yuseuhoseutel |
| my friend's house | 제 친구 집 je chingu jip |

| B I haven't decided yet. | 아직 정하지 않았어요.<br>ajik jeonghaji anasseoyo |
| A How long are you staying? | 얼마나 머무를 예정이에요?<br>eolmana meomureul yejeongieyo |
| B I'm staying for 3 days. | 3일이요.<br>sam-iriyo |
| I'm traveling <u>alone</u>. | <u>혼자</u> 여행하고 있어요.<br><u>honja</u> yeohaenghago isseoyo |

| alone | 혼자 honja |
| with my husband | 남편과 nampyeongwa |
| with my wife | 아내와 anaewa |
| with my family | 가족과 gajokgwa |
| with my friend | 친구와 chinguwa |

| I don't speak Korean well. | 전 한국어를 잘 못해요.<br>jeon hangugeoreul jal motaeyo |

| Can I get a translator, please? | 통역사 좀 불러 주시겠어요?<br>tongyeoksa jom bulleo jusigesseoyo |
| How much cash do you have with you? | 현금은 얼마나 가지고 계세요?<br>hyeongeumeun eolmana gajigo gyeseyo |
| A Is this your first visit? | 이 나라는 처음이에요?<br>i naraneun cheo-eumieyo |
| B Yes, it is. | 네, 처음이에요.<br>ne cheo-eumieyo |
| A Do you have a return ticket? | 돌아가는 항공권은 가지고 있어요?<br>doraganeun hanggonggwoneun gajigo isseoyo |
| B Yes, I do. | 네, 있어요.<br>ne isseoyo |

## BAGGAGE CLAIM

| Where is the baggage claim area? | 수하물은 어디에서 찾아요?<br>suhamureun eodieseo chajayo |
| That's mine. | 그건 제 거예요.<br>geugeon je geoyeyo |
| Get that black suitcase for me, please. | 저 까만 가방 좀 주시겠어요?<br>jeo kkaman gabang jom jusigesseoyo |

| black | 까만 kkaman |
| white | 하얀 hayan |
| red | 빨간 ppalgan |
| big | 큰 keun |
| small | 작은 jageun |

* Refer to the page 368 for colors.

| Is the baggage from KE 608 on the carousel? | KE 608편 짐은 나왔어요?<br>keii yukgongpal-pyeon jimeun nawasseoyo |
| I can't find my luggage. | 제 수하물이 안 보이는데요.<br>je suhamuri an boineundeyo |
| Where's my luggage? | 제 수하물은 어디에 있어요?<br>je suhamureun eodie isseoyo |
| The airline lost my luggage. | 제 수하물이 없어졌어요.<br>je suhamuri eopseojyeosseoyo |
| One of my bags is missing. | 가방 한 개가 없어졌어요.<br>gabang han gaega eopseojyeosseoyo |
| Please help me find my baggage. | 제 짐 찾는 것 좀 도와주세요.<br>je jim channeun geot jom dowajuseyo |
| I've lost a small red bag. | 없어진 짐은 빨간 작은 가방이에요.<br>eopseojin jimeun ppalgan jageun gabangieyo |
| Could I see your baggage claim tag? | 수하물표를 좀 보여 주시겠어요?<br>suhamulpyoreul jom boyeo jusigesseoyo |

| | |
|---|---|
| Where is the Lost and Found? | 분실물 신고 창구는 어디예요?<br>bunsilmul singo changguneun eodiyeyo |
| A What flight did you arrive on? | 어떤 비행기를 타셨어요?<br>eotteon bihaenggireul tasyeosseoyo |
| B KE 708. | KE 항공 708편이에요.<br>keii hanggong chilgongpal-pyeonieyo |
| Please fill out this form. | 이 양식을 작성해 주세요.<br>i yangsigeul jakseonghae juseyo |
| How long will it take to find it? | 찾는데 시간이 얼마나 걸립니까?<br>channeunde sigani eolmana geollimnikka |
| I'm sorry, but I think your bag is on the next plane. | 죄송합니다만, 손님의 가방은 다음 비행기로 올 것 같습니다.<br>joesonghamnidaman, sonnimui gabangeun da-eum bihaenggiro ol geot gasseumnida |
| A How long will I have to wait for it? | 얼마나 기다려야 해요?<br>eolmana gidaryeoya haeyo |
| B It shouldn't be more than <u>three</u> hours. | 세 시간은 안 넘습니다.<br><u>se</u> siganeun an neomseumnida<br>* Refer to page 345 for numerals.<br>* Refer to page 356 for times. |
| Please call me when you find my baggage. | 제 수하물을 찾으면 제게 전화해 주세요.<br>je suhamureul chajeumyeon jege jeonhwahae juseyo |

| Please send it to the hotel as soon as you find the bag. | 짐을 찾는 대로 호텔로 보내 주세요.<br>jimeul channeun daero hotello bonae juseyo |
|---|---|
| A We'll send it to your hotel as soon as it arrives. | 도착하는 대로 저희가 호텔로 보내드리겠습니다.<br>dochakaneun daero jeohuiga hotello bonaedeurigesseumnida |
| B Alright, thanks for your help. | 알겠습니다. 도와 주셔서 감사합니다.<br>algesseumnida dowa jusyeoseo gamsahamnida |

If your luggage is missing at the airport, report it to the baggage claim center. Have the airline crew check the cargo compartment. Just in case, keep the claim tag with you. If you can't find your baggage, report it to the airline service center. Put a name tag with your name, address and phone number on your bag.

## CUSTOMS

| A Can I have your customs declaration card? | 세관신고서를 보여주시겠어요?<br>segwansingoseoreul boyeojusigesseoyo |
|---|---|
| B I don't have a customs declaration card. | 세관신고서를 가지고 있지 않아요.<br>segwansingoseoreul gajigo itji anayo |

| | |
|---|---|
| What's in it? | 안에 뭐가 있나요?<br>ane mwoga innayo |
| Please open this bag. | 가방 좀 열어주시겠어요?<br>gabang jom yeoreojusigesseoyo |
| These are my personal belongings. | 제 소지품입니다.<br>je sojipumimnida |
| It's not new. | 새 물건이 아니에요.<br>sae mulgeoni anieyo |
| I've been using this <u>camera</u>. | 이 <u>카메라</u>는 제가 사용하던 거예요.<br>i <u>kameraneun</u> jega sayonghadeon geoyeyo |

. . . . . . . . . . . . . . . . . . . . . . . . . . . . . . . . . . . . . . . . . .

| | |
|---|---|
| camera | 카메라는 kameraneun |
| bag | 가방은 gabang-eun |
| watch | 시계는 sigyeneun |

. . . . . . . . . . . . . . . . . . . . . . . . . . . . . . . . . . . . . . . . . .

| | |
|---|---|
| These are gifts. | 이건 선물이에요.<br>igeon seonmurieyo |
| These are presents for my <u>friends</u>. | <u>친구</u>에게 줄 선물이에요.<br><u>chingu</u>ege jul seonmurieyo |

. . . . . . . . . . . . . . . . . . . . . . . . . . . . . . . . . . . . . . . . . .

| | |
|---|---|
| friends | 친구 chin-gu |
| family | 가족 gajok |

. . . . . . . . . . . . . . . . . . . . . . . . . . . . . . . . . . . . . . . . . .

| | |
|---|---|
| May I close my bag now? | 이제 가방을 닫아도 돼요?<br>ije gabang-eul dadado dwaeyo |

| Do I have to pay any duty? | 관세를 물어야 해요? |
| | gwansereul mureoya haeyo |
| You will have to pay duty on this. | 이건 세금을 내셔야 합니다. |
| | igeon segeumeul naesyeoya hamnida |
| How much do I need to pay? | 얼마를 내야 해요? |
| | eolmareul naeya haeyo |
| Where do I pay? | 어디에서 내야 해요? |
| | eodieseo naeya haeyo |
| Can I pay with dollars? | 달러로 내도 돼요? |
| | dalleoro naedo dwaeyo |
| This is my luggage. | 이게 제 수하물이에요. |
| | ige je suhamurieyo |
| This is all I have. | 이게 전부예요. |
| | ige jeonbuyeyo |
| A Do you have anything to declare? | 신고할 것이 있습니까? |
| | singohal geosi isseumnikka |
| B I have nothing to declare. | 신고할 게 없어요. |
| | singohal ge eopseoyo |
| I have two cartons of cigarettes. | 담배 두 보루가 있어요. |
| | dambae du boruga isseoyo |

| two cartons of cigarettes | 담배 두 보루가 dambae du boruga |
| three bottles of whiskey | 위스키 세 병이 wiseuki se byeong-i |
| four bottles of gin | 진 네 병이 jin ne byeong-i |
| five bottles of wine | 와인 다섯 병이 wain daseot byeong-i |

\* Refer to page 349 for countings.

| Where's customs? | 세관이 어디에 있어요? |
| | segwani eodie isseoyo |

| Here's my customs declaration form. | 제 세관 서류예요. |
| | je segwan seoryuyeyo |

---

You must present your bags for customs inspection, and they may be opened. An oral declaration of your personal belongings will be sufficient except in some circumstances, in which case, you'll have to fill out a written declaration: arrival by ship or articles in excess of the duty-free allowance.

---

## TOURIST INFORMATION CENTER

| Where is the tourist information center? | 관광 안내소는 어디에 있어요? |
| | gwangwang annaeseoneun eodie isseoyo |

| May I have a guidebook? | 안내서를 얻을 수 있을까요? |
| | annaeseoreul eodeul su isseulkkayo |

| | |
|---|---|
| Are there English guidebooks for <u>Seoul</u>? | 영어로 된 서울 여행안내서 있나요?<br>yeong-eoro doen <u>seoul</u><br>yeohaeng-annaeseo innayo |
| Seoul<br>Jejudo | 서울 seoul<br>제주도 jejudo |

* Refer to page 365 for cities.

| | |
|---|---|
| Which guidebook would you recommend? | 어떤 여행안내서가 좋을까요?<br>eotteon yeohaeng-annaeseoga<br>jo-eulkkayo |
| Where can I buy a guidebook? | 여행안내서를 어디서 살 수 있어요?<br>yeohaeng-annaeseoreul eodiseo sal<br>su isseoyo |
| A sightseeing map, please. | 관광지도 한 장 주세요.<br>gwangwangjido han jang juseyo |
| Can I have a subway map? | 지하철 노선도를 얻을 수 있을까요?<br>jihacheol noseondoreul eodeul su<br>isseulkkayo |
| A list of hotels, please. | 호텔 목록 한 장 주세요.<br>hotel mongnok han jang juseyo |
| Can you recommend a cheap hotel? | 값싼 호텔 한 군데 추천해 주시겠어요?<br>gapssan hotel han gunde<br>chucheonhae jusigesseoyo |
| Can I reserve a hotel room here? | 여기서 호텔을 예약할 수 있어요?<br>yeogiseo hotereul yeyakal su isseoyo |

| Can you make a reservation for me? | 예약 좀 해 주시겠어요?<br>yeyak jom hae jusigesseoyo |
|---|---|
| How can I get to the youth hostel? | 유스호스텔까지 어떻게 가면 돼요?<br>yuseuhoseutelkkaji eotteoke gamyeon dwaeyo |
| Could you draw me a map? | 약도를 그려 주시겠어요?<br>yakdoreul geuryeo jusigesseoyo |
| Can I use the telephone? | 전화를 좀 쓸 수 있을까요?<br>jeonhwareul jom sseul su isseulkkayo |
| A What is the best place to see? | 구경하기 제일 좋은 곳이 어디예요?<br>gugyeonghagi jeil jo-eun gosi eodiyeyo |
| B Jejudo Island is a good place. | 제주도가 좋아요.<br>jejudoga joayo |
| A Can you recommend some interesting places? | 불만한 곳을 알려 주시겠어요?<br>bolmanhan goseul allyeo jusigesseoyo |
| B I recommend <u>Gyeongju</u>. | <u>경주를</u> 권해 드리고 싶어요.<br><u>gyeongjureul</u> gwonhae deurigo sipeoyo |

\* Refer to page 365 for cities.

| How can I get there? | 거기는 어떻게 가요?<br>geogineun eotteoke gayo |
|---|---|
| Can I get there on foot? | 걸어서 갈 수 있어요?<br>georeoseo gal su isseoyo |

| You'd better take a bus. | 버스를 타는 게 좋을 거예요. |
| | beoseureul taneun ge joeul geoyeyo |
| Where can I go for a day trip? | 하루만에 다녀올 만한 곳이 어딘가요? |
| | harumane danyeo-ol manhan gosi eodingayo |
| Could you call a taxi for me? | 택시를 한 대 불러 주세요. |
| | taeksireul han dae bulleo juseyo |
| I'd like to rent a car. | 차를 빌리고 싶어요. |
| | chareul billigo sipeoyo |

## TRANSPORTATION

| I want to go to Namsan in Seoul. | 서울 남산에 가려고 해요. |
| | seoul namsane garyeogo haeyo |

| Namsan | 남산 namsan |
| Namdaemun | 남대문 namdaemun |
| Dongdaemun | 동대문 dongdaemun |
| Myeong-dong | 명동 myeongdong |
| Insa-dong | 인사동 insadong |

| What's the best way to go there? | 어떻게 가는 게 가장 좋아요? |
| | eotteoke ganeun ge gajang joayo |
| It says on the sign there. | 저쪽 안내표지판을 보시면 알 수 있어요. |
| | jeojjok annaepyojipaneul bosimyeon al su isseoyo |

| | |
|---|---|
| Where do I get on? | 어디서 탈 수 있어요?<br>eodiseo tal su isseoyo |
| How long does it take? | 얼마나 걸려요?<br>eolmana geollyeoyo |

## Bus

| | |
|---|---|
| Where can I take the bus to downtown? | 시내로 가는 버스를 타는 곳이 어디예요?<br>sinaero ganeun beoseureul taneun gosi eodiyeyo |
| Where is the bus stop? | 버스 정류장은 어디에 있어요?<br>beoseu jeongnyujangeun eodie isseoyo |
| When does the next one leave? | 다음 차는 언제 가요?<br>da-eum chaneun eonje gayo |
| How much is the fare? | 요금은 얼마예요?<br>yogeumeun eolmayeyo |
| I want to go to the airport bus counter. | 공항버스 카운터에 가려고 해요.<br>gonghangbeoseu kaunteo-e garyeogo haeyo |
| Is there an airport bus to the city? | 시내로 가는 공항버스가 있어요?<br>sinaero ganeun gonghangbeoseuga isseoyo |
| Is there a bus to <u>Seoul Hotel</u>? | <u>서울 호텔</u> 가는 버스가 있나요?<br><u>seoul hotel</u> ganeun beoseuga innayo |

| | |
|---|---|
| Lotte Hotel | 롯데 호텔 lotte hotel |
| Shilla Hotel | 신라 호텔 shilla hotel |

| Please let me know where to get off. | 내릴 때가 되면 좀 알려 주시겠어요?<br>naeril ttaega doemyeon jom allyeo jusigesseoyo |
|---|---|
| I am getting off at the next stop. | 다음 정류장에서 내려요.<br>da-eum jeongnyujangeseo naeryeoyo |
| I took the wrong bus. | 버스를 잘못 탔어요.<br>beoseureul jalmot tasseoyo |
| I missed my stop. | 내릴 곳을 지나쳤어요.<br>naeril goseul jinachyeosseoyo |

## Taxi

| Where's the taxi stand? | 택시 타는 곳이 어디예요?<br>taeksi taneun gosi eodiyeyo |
|---|---|
| A Where would you like to go? | 어디로 가세요?<br>eodiro gaseyo |
| B Take me to Seoul Hotel, please. | 서울 호텔로 가 주세요.<br>seoul hotello ga juseyo |
| B Take me to this address, please. | 이 주소로 가 주세요.<br>i jusoro ga juseyo |
| Can I put my bag in the trunk? | 트렁크에 짐을 실을 수 있어요?<br>teureongkeue jimeul sireul su isseoyo |
| How long is it to Seoul? | 서울까지는 얼마나 걸려요?<br>seoulkkajineun eolmana geollyeoyo |

I'm running late.
Could you go a little
faster, please.

늦었어요. 서둘러 주세요.
neujeosseoyo seodulleo juseyo

Please slow down.

천천히 가 주세요.
cheoncheonhi ga juseyo

How much will it cost?

요금은 얼마나 나와요?
yogeumeun eolmana nawayo

Could you wait for me
for a while?

여기서 잠시만 기다려 주세요.
yeogiseo jamsiman gidaryeo juseyo

Please pull over here.

여기에 세워 주세요.
yeogie sewo juseyo

How much is it?

요금은 얼마예요?
yogeumeun eolmayeyo

Here we are.

호텔에 다 왔습니다.
hotere da wasseumnida

Thank you. Keep the
change.

감사합니다. 잔돈은 가지세요.
gamsahamnida jandoneun gajiseyo

Thank you for the ride.

태워 주셔서 감사합니다.
taewo jusyeoseo gamsahamnida

## Subway

Where is the subway
station?

지하철역은 어디에 있어요?
jihacheollyeogeun eodie isseoyo

| What is the nearest subway station from here? | 여기에서 가장 가까운 지하철역은 어디예요? |
| | yeogieseo gajang gakkaun jihacheollyeogeun eodiyeyo |
| How can I get to downtown? | 시내까지 가려면 어떻게 가야 해요? |
| | sinaekkaji garyeomyeon eotteoke gaya haeyo |
| Can I get a subway map? | 지하철 노선도를 얻을 수 있어요? |
| | jihacheol noseondoreul eodeul su isseoyo |
| Where is the ticket booth? | 매표소는 어디에 있나요? |
| | maepyosoneun eodie innayo |
| How much is the fare? | 요금이 얼마예요? |
| | yogeumi eolmayeyo |
| Where can I buy a ticket? | 표는 어디에서 사요? |
| | pyoneun eodieseo sayo |
| Where is the ticket machine? | 표 판매기가 어디에 있어요? |
| | pyo panmaegiga eodie isseoyo |
| Which machine should I use? | 어떤 기계를 사용해야 해요? |
| | eotteon gigyereul sayonghaeya haeyo |
| Where can I buy a single-use ticket? | 일회용 교통카드 발매기는 어디에 있어요? |
| | ilhoeyong gyotongkadeu balmaegineun eodie isseoyo |

| How do I use this machine? | 이것은 어떻게 사용해요? |
| | igeoseun eotteoke sayonghaeyo |

| How many stations is it from here? | 몇 정거장 가야 돼요? |
| | myeot jeonggeojang gaya dwaeyo |

| Do I need to transfer? | 갈아타야 해요? |
| | garataya haeyo |

| How many times do I need to transfer? | 몇 번이나 갈아타야 해요? |
| | myeot beonina garataya haeyo |

| Where do I need to transfer? | 어디에서 갈아타야 해요? |
| | eodieseo garataya haeyo |

| Get off at the second stop. | 두 번째 정거장에서 내리세요. |
| | du beonjjae jeonggeojangeseo naeriseyo |

---

| first | 첫 cheot |
| second | 두 du |
| third | 세 se |

* Refer to page 345 for ordinal numerals.

---

| Which line do I change to? | 몇 호선으로 갈아타야 해요? |
| | myeot hoseoneuro garataya haeyo |

| What's the next station? | 다음 역은 어디예요? |
| | da-eum yeogeun eodiyeyo |

| Could you tell me when to get off? | 내릴 곳에서 좀 알려 주시겠어요? |
| | naeril goseseo jom allyeo jusigesseoyo |

# Car Rent

| I want to rent a car. | 차를 렌트하고 싶어요. |
| | chareul renteuhago sipeoyo |

| A What kind of car do you want? | 어떤 차를 원하세요? |
| | eotteon chareul wonhaseyo |

| B I would like to rent a <u>compact car</u>. | <u>소형차</u>를 빌리고 싶어요. |
| | <u>sohyeongchareul</u> billigo sipeoyo |

- - - - - - - - - - - - - - - - - - - - - - - - - - - - - - - - - - - -

| compact car | 소형차를 sohyeongchareul |
| sedan | 승용차를 seungyongchareul |
| limousine | 리무진을 rimujineul |
| van | 승합차를 / 밴을 |
| | seunghapchareul / baeneul |

- - - - - - - - - - - - - - - - - - - - - - - - - - - - - - - - - - - -

| Please have a look at this list. | 이 목록을 보세요. |
| | i mongnogeul boseyo |

| Do you have an international driver's license? | 국제 면허증이 있으세요? |
| | gukje myeonheojeung-i isseuseyo |

| I would like to rent a car for <u>a week</u>. | 차를 <u>일주일</u> 동안 빌리려고 해요. |
| | chareul <u>iljuil</u> dongan billiryeogo haeyo |
| | * Refer to page 356 for times. |

| How much is it to rent a car? | 렌트 요금이 얼마예요? |
| | renteu yogeumi eolmayeyo |

What's the rate per day?

하루에 얼마예요?

harue eolmayeyo

Do I need to leave a deposit?

보증금이 필요한가요?

bojeunggeumi piryohangayo

I'd like to rent this car for three days.

이 차로 3일간 빌리고 싶은데요.

i charo sam-ilgan billigo sipeundeyo

I would like to buy insurance.

보험을 들어 주세요.

boheomeul deureo juseyo

Can I return the car to a different location?

다른 장소에 반납할 수 있나요?

dareun jangsoe bannapal su innayo

# MONEY EXCHANGE

## LOCATING MONEY EXCHANGE

| | |
|---|---|
| Where is the currency exchange? | 환전소가 어디에 있어요?<br>hwanjeonsoga eodie isseoyo |
| Where can I change <u>money</u>? | 돈 바꾸는 곳이 어디에 있어요?<br><u>don</u> bakkuneun gosi eodie isseoyo |

| | |
|---|---|
| money | 돈 don |
| dollar | 달러 dalleo |
| euro | 유로화 yurohwa |
| traveler's check | 여행자 수표 yeohaengja supyo |
| personal check | 개인용 수표 gaeinnyong supyo |

| | |
|---|---|
| Excuse me, where is the nearest currency exchange counter from here? | 실례합니다만 여기에서 가장 가까운 환전소가 어디에 있나요?<br>sillyehamnidaman yeogieseo gajang gakkaun hwanjeonsoga eodie innayo |
| I want to exchange money, but are there any banks nearby? | 환전을 하려고 하는데 이 근처에 은행이 있나요?<br>hwanjeoneul haryeogo haneunde i geuncheo-e eunhaeng-i innayo |
| Can you show me the way to get to the currency exchange counter? | 환전소로 가는 길 좀 알려 주시겠어요?<br>hwanjeonsoro ganeun gil jom allyeo jusigesseoyo |

| How can I get to the currency exchange counter? | 환전소까지 어떻게 가야 해요?<br>hwanjeonsokkaji eotteoke gaya haeyo |
| --- | --- |
| How long does it take to get to the currency exchange counter? | 환전소까지 얼마나 걸려요?<br>hwanjeonsokkaji eolmana geollyeoyo |
| Is the currency exchange open? | 환전소 열었어요?<br>hwanjeonso yeoreosseoyo |
| How late is the currency exchange counter open? | 그 환전소는 몇 시까지 문을 열어요?<br>geu hwanjeonsoneun myeot sikkaji muneul yeoreoyo |
| Can I get to the currency exchange counter on foot? | 환전소까지 걸어갈 수 있어요?<br>hwanjeonsokkaji georeogal su isseoyo |

## AT THE MONEY EXCHANGE

| Can I exchange money here? | 여기서 환전할 수 있나요?<br>yeogiseo hwanjeonhal su innayo |
| --- | --- |
| Which window is for currency exchange? | 환전 창구가 어디에 있습니까?<br>hwanjeon changguga eodie isseumnikka |
| How much money can I exchange? | 얼마까지 환전할 수 있어요?<br>eolmakkaji hwanjeonhal su isseoyo |

|  |  |
|---|---|
| What should I bring with me when I exchange money? | 환전을 할 때 뭐가 필요해요?<br>hwanjeoneul hal ttae mwoga piryohaeyo |
| Do I need to fill out a form? | 서류를 써야 하나요?<br>seoryureul sseoya hanayo |
| A May I see your passport, please? | 여권을 보여 주시겠어요?<br>yeogwoneul boyeo jusigesseoyo |
| B Here's my passport. | 제 여권이에요.<br>je yeogwonieyo |
| May I cash traveler's checks here? | 여행자 수표를 현금으로 바꿀 수 있어요?<br>yeohaengja supyoreul hyeon-geumeuro bakkul su isseoyo |
| Cash a traveler's check, please. | 여행자 수표를 현금으로 바꿔 주세요.<br>yeohaengja supyoreul hyeon-geumeuro bakkwo juseyo |
| I'd like to change <u>dollar</u> into won. | <u>달러</u>를 원화로 바꾸고 싶어요.<br><u>dalleoreul</u> wonhwaro bakkugo sipeoyo |

| | |
|---|---|
| dollar | 달러를 dalleoreul |
| pound | 파운드를 paundeureul |
| euro | 유로화를 yurohwareul |

| | |
|---|---|
| What's today's dollar to won exchange rate? | 오늘 달러와 원화 환율이 얼마예요?<br>oneul dalleowa wonhwa hwanyuri eolmayeyo |

90

| I'd like to change <u>100</u> dollars to won. | <u>100달러를 원화로 바꾸고 싶습니다.</u><br>baek-dalleoreul wonhwaro bakkugo sipseumnida |
|---|---|

| 100 | 백 baek |
|---|---|
| 200 | 이백 ibaek |
| 300 | 삼백 sambaek |
| 400 | 사백 sabaek |
| 500 | 오백 obaek |
| 600 | 육백 yukbaek |
| 700 | 칠백 chilbaek |
| 800 | 팔백 palbaek |
| 900 | 구백 gubaek |

| I'd like the money in <u>large bills</u>. | <u>고액권으로 주세요.</u><br>goaekgwoneuro juseyo |
|---|---|

| in large bills | 고액원으로 goaekgwoneuro |
|---|---|
| in small bills | 소액권으로 soaekgwoneuro |

| Please exchange twenty <u>100,000</u> won notes, ten <u>50,000</u> won notes, and ten <u>10,000</u> won notes. | <u>100,000원 권 20장, 50,000원 권 10장,</u><br><u>10,000원 권 10장으로 바꿔 주세요.</u><br>simman-won gwon isipjang oman-won gwon yeoljang <u>man</u>-won gwon yeoljang-euro bakkwo juseyo<br>* Refer to page 95 for money. |
|---|---|

| Could you change this bill into coins? | 이 지폐를 동전으로 바꿔 주시겠어요?<br>i jipyereul dongjeoneuro bakkwo jusigesseoyo |
|---|---|

| | |
|---|---|
| Could you include coins? | 동전도 함께 섞어서 주시겠어요?<br>dongjeondo hamkke seokkeoseo jusigesseoyo |
| How much can I withdraw with this international bank card? | 이 국제현금카드로 얼마까지 인출할 수 있어요?<br>i gukjehyeon-geumkadeuro eolmakkaji inchulhal su isseoyo |
| How much will this be in won? | 이 금액을 원화로 바꾸면 얼마예요?<br>i geumaegeul wonhwaro bakkumyeon eolmayeyo |
| Is this exchange coupon available? | 이 환율 우대 쿠폰을 사용할 수 있나요?<br>i hwanyul udae kuponeul sayonghal su innayo? |
| How much does it cost to exchange money? | 환전하는 데 수수료가 얼마예요?<br>hwanjeonhaneun de susuryoga eolmayeyo |
| Where can I get the lowest exchange costs? | 환전수수료 비용이 저렴한 곳이 어디예요?<br>hwanjeonsusuryo biyong-i jeoryeomhan gosi eodiyeyo |
| May I have a receipt, please? | 영수증을 주실래요?<br>yeongsujeung-eul jusillaeyo |
| The amount is not correct. | 돈이 맞지 않아요.<br>doni matji anayo |

# Korean Money

Toegye Yi Hwang (1501~1570)

Toegye Yi Hwang was a scholor in Joseon Dynasty. He founded Dosan Seowon School where he fostered young scholoars.

Yulgok Yi Yi (1536~1584)

Yulgok Yi Yi was a scholar in the Joseon Dynasty. He insisted on having one hundred thousand soldiers to protect the country. He was wise and visionary.

King Sejong the Great (1397~1450)

King Sejong the Great invented Hangeul, or the Korean alphabet. He also made many contributions to national security, science, economics, and culture.

Shin Saimdang (1504~1551)

Shin Saimdang was a mother of Yulgok Yi Yi, and a symbol of a wise wife. As a female artist, she left many splendid poems and paintings.

Dabotap Pagoda

Dabotap Pagoda is in Bulguksa Temple in Gyeongju. It is a representative structure of ancient Shilla. It has a structural beauty.

Ear of rice

The coin is to celebrate World Food Day made by International Food and Agriculture Organization. Rice is a main dish of Korean people.

Admiral Yi Sunshin

Yi Sunshin was a general in the Joseon Dynasty. He devised *geobukseon*, or Turtle Ship and led victorious sea battles.

Crane

A Crane is a symbol of a scholar. It is considered sacred.

## Currency Unit

| | |
|---|---|
| 10 won | 10원 sip-won |
| 50 won | 50원 osip-won |
| 100 won | 100원 baek-won |
| 500 won | 500원 obaek-won |
| 1,000 won | 1,000원 cheon-won |
| 5,000 won | 5,000원 ocheon-won |
| 10,000 won | 10,000원 man-won |
| 50,000 won | 50,000원 oman-won |
| 100,000 won | 100,000원 simman-won |
| 500,000 won | 500,000원 osimman-won |
| 1,000,000 won | 1,000,000원 baengman-won |
| 5,000,000 won | 5,000,000원 obaengman-won |

## Exchange List

Please exchange like this.
이렇게 환전 좀 해 주세요.
ireoke hwanjeon jom hae juseyo

| | |
|---|---|
| 10원짜리 _____개 | sip-wonjjari _____gae |
| 50원짜리 _____개 | osip-wonjjari _____gae |
| 100원짜리 _____개 | baek-wonjjari _____gae |
| 500원짜리 _____개 | obaek-wonjjari _____gae |
| 1,000원짜리 _____장 | cheon-wonjjari _____jang |
| 5,000원짜리 _____장 | ocheon-wonjjari _____jang |
| 10,000원짜리 _____장 | man-wonjjari _____jang |
| 50,000원짜리 _____장 | oman-wonjjari _____jang |

* Refer to page 345 for numerals.

# AT THE HOTEL

## TO THE HOTEL

I'd like to go to the
Seoul Hotel.

서울 호텔로 가려고 해요.
seoul hotello garyeogo haeyo

Where is the bus
stop?

버스 정류장이 어디예요?
beoseu jeongnyujang-i eodiyeyo

Which buses go into
town?

어떤 버스가 시내로 가요?
eotteon beoseuga sinaero gayo

Where can I get a taxi?

택시를 어디서 타요?
taeksireul eodiseo tayo

How much is the fare?

요금은 얼마예요?
yogeumeun eolmayeyo

## RESERVATION

I'd like to book
a room.

방을 예약하고 싶은데요.
bangeul yeyakago sipeundeyo

I'm calling to make
a reservation for two
rooms.

방 두 개를 예약하려고 합니다.
bang du gaereul yeyakaryeogo
hamnida

* Refer to page 349 for countings.

96

| My name is _____. | 제 이름은 _____입니다. |
| | je ireumeun_____ imnida |

| My card number is 1111-2222-3333-4444. | 카드번호는 1111-2222-3333-4444입니다. |
| | kadeubeonhoneun il-il-il-il i-i-i-i sam-sam-sam-sam sa-sa-sa-sa imnida |

* Refer to page 345 for numerals.

| What type of room would you like? | 어떤 방을 원하세요? |
| | eotteon bang-eul wonhaseyo |

| How many in your group? | 몇 분이십니까? |
| | myeot bunisimnikka |

| What's the daily rate? | 하루 숙박료가 얼마예요? |
| | haru sukbangnyoga eolmayeyo |

| A What's your arrival date? | 도착하시는 날짜가 언제입니까? |
| | dochakasineun naljjaga eonjeimnikka |

| B September 9th. | 9월 9일입니다. |
| | gu-wol gu-irimnida |

* Refer to page 353 for dates.

| A How long will you be staying? | 얼마나 계실 겁니까? |
| | eolmana gyesil geomnikka |

| B Three nights, please. | 3일간 묵으려고 합니다. |
| | sam-ilgan mugeuryeogo hamnida |

| I'm planning to stay for two nights next week. | 다음주에 2일간 숙박할 예정이에요. |
| | da-eumjue i-ilgan sukbakal yejeong-ieyo |

AT THE HOTEL

**A** How would you like to pay?

숙박비는 어떻게 지불하시겠습니까?

sukbakbineun eotteoke jibulhasigesseumnikka

**B** I'll pay with credit card.

신용카드로 계산하겠습니다.

sinyongkadeuro gyesanhagesseumnida

Do I need to leave a deposit?

선금을 내야 합니까?

seongeumeul naeya hamnikka

Will you give me a discount if I stay longer?

장기 투숙하면 할인 되나요?

janggi tusukamyeon harin doenayo

Isn't there any other way? Please, help me.

방법이 없을까요? 좀 도와주세요.

bangbeobi eopseulkkayo jom dowajuseyo

Isn't there other hotels around? Can you recommend one?

근처에 다른 호텔이 있어요? 한 곳 추천해 주세요.

geuncheo-e dareun hoteri isseoyo han got chucheonhae juseyo

Do you have any cheaper rooms?

좀 싼 방 있어요?

jom ssan bang isseoyo

I need a room with Internet access.

인터넷이 되는 방으로 부탁해요.

inteonesi doeneun bang-euro butakaeyo

Does the rate include any service charges?

숙박료에 봉사료가 포함돼요?

sukbangnyoe bongsaryoga pohamdwaeyo

| Does that include breakfast? | 숙박료에 아침 식사가 포함됩니까?<br>sukbangnyoe achim siksaga pohamdoemnikka |
| --- | --- |
| Do you have any special packages? | 패키지 상품이 있어요?<br>paekiji sangpumi isseoyo |
| Does this price include all the service charges? | 서비스 요금을 모두 포함한 가격이에요?<br>seobiseu yogeumeul modu pohamhan gagyeogieyo |
| Is there a discount for children? | 아이들은 요금 할인이 있나요?<br>aideureun yogeum harini innayo |
| Is there a charge for babies? | 아기도 요금 받아요?<br>agido yogeum badayo |

## CHECKING-IN

| I'm checking in. | 체크인하려고 하는데요.<br>chekeu-inharyeogo haneundeyo |
| --- | --- |
| A Do you have a reservation? | 예약하셨어요?<br>yeyakasyeosseoyo |
| B I have a reservation. | 예약을 했어요.<br>yeyageul haesseoyo |
| B I don't have a reservation. | 예약을 하지 않았어요.<br>yeyageul haji anasseoyo |
| What name is it under? | 어느 분 성함으로 예약하셨어요?<br>eoneu bun seonghameuro yeyakasyeosseoyo |

| This is my confirmation paper. | 예약 확인서입니다. |
| | yeyak hwaginseoimnida |

| I don't have a reservation, but can I get a room? | 예약은 안 했는데 방 있어요? |
| | yeyageun an haenneunde bang isseoyo |

| A How many are there in your group? | 몇 분이세요? |
| | myeot buniseyo |

| B Two adults. | 어른 두 명이에요. |
| | eoreun du myeongieyo |

\* Refer to page 349 for countings.

| I'd like a single room. | 싱글룸 하나 부탁합니다. |
| | singgeullum hana butakamnida |

........................................................

a single room 싱글룸 하나 singgeullum hana
two single rooms 일인용 방 둘 irinnyong bang dul
a suite 스위트 하나 seuwiteu hana

........................................................

| I'd like a room with a doule bed. | 더블 베드가 있는 방 하나 부탁합니다. |
| | deobeul bedeuga inneun bang hana butakamnida |

........................................................

with twin beds 트윈 베드가 있는 teuwin bedeuga inneun
with a shower 샤워실이 있는 syawosiri inneun
with a nice view 전망이 좋은 jeonmang-i jo-eun
facing the mountain 산이 보이는 sani boineun
facing the ocean 바다가 보이는 badaga boineun
facing the street 도로가 보이는 doroga boineun
facing the courtyard 정원이 보이는 jeongwoni boineun

........................................................

| I need a baby crib in the room, please. | 유아용 침대 좀 부탁해요. |
| | yuayong chimdae jom butakaeyo |
| How many days will you be staying? | 얼마 동안 계실 겁니까? |
| | eolma dong-an gyesil geomnikka |
| I'll be staying just for tonight. | <u>오늘 밤만</u> 머물 겁니다. |
| | oneul bamman meomul geomnida |

---

| just for tonight | 오늘 밤만 oneul bamman |
| for a week | 일주일 동안 iljuil dong-an |
| at least for a week | 적어도 일주일은 jeogeodo iljuireun |

---

| Do you have a room? | 빈 방 있어요? |
| | bin bang isseoyo |
| May I see the room? | 방 좀 보여 주시겠어요? |
| | bang jom boyeo jusigesseoyo |
| Please fill out the registration card. | 숙박카드를 기입해 주세요. |
| | sukbak-kadeureul giipae juseyo |
| Could you tell me how to fill out a registration card? | 숙박카드는 어떻게 기입해야 해요? |
| | sukbak-kadeuneun eotteoke giipaeya haeyo |
| Please fill out this form and sign here. | 이 양식에 기입하신 후에 사인해 주세요. |
| | i yangsige giipasin hue sainhae juseyo |
| What do I have to fill out? | 어떤 것을 써야 해요? |
| | eotteon geoseul sseoya haeyo |

| Can I write it like this? | 이렇게 쓰면 돼요?<br>ireoke sseumyeon dwaeyo |
|---|---|
| What time do I have to check out? | 몇 시에 체크아웃을 해야 해요?<br>myeot sie chekeuauseul haeya haeyo |
| What floor is it on? | 몇 층에 있어요?<br>myeot cheung-e isseoyo |
| Can I use the room right now? | 방에 지금 들어갈 수 있어요?<br>bang-e jigeum deureogal su isseoyo |
| I need some help with my bags. | 짐을 방으로 옮겨 주세요.<br>jimeul bang-euro omgyeo juseyo |
| Could you hold my baggage for me before I check in? | 방을 이용할 수 있을 때까지 제 짐 좀 보관해 주시겠어요?<br>bang-eul iyonghal su isseul ttaekkaji je jim jom bogwanhae jusigesseoyo |
| Could you check again? | 다시 한 번 확인 부탁드려요.<br>dasi han beon hwagin butakdeuryeoyo |
| I'd like to cancel my reservation. | 예약을 취소하고 싶어요.<br>yeyageul chwisohago sipeoyo |
| Please don't cancel my reservation. | 예약을 취소하지 마세요.<br>yeyageul chwisohaji maseyo |
| Is there another hotel nearby? | 이 근처에 다른 호텔이 있어요?<br>i geuncheo-e dareun hoteri isseoyo |

Check-in time is usually after 2 p.m. If you arrive at the hotel before check-in time, use their baggage hold service. You can walk around the hotel or go shopping. If you arrive a lot later than check-in time without having paid for your room, call the hotel so that you don't lose your reservation.

## CHANGING ROOMS

| | |
|---|---|
| It's too <u>big</u>. | 너무 <u>큰</u>데요.<br>neomu <u>keun</u>deyo |

| | |
|---|---|
| big | 큰 keun |
| small | 작은 jageun |
| dark | 어두운 eoduun |
| noisy | 시끄러운 sikkeureoun |

| | |
|---|---|
| Could I get a different room? | 다른 방으로 바꿀 수 있어요?<br>dareun bang-euro bakkul su isseoyo |
| Do you have a <u>better</u> room? | <u>더 좋은</u> 방 있어요?<br><u>deo jo-eun</u> bang isseoyo |

| | |
|---|---|
| better | 더 좋은 deo jo-eun |
| larger | 더 큰 deo keun |
| smaller | 더 작은 deo jageun |
| quieter | 더 조용한 deo joyonghan |

| Do you have a room with a better view? | 전망이 더 좋은 방 있어요? |
| | jeonmang-i deo jo-eun bang isseoyo |
| I'd like a room with more light. | 햇빛이 더 잘 드는 방 좀 부탁합니다. |
| | haetbichi deo jal deuneun bang jom butakamnida |

| with more light | 햇빛이 더 잘 드는 |
| | haetbichi deo jal deuneun |
| on a higher floor | 더 높은 층에 있는 |
| | deo nopeun cheung-e inneun |
| on a lower floor | 더 낮은 층에 있는 |
| | deo najeun cheung-e inneun |

## WITH THE DESK CLERK

| The key for Room 200, please. | 200호실 열쇠 좀 주세요. |
| | ibaek-hosil yeolsoe jom juseyo |
| | *Refer to page 345 for numerals. |
| Are there any messages for me? | 제게 온 메시지가 있나요? |
| | jege on mesijiga innayo |

| messages | 메시지 mesiji |
| letters | 편지 pyeonji |

| Could you keep this in your safe? | 이것 좀 금고에 넣어 주세요. |
| | igeot jom geumgo-e neoeo juseyo |

| I'd like to take my things out of your safe. | 제 물건 좀 금고에서 꺼내 주세요. |
| | je mulgeon jom geumgo-eseo kkeonae juseyo |
| Can I rent a laptop computer? | 노트북을 빌릴 수 있을까요? |
| | noteubugeul billil su isseulkkayo |
| Can I use a computer? | 컴퓨터를 사용할 수 있어요? |
| | keompyuteoreul sayonghal su isseoyo |

| a computer | 컴퓨터를 keompyuteoreul |
| a printer | 프린터를 peurinteoreul |
| the Internet | 인터넷을 inteoneseul |
| a fax machine | 팩스를 paekseureul |
| the business room | 비즈니스 룸을 bijeuniseu rumeul |

| Where's the elevator? | 엘리베이터가 어디에 있어요? |
| | ellibeiteoga eodie isseoyo |

| elevator | 엘리베이터가 ellibeiteoga |
| telephone | 전화가 jeonhwaga |
| bathroom | 욕실이 yoksiri |
| ladies' room | 여자 화장실이 yeoja hwajangsiri |
| men's room | 남자 화장실이 namja hwajangsiri |

| How do I control the air conditioner? | 에어컨은 어떻게 조절해요? |
| | e-eokeoneun eotteoke jojeolhaeyo |

| | |
|---|---|
| air conditioner | 에어컨은 e-eokeoneun |
| heater | 히터는 hiteoneun |

| | |
|---|---|
| Where can I plug in my <u>electric razor</u>? | <u>전기 면도기를 어디에 꽂아요?</u><br><u>jeon-gi myeondogireul eodie kkojayo</u> |

| | |
|---|---|
| electric razor | 전기 면도기를 jeon-gi myeondogireul |
| hairdryer | 헤어 드라이어를 he-eo deuraieoreul |

| | |
|---|---|
| Do you have an <u>adapter plug</u>? | <u>어댑터 플러그 있어요?</u><br><u>eodaepteo peulleogeu isseoyo</u> |

| | |
|---|---|
| adapter plug | 어댑터 플러그 eodaepteo peulleogeu |
| electric transformer | 변압기 byeonapgi |

| | |
|---|---|
| How does the shower work? | 샤워기는 어떻게 사용해요?<br>syawogineun eotteoke sayonghaeyo |
| Will you make my room warmer? | 방을 좀 더 따뜻하게 해 주시겠어요?<br>bang-eul jom deo ttatteutage hae jusigesseoyo |
| I need a bellhop. | 사람 좀 보내 주세요.<br>saram jom bonae juseyo |
| Please send <u>some towels</u> to my room. | 이 방에 <u>수건</u> 좀 보내 주세요.<br>i bang-e sugeon jom bonae juseyo |

| some towels | 수건 sugeon |
| some soap | 비누 binu |
| some hangers | 옷걸이 otgeori |
| a pillow | 베개 begae |
| a blanket | 담요 damnyo |
| some ice | 얼음 eoreum |
| some ice water | 냉수 naengsu |
| an ashtray | 재떨이 jaetteori |
| some toilet paper | 화장지 hwajangji |
| a luggage rack | 수화물대 suhwamuldae |

| Is room service available? | 룸서비스가 되나요?<br>rumseobiseuga doenayo |
| Untill when is room service available? | 룸서비스는 몇 시까지 하죠?<br>rumseobiseuneun myeot sikkaji hajyo |
| Is a babysitter available? | 애 보는 사람이 있어요?<br>ae boneun sarami isseoyo |
| Where is the emergency exit? | 비상구는 어디에 있어요?<br>bisangguneun eodie isseoyo |
| Are there any English-speaking staff? | 영어를 할 수 있는 직원이 있어요?<br>yeong-eoreul hal su inneun jigwoni isseoyo |
| Can I make a collect call? | 수신자 요금 부담으로 전화하고 싶습니다.<br>susinja yogeum budameuro jeonhwahago sipseumnida |

| Leave them on the counter, please. | 카운터에 맡겨 주세요. |
| | kaunteo-e matgyeo juseyo |
| Can I have a business card of the hotel? | 호텔 명함을 한 장 주세요. |
| | hotel myeonghameul han jang juseyo |

## USING FACILITIES

| Is there a <u>gym</u>? | <u>체육관이</u> 있어요? |
| | <u>cheyukgwani</u> isseoyo |

| gym | 체육관이 cheyukgwani |
| fitness center | 헬스 클럽이 helseu keulleobi |
| sauna | 사우나가 saunaga |
| swimming pool | 수영장이 suyeongjang-i |
| tennis court | 테니스 코트가 teniseu koteuga |

| What time does it open? | 몇 시에 열어요? |
| | myeot sie yeoreoyo |
| Is there a charge? | 입장료가 있어요? |
| | ipjangnyoga isseoyo |
| Does the hotel provide swimming suit rentals? | 수영복을 빌릴 수 있어요? |
| | suyeongbogeul billil su isseoyo |
| Do you have a separate swimming pool for kids? | 유아용 풀장이 따로 있어요? |
| | yuayong puljang-i ttaro isseoyo |

| What time is breakfast? | 아침 식사 시간은 몇 시예요? |
| | achim siksa siganeun myeot siyeyo |

| How late is the bar open? | 바는 언제까지 열어요? |
| | baneun eonjekkaji yeoreoyo |

| Which floor is the convention hall on? | 연회장은 몇 층이에요? |
| | yeonhoejang-eun myeot cheungieyo |

| Is there a <u>restaurant</u> in the hotel? | 호텔 안에 <u>식당</u>이 있어요? |
| | hotel ane <u>sikdang</u>-i isseoyo |

| restaurant | 식당이 sikdang-i |
| bar | 바가 baga |
| coffee shop | 커피숍이 keopisyobi |
| barbershop | 이발소가 ibalsoga |
| beauty parlor | 미용실이 miyongsiri |
| pharmacy | 약국이 yakgugi |
| snack bar | 스낵바가 seunaekbaga |

| Where is it? | 거기가 어디예요? |
| | geogiga eodiyeyo |

## IN THE ROOM

| I need <u>room service</u>, please. | <u>룸서비스</u> 좀 부탁합니다. |
| | <u>rumseobiseu</u> jom butakamnida |

| room service | 룸서비스 rumseobiseu |
| a masseur / a masseuse | 안마사 anmasa |
| a babysitter | 애 보는 사람 ae boneun saram |

Caffeine-free drink, please.
카페인 없는 음료를 부탁해요.
kapein eomneun eumnyoreul butakaeyo

Are there any snacks available?
간단한 식사를 할 수 있어요?
gandanhan siksareul hal su isseoyo

I'd like to order breakfast, please.
아침 식사를 부탁해요.
achim siksareul butakaeyo

A What time shall we bring it?
몇 시에 가져다 드릴까요?
myeot sie gajyeoda deurilkkayo

B At 8:00, please.
8시에 부탁합니다.
yeodeol-sie butakamnida

\* Refer to page 356 for times.

I need a wake-up call, please.
모닝콜 좀 부탁합니다.
moningkol jom butakamnida

Who is it?
누구세요?
nuguseyo

Just a minute.
잠깐만 기다리세요.
jamkkanman gidariseyo

Come in.
들어오세요.
deureo-oseyo

| Put it on the <u>table</u>, please. | 테이블 위에 놓아 주세요. |
| | <u>teibeul</u> wie noa juseyo |

---

| table | 테이블 teibeul |
| bed | 침대 chimdae |

| I didn't order this. | 전 이거 주문하지 않았는데요. |
| | jeon igeo jumunhaji ananneundeyo |

| Please charge it to my room. | 계산은 제 방으로 달아 주세요. |
| | gyesaneun je bang-euro darajuseyo |

| Here's your tip. | 이건 팁이에요. |
| | igeon tibieyo |

| I'm still waiting for the wine. | 아까 부탁한 와인이 안 와요. |
| | akka butakan waini an wayo |

| When do you clean my room? | 언제 방청소를 해주나요? |
| | eonje bangcheongsoreul haejunayo |

| Please clean my room while I'm out. | 외출한 동안 방청소를 해 주세요. |
| | oechulhan dongan bangcheongsoreul hae juseyo |

| Please don't clean up my room. | 방청소를 하지 마세요. |
| | bangcheongsoreul haji maseyo |

| Can I have food delievered to my room from outside? | 호텔 밖에서 음식 배달을 주문할 수 있어요? |
| | hotel bakkeseo eumsik baedareul jumunhal su isseoyo |

## PROBLEMS

| The door is locked. | 문이 잠겼어요.<br>muni jamgyeosseoyo |
|---|---|
| I lost my key. | 방 열쇠를 잃어버렸어요.<br>bang yeolsoereul ireobeoryeosseoyo |
| I locked myself out of the room. | 열쇠를 방 안에 놓고 나왔어요.<br>yeolsoereul bang ane noko nawasseoyo |
| I don't know how to use this electronic key card. | 카드키 사용법을 잘 모르겠어요.<br>kadeuki sayongbeobeul jal moreugesseoyo |
| The bathtub is clogged. | 욕조물이 잘 안 빠져요.<br>yokjomuri jal an ppajyeoyo |
| The bath plug is broken. | 욕조의 물마개가 망가졌어요.<br>yokjoui mulmagaega manggajyeosseoyo |
| There's no running <u>water</u>. | <u>물</u>이 안 나와요.<br><u>muri</u> an nawayo |

.................................................................

| water<br>hot water | 물이 muri<br>더운 물이 deoun muri |

.................................................................

| The shower is not working. | 샤워기가 고장 났어요.<br>syawogiga gojang nasseoyo |

| The toilet is overflowing. | 변기 물이 넘치려고 해요.<br>byeon-gi muri neomchiryeogo haeyo |
| The <u>toilet</u> is clogged. | 변기가 막혔어요.<br><u>byeon-gi</u>ga makyeosseoyo |

---

| toilet | 변기 byeon-gi |
| sink | 싱크대 singkeudae |

---

| I need a new light bulb. | 새 전구가 필요해요.<br>sae jeon-guga piryohaeyo |
| The window won't open. | 창문이 안 열려요.<br>changmuni an yeollyeoyo |
| The window won't close. | 창문이 안 닫혀요.<br>changmuni an dachyeoyo |
| The shades won't open. | 블라인드가 안 걷혀요.<br>beullaindeuga an geochyeoyo |
| The shades won't close. | 블라인드가 안 내려져요.<br>beullaindeuga an naeryeojyeoyo |
| There's no electricity. | 전기가 안 들어와요.<br>jeon-giga an deureowayo |
| The <u>TV</u> doesn't work. | <u>TV</u>가 안 나와요.<br><u>tibeui</u>ga an nawayo |

| | |
|---|---|
| TV | TV tibeui |
| radio | 라디오 radio |
| DVD player | DVD dibeuidi |

| | |
|---|---|
| The light doesn't work. | 불이 안 들어와요.<br>buri an deureowayo |
| The air conditioning doesn't work. | 에어컨 작동이 안 돼요.<br>e-eokeon jakdong-i an dwaeyo |
| There's no heat. | 난방이 안돼요.<br>nanbang-i andwaeyo |
| The ventilation is out of order. | 환풍기가 고장 났어요.<br>hwanpunggiga gojang nasseoyo |
| My room hasn't been cleaned yet. | 방청소가 되어 있지 않아요.<br>bangcheongsoga doe-eo itji anayo |
| My bed sheets are dirty. Can I get new ones? | 침대 시트가 더러워요. 바꿔주시겠어요?<br>chimdae siteuga deoreowoyo<br>bakkwojusigesseoyo |

| | |
|---|---|
| bed sheets | 침대 시트가 chimdae siteuga |
| towels | 수건이 sugeoni |

| | |
|---|---|
| The next room is very noisy. | 옆방이 너무 시끄러워요.<br>yeopbang-i neomu sikkeureowoyo |
| There's no soap. | 비누가 없어요.<br>binuga eopseoyo |

| soap | 비누가 binuga |
| towel | 수건이 sugeoni |
| toilet paper | 휴지가 hyujiga |
| hanger | 옷걸이가 otgeoriga |

| I smell something in my room. | 방에서 냄새가 나요.<br>bang-eseo naemsaega nayo |

There are English speaking staff members in most of large hotels. If there is a problem, don't hesitate to call the front desk to ask for help.

## SERVICE

### With the Operator

| I'd like an outside line. | 외부에 전화 좀 하고 싶어요.<br>oebue jeonhwa jom hago sipeoyo |
| Hello. I'd like to make a long-distance call. | 여보세요. 장거리 전화를 좀 하고 싶어요.<br>yeoboseyo janggeori jeonhwareul jom hago sipeoyo |
| The number is 055-244-4567. | 번호는 055-244-4567이에요.<br>beonhoneun gong-o-o i-sa-sa sa-o-yuk-chirieyo |

* Refer to page 345 for numerals.

| Hello. I was cut off. | 여보세요. 전화가 끊어졌어요. |
| | yeoboseyo jeonhwaga kkeuneojyeosseoyo |
| Could you try it again? | 다시 한 번 해 보시겠어요? |
| | dasi han beon hae bosigesseoyo |

## Laundry Service

| Do you have laundry service? | 세탁 서비스가 있어요? |
| | setak seobiseuga isseoyo |
| I have some laundry. | 세탁할 게 있어요. |
| | setakal ge isseoyo |
| I'd like my clothes dry-cleaned. | 드라이클리닝 좀 부탁해요. |
| | deuraikeullining jom butakaeyo |
| Have this pressed, please. | 이것을 다림질해 주세요. |
| | igeoseul darimjilhae juseyo |
| I'd like to have a <u>shirt</u> ironed. | <u>셔츠</u> 한 장 다림질 좀 부탁합니다. |
| | syeocheu han jang darimjil jom butakamnida |

| shirt | 셔츠 syeocheu |
| dress shirt | 와이셔츠 waisyeocheu |
| blouse | 블라우스 beullauseu |
| pants | 바지 baji |
| skirt | 치마 chima |

| When will it be done by? | 언제까지 돼요? |
| | eonjekkaji dwaeyo |

| Will it be ready today? | 오늘 중으로 돼요?<br>oneul jung-euro dwaeyo |
| --- | --- |
| Will it be ready by tomorrow morning? | 내일 아침까지 될까요?<br>naeil achimkkaji doelkkayo |
| Could you bring it to my room, please? | 제 방으로 가져다 주세요.<br>je bang-euro gajyeoda juseyo |
| How much does it cost? | 요금은 얼마예요?<br>yogeumeun eolmayeyo |
| This laundry isn't mine. | 이 세탁물은 제 것이 아니에요.<br>i setangmureun je geosi anieyo |
| Could you bring an iron up to my room? | 다리미를 방으로 갖다 주시겠어요?<br>darimireul bang-euro gatda jusigesseoyo |
| My room number is 324. | 제 방 번호는 324호예요.<br>je bang beonhoneun sambaegisipsa-hoyeyo |
| A How long will it take? | 얼마나 걸려요?<br>eolmana geollyeoyo |
| B It won't take long. It will be done in two hours. | 오래 걸리지 않아요. 두 시간이면 됩니다.<br>orae geolliji anayo du siganimyeon deomnida |

## Hair Shop

| I'd like to make a reservation at <u>3:00</u> this afternoon. | 오늘 오후 <u>3시</u>에 예약을 하고 싶어요.<br>oneul ohu <u>se-sie</u> yeyageul hago sipeoyo |
| --- | --- |

* Refer to page 356 for times.

| | |
|---|---|
| I'd like to get a haircut. | 머리 좀 잘라주세요.<br>meori jom jalla juseyo |
| I'd like to get a shave. | 면도 좀 부탁해요.<br>myeondo jom butakaeyo |
| Please don't make it too short. | 너무 짧게 자르지 마세요.<br>neomu jjalge jareuji maseyo |
| I'd like to get a perm. | 파마해 주세요.<br>pamahae juseyo |
| I'd like to get my hair dyed <u>black</u>. | <u>까만색</u>으로 염색해 주세요.<br>kkamansaegeuro yeomsaekae juseyo<br>* Refer to page 368 for colors. |
| I just need to shampoo. | 머리만 감겨 주세요.<br>meoriman gamgyeo juseyo |
| I just need a blow-dry. | 드라이만 해 주세요.<br>deuraiman hae juseyo |
| How much does it cost? | 요금은 얼마예요?<br>yogeumeun eolmayeyo |
| Does the price include a service charge? | 봉사료가 포함된 금액이에요?<br>bongsaryoga pohamdoen geumaegieyo |
| Is an English-language interpreter available? | 영어 통역이 있어요?<br>yeong-eo tongyeogi isseoyo |

## ORDERING

### Breads

| | |
|---|---|
| toast | 토스트 toseuteu |
| bread roll | 롤빵 rolppang |
| croissant | 크루아상 keuruasang |
| muffin | 머핀 meopin |
| pastry | 패스트리 paeseutri |
| doughnut | 도넛 doneot |

### Meats

| | |
|---|---|
| bacon | 베이컨 beikeon |
| ham | 햄 haem |
| sausage | 소시지 sosiji |

### Cereals

| | |
|---|---|
| cereal | 콘플레이크 konpeulleikeu |
| oatmeal | 오트밀 oteumil |

## Eggs

scrambled egg     스크램블 에그 seukeuraembeul egeu

fried egg     계란 프라이 gyeran peurai

soft-boiled egg     계란 반숙 gyeran bansuk

omelet     오믈렛 omeullet

## Other Hot Dishes

pancake     팬케이크 paenkeikeu

waffle     와플 wapeul

pie     파이 pai

## Condiments

jam     잼 jaem

marmalade     마멀레이드 mameolleideu

honey     꿀 kkul

syrup     시럽 sireop

## Combinations

ham and egg     햄 에그 haem egeu

bacon and egg     베이컨 에그 beikeon egeu

| sausage and egg | 소시지 에그 sosiji egeu |
| ham omelet | 햄 오믈렛 haem omeullet |
| cheese omelet | 치즈 오믈렛 chijeu omeullet |

## Beverages

| coffee | 커피 keopi |
| black tea | 홍차 hongcha |
| milk | 우유 uyu |
| warm milk | 따뜻한 우유 ttatteutan uyu |
| hot chocolate | 코코아 kokoa |
| juice | 주스 juseu |

## Fruits

| watermelon | 수박 subak |
| apple | 사과 sagwa |
| orange | 오렌지 orenji |
| melon | 멜론 mellon |
| pear | 배 bae |
| strawberry | 딸기 ttalgi |

| pineapple | 파인애플 painaepeul |
|-----------|--------------------|
| tomato | 토마토 tomato |

## Special Requests

| decaffeinated coffee | 카페인 없는 커피<br>kapein eomneun keopi |
|----------------------|------------------------------------------|
| decaffeinated tea | 카페인 없는 차<br>kapein eomneun cha |
| sugar-free | 무설탕 / 무가당<br>museoltang / mugadang |
| I'd like it cooked without <u>salt</u>, please. | <u>소금을</u> 넣지 말고 해 주세요.<br><u>sogeumeul</u> neochi malgo hae juseyo |

| salt | <u>소금을</u> sogeumeul |
|------|------------------------|
| butter | 버터를 beoteoreul |
| oil | 기름을 gireumeul |

## CHECKING-OUT

| When is the latest I can check out? | 체크아웃 시간은 몇 시까지예요?<br>chekeuaut siganeun myeot sikkajiyeyo |
|-------------------------------------|-----------------------------------------------------------------------|

| I'm checking out __this morning.__ | <u>오늘 아침에 나갈 거예요.</u> |
|---|---|
| | <u>oneul achime</u> nagal geoyeyo |

| this morning | 오늘 아침에 oneul achime |
|---|---|
| around noon | 정오쯤에 jeongojjeume |
| early tomorrow | 내일 일찍 naeil iljjik |
| tomorrow morning | 내일 아침에 naeil achime |

| Please have my bill ready. | 계산서 좀 준비해 주세요. |
|---|---|
| | gyesanseo jom junbihae juseyo |

| I'm ready to check out. | 체크아웃하려고 하는데요. |
|---|---|
| | chekeuautaryeogo haneundeyo |

| May I have my bill, please. My room is 600. | 계산서 좀 부탁합니다. 600호실입니다. |
|---|---|
| | gyesanseo jom butakamnida yukbaek-hosirimnida |

| Can I extend my stay one more night? | 하루 더 묵을 수 있어요? |
|---|---|
| | haru deo mugeul su isseoyo |

| A Can I check out a day earlier than scheduled? | 체크아웃을 하루 앞당길 수 있어요? |
|---|---|
| | chekeuauseul haru apdanggil su isseoyo |

| B Your name and room number, please. | 성함과 방 번호를 알려주세요. |
|---|---|
| | seonghamgwa bang beonhoreul allyeojuseyo |

| Would you give me the key, please? | 열쇠를 주시겠습니까? |
|---|---|
| | yeolsoereul jusigesseumnikka |

| I had nothing from the minibar. | 미니바는 이용하지 않았어요. |
|---|---|
| | minibaneun iyonghaji anasseoyo |

| | |
|---|---|
| I don't have much time. Could you hurry, please? | 시간이 없으니 서둘러 주세요.<br>sigani eopseuni seodulleo juseyo |
| Can I have the bill? | 계산서를 보여주시겠어요?<br>gyesanseoreul boyeojusigesseoyo |
| Does this include the tax and service charges? | 세금과 봉사료가 포함된 거예요?<br>segeumgwa bongsaryoga pohamdoen geoyeyo |
| Does the price include the phone call charges? | 전화요금도 포함된 비용이에요?<br>jeonhwayogeumdo pohamdoen biyongieyo |
| What's this bill for? | 이건 무슨 비용이에요?<br>igeon museun biyongieyo |
| There seems to be a mistake with the bill. | 계산서가 잘못된 것 같은데요.<br>gyesanseoga jalmotdoen geot gateundeyo |
| Could you check it again? | 다시 한 번 확인해 주세요.<br>dasi han beon hwaginhae juseyo |
| Could you explain this item on the bill? | 이 항목을 설명해 주시겠어요?<br>i hangmogeul seolmyeonghae jusigesseoyo |
| A How would you like to pay? | 어떻게 지불하시겠어요?<br>eotteoke jibulhasigesseoyo |
| B I will pay in cash. | 현금으로 계산할게요.<br>hyeongeumeuro gyesanhalgeyo |

| | |
|---|---|
| in cash | 현금으로 hyeongeumeuro |
| by credit card | 신용카드로 sinyongkadeuro |

| | |
|---|---|
| Haven't you forgotten anything? | 잊으신 물건은 없습니까?<br>ijeusin mulgeoneun eopseumnikka |
| I'd like to get my valuables back. | 맡겨 둔 귀중품을 찾고 싶어요.<br>matgyeo dun gwijungpumeul chatgo sipeoyo |
| Please give me my things from the safe. | 금고에 맡긴 물건을 돌려주세요.<br>geumgo-e matgin mulgeoneul dollyeojuseyo |
| I left something in the room. | 방에 물건을 두고 왔어요.<br>bang-e mulgeoneul dugo wasseoyo |
| Could you call a taxi, please? | 택시 좀 불러 주시겠어요?<br>taeksi jom bulleo jusigesseoyo |
| Is my baggage coming down? | 제 짐은 내려 왔어요?<br>je jimeun naeryeo wasseoyo |
| Would you send someone to bring my luggage down? | 짐 들 사람 좀 불러 주세요.<br>jim deul saram jom bulleo juseyo |
| Can you keep my baggage untill <u>noon</u>? | 제 짐을 <u>정오</u>까지 좀 맡아 주세요.<br>je jimeul <u>jeongo</u>kkaji jom mata juseyo |

| | |
|---|---|
| noon | 정오 jeong-o |
| evening | 저녁 jeonyeok |

When you check out, the hotel charges you for room service along with any telephone calls and bills from the other facilities in the hotel. Keep in mind that the drinks and liquor in the minibar in the room are not complimentary. If you take any, you have to pay for them when you check out.

Check out time is 12 p.m. at most hotels. But some hotels have different policies, so please check beforehand. You might have to pay for extra hours if you check out late.

## YOUTH HOSTEL

| | |
|---|---|
| How many people does a room accomodate? | 한 방을 몇 명이 쓰죠?<br>han bang-eul myeot myeong-i sseujyo |
| Can I stay here? I'm a member. | 회원인데요. 여기서 머물 수 있어요?<br>hoewonindeyo yeogiseo meomul su isseoyo |
| I have a membership card. | 회원증을 갖고 있어요.<br>hoewonjeung-eul gatgo isseoyo |
| Here's my membership card. | 제 회원증이에요.<br>je hoewonjeung-ieyo |
| Where can I take a shower? | 샤워는 어디서 할 수 있어요?<br>syawoneun eodiseo hal su isseoyo |
| Is there a time when I can take a bath? | 목욕 시간이 정해져 있어요?<br>mogyok sigani jeonghaejyeo isseoyo |

| | |
|---|---|
| When is the meal time? | 식사 시간은 언제예요?<br>siksa siganeun eonjeyeyo |
| Where's the dinning room? | 식당은 어디예요?<br>sikdang-eun eodiyeyo |
| Can I cook for myself? | 취사가 가능한가요?<br>chwisaga ganeunghangayo |
| Can I borrow a pan and a burner? | 냄비와 버너를 빌려 주세요.<br>naembiwa beoneoreul billyeo juseyo |
| Can I borrow blankets? | 담요를 빌릴 수 있어요?<br>damnyoreul billil su isseoyo |
| I need some extra blankets, please. | 담요를 더 갖다 주시겠어요?<br>damnyoreul deo gatda jusigesseoyo |
| Try not to be too loud in the room. | 방에서 너무 떠들지 마세요.<br>bang-eseo neomu tteodeulji maseyo |
| Is there a curfew? | 문 닫는 시간이 있어요?<br>mun danneun sigani isseoyo |
| When is "lights out"? | 소등은 언제 해요?<br>sodeung-eun eonje haeyo |
| When do we have to get up? | 기상 시간이 언제예요?<br>gisang sigani eonjeyeyo |

# Accommodations

When you stay in Korea, you have a choice between Western-style and Korean-style accommodations. The terms "Western-style" and "Korean-style" categorize both the facilities and the service that each type of lodging offers. In each of the two broad categories, you'll find a wide range of possibilities, from costly and luxurious to inexpensive and simple. You might stay at a Western-style hotel when you first arrive, and then a Korean-style inn, or *yeogwan* for a few nights as you travel around. Sometimes it's possible to have a bit of both world: some Western-style hotels have a few Korean-style rooms or suites, and some Korean-style hotels may have a few guest rooms with beds.

## Hotels

First-class hotels in Korea may equal fine hotels anywhere for facilities, quality service and the rate as well. Korea has a great many Western-style hotels of various types and standards.

## *Yeogwan*; Korean Inns

Staying at a *yeogwan* is a good way to experience everyday Korean customs firsthand. These inns offer traditional and authentic Korean flavor, from the architecture and furnishings to the pace and style of life. You'll have everything you need to be comfortable. If you do decide to stay at a *yeogwan*, there is a range in quality and price (as with Western-style hotels) from luxurious to simple.

## Youth Hostel

They offer rather low-priced accommodation for students, foreign athletes, and other economic minded travelers. The Korea Youth Hostel Association (Tel. 02-725-3031) will help you with all the necessary informations including listings of facilities.

# MOVING AROUND TOWN

## BY TAXI

A Where can I get
a taxi?

택시 타는 곳이 어디예요?
taeksi taneun gosi eodiyeyo

B Go this way.

이쪽으로 가세요.
ijjogeuro gaseyo

A Would you call
a taxi, please?

택시 좀 불러 주시겠어요?
taeksi jom bulleo jusigesseoyo

B Sure, one moment,
please.

그럼요, 잠시만 기다려 주세요.
geureomnyo jamsiman gidaryeo
juseyo

It will be here in
10 minutes.

10분 후에 올 거예요.
sip-bun hue ol geoyeyo

Sorry, there are no
taxis available at the
moment.

죄송합니다만 지금 택시가 없네요.
joesonghamnidaman jigeum
taeksiga eomneyo

Could you load this
luggage?

이 짐 좀 실어 주시겠어요?
i jim jom sireo jusigesseoyo

Take me to Myeong-
dong, please.

명동으로 가 주세요.
myeongdongeuro ga juseyo

| Hongdae | 홍대 hongdae |
| Sinchon | 신촌 sinchon |

* Refer to page 366 for areas.

| I'd ilke to go near Gwanghwamun. | 광화문쪽으로 가 주세요. |
| | gwanghwamunjjogeuro ga juseyo |

| Can you take me to this address? | 이 주소로 가 주시겠어요? |
| | i juso ro ga jusigesseoyo |

| A How much will a taxi costs to the City Hall? | 시청까지 택시 요금이 얼마나 나올까요? |
| | sicheongkkaji taeksi yogeumi eolmana naolkkayo |

| B It will cost you about 8,000 won. | 8,000원 정도 나올 거예요. |
| | palcheon-won jeongdo naol geoyeyo |

* Refer to page 95 for money.

| A How long does it take to Itaewon by taxi? | 이태원까지 택시로 얼마나 걸려요? |
| | itaewonkkaji taeksiro eolmana geollyeoyo |

| B It takes about 20 minutes to get there. | 20분쯤 걸릴 거예요. |
| | isip-bunjjeum geollil geoyeyo |

* Refer to page 357 for times.

| Can I get there by 1 o'clock? | 1시까지 도착할 수 있을까요? |
| | han-sikkaji dochakal su isseulkkayo |

| Please take me there as quickly as possible. | 최대한 빨리 가 주세요. |
| | choedaehan ppalli ga juseyo |

| Please go slowly. | 좀 천천히 가 주세요. |
| | jom cheoncheonhi ga juseyo |

MOVING AROUND TOWN

131

| Go straight, please. | 직진해 주세요.<br>jikjinhae juseyo |
| Could you go a little ahead, please? | 조금만 더 가 주시겠어요?<br>jogeumman deo ga jusigesseoyo |
| Would you mind going back a little? | 조금만 되돌아 가 주시겠어요?<br>jogeumman doedora ga jusigesseoyo |
| I think it's around here. | 이 근처인 것 같은데요.<br>i geuncheoin geot gateundeyo |
| Isn't this the long way? | 이쪽으로 가면 돌아가는 거 아니에요?<br>ijjogeuro gamyeon doraganeun geo anieyo |
| <u>Right turn</u> at the next corner, please. | 다음 코너에서 <u>우회전</u> 해 주세요.<br>da-eum koneo-eseo <u>uhoejeon</u> hae juseyo |

. . . . . . . . . . . . . . . . . . . . . . . . . . . . . . . . . . . . . . . . . . . . . . . . . . . . . .

| right turn<br>left turn | 우회전 uhoejeon<br>좌회전 jwahoejeon |

. . . . . . . . . . . . . . . . . . . . . . . . . . . . . . . . . . . . . . . . . . . . . . . . . . . . . .

| Stop the car here, please. | 여기서 세워 주세요.<br>yeogiseo sewo juseyo |
| Drop me off at the corner. | 저 모퉁이에서 내려 주세요.<br>jeo motungieseo naeryeo juseyo |
| A How much is the fare? | 요금이 얼마예요?<br>yogeumi eolmayeyo |

**B** It's 9,000 won.      9,000원입니다.
gucheon-wonimnida

* Refer to page 95 for money.

Here you are.      여기 있습니다. 잔돈은 괜찮아요.
Keep the change.    yeogi isseummida jandoneun
gwaenchanayo

**A** Can I get a receipt,    영수증을 받을 수 있을까요?
please?       yeongsujeung-eul badeul su
isseulkkayo

**B** Here is the receipt.   영수증 여기 있습니다.
yeongsujeung yeogi isseumnida

## BY BUS

**A** Which bus do     이태원에 가려면 몇 번 버스를 타야 해요?
I need to take to get  itaewone garyeomyeon myeot beon
to Itaewon?      beoseureul taya haeyo

Daehangno       대학로 daehangno
Gwanghwamun    광화문 gwanghwamun

* Refer to page 366 for areas.

**B** Take bus number   건너편에서 149번 버스를 타세요.
149 across the    geonneopyeoneseo baeksasipgu-
streets.        beon beoseureul taseyo

* Refer to page 345 for numerals.

133

Where should I get a bus to <u>City Hall</u>?

시청 가는 버스는 어디에서 타요?

sicheong ganeun beoseuneun eodieseo tayo

* Refer to page 366 for areas.

A Where's the nearest bus stop?

여기에서 가장 가까운 버스 정류장이 어디예요?

yeogieseo gajang gakkaun beoseu jeongnyujang-i eodiyeyo

B You can see it if you go <u>100</u> meters this way.

이쪽으로 100미터 정도 가면 있어요.

ijjogeuro baek-miteo jeongdo gamyeon isseoyo

* Refer to page 345 for numerals.

B There's no bus stop around here.

이 근처에는 버스 정류장이 없어요.

i geuncheo-eneun beoseu jeongnyujang-i eopseoyo

A Does this bus go to Apgujeong?

이 버스 압구정에 가요?

i beoseu apgujeong-e gayo

B Yes, it goes to Apgujeong.

네, 압구정까지 갑니다.

ne apgujeongkkaji gamnida

B No, take the number 6800 bus.

아니요, 6800번 버스를 타세요.

aniyo yukcheonpalbaek-beon beoseureul taseyo

A Where do I put the fare?

요금을 어디에 넣어야 해요?

yogeumeul eodie neo-eoya haeyo

B Put it here.

여기에 넣으세요.

yeogie neo-euseyo

How long does it take from here to <u>Gangnam Station</u>?

여기서 <u>강남역</u>까지 얼마나 걸려요?

yeogiseo <u>gangnamyeok</u>-kkaji eolmana geollyeoyo

* Refer to page 366 for subway stations.

A How many more stops left from here to <u>Namsan</u>?

여기서 <u>남산</u>까지 몇 정거장이에요?

yeogiseo <u>namsan</u>kkaji myeot jeonggeojangieyo

* Refer to page 366 for areas.

B <u>Three</u> more stops to go.

<u>세</u> 정거장 남았어요.

<u>se</u> jeonggeojang namasseoyo

* Refer to page 345 for numerals.

Could you tell me where I should be getting off?

내릴 곳에서 좀 알려 주시겠어요?

naeril goseseo jom allyeo jusigesseoyo

Where do I get off to go to Dongdaemun Market?

동대문 시장에 가려면 어디서 내려야 해요?

dongdaemun sijang-e garyeomyeon eodiseo naeryeoya haeyo

A What's the next stop?

다음 정류장이 어디예요?

da-eum jeongnyujang-i eodiyeyo

B The next stop is Hoegi Station.

다음 정류장은 회기역이에요.

da-eum jeongnyujangeun hoegiyeogieyo

## BY SUBWAY

### Asking About Lines and Directions

| | |
|---|---|
| Where is the nearest subway station? | 근처에 가장 가까운 지하철역은 어디에 있어요?<br>geuncheo-e gajang gakkaun jihacheollyeogeun eodie isseoyo |
| A Where is a Line <u>1</u> station? | 1호선 지하철역이 어디에 있어요?<br>il-hoseon jihacheollyeogi eodie isseoyo<br>* Refer to page 345 for numerals. |
| B It's <u>right over there</u>. | <u>바로 저기에</u> 있어요.<br><u>baro jeogie</u> isseoyo |

. . . . . . . . . . . . . . . . . . . . . . . . . . . . . . . . . . . . . .

| | |
|---|---|
| right over there | 바로 저기에 baro jeogie |
| down this road | 이 길로 쭉 내려가면<br>i gillo jjuk naeryeogamyeon |
| at the corner of this street | 이 길 모퉁이에 i gil motung-ie |
| behind you | 뒤쪽에 dwijjoge |
| a little far away | 좀 먼 곳에 jom meon gose |

. . . . . . . . . . . . . . . . . . . . . . . . . . . . . . . . . . . . . .

| | |
|---|---|
| It's not around here. | 이 근처에는 없어요.<br>i geuncheo-eneun eopseoyo |
| A Which line should I take to get to <u>Suwon</u>? | <u>수원</u>에 가려면 몇 호선을 타야 해요?<br><u>suwone</u> garyeomyeon myeot hoseoneul taya haeyo<br>* Refer to page 365 cities. |

**B** Take Line 1.

1호선을 타세요.
il-hoseoneul taseyo

* Refer to page 345 for numerals.

How long does it take to get to Jonggak Station?

종각역까지 얼마나 걸려요?
jonggakyeok-kkaji eolmana geollyeoyo

* Refer to page 366 for subway stations.

**A** How many stops do I have to go to get to Itaewon Station?

이태원역까지 몇 정거장 더 가야 해요?
itaewonnyeok-kkaji myeot jeonggeojang deo gaya haeyo

**B** You have to go two more stops.

두 정거장 더 가야 해요.
du jeonggeojang deo gaya haeyo

Where is the platform for the train to Dongdaemun?

동대문에 가려면 어느 홈에서 타야 해요?
dongdaemune garyeomyeon eoneu homeseo taya haeyo

* Refer to page 366 for areas.

**A** Is this the right platform for the train to Express Bus Terminal?

고속터미널에 가려면 이 홈에서 타면 돼요?
gosokteomineore garyeomyeon i homeseo tamyeon dwaeyo

**B** Take the train on the other side.

반대편에서 타세요.
bandaepyeoneseo taseyo

# Buying Tickets & Charging a Transportation Card

**A** Can I buy a transportation card here?

여기 교통 카드 팔아요?
yeogi gyotong kadeu parayo

**B** Yes, we have it here.

네, 판매합니다.
ne panmaehamnida

**B** No, we don't have transportation cards.

아니요, 교통 카드는 판매하지 않아요.
aniyo gyotong kadeuneun panmaehaji anayo

Can I charge my transportation card here?

교통 카드 충전할 수 있나요?
gyotong kadeu chungjeonhal su innayo

Please put 10,000 won on this card.

이 카드에 10,000원어치 충전 좀 부탁합니다.
i kadeue man-woneochi chungjeon jom butakamnida

5,000 won
10,000 won
15,000 won
20,000 won

5,000원  ocheon-won
10,000원  man-won
15,000원  manocheon-won
20,000원  iman-won

Where is the ticket machine?

승차권 판매기가 어디에 있어요?
seungchagwon panmaegiga eodie isseoyo

ticket machine
transportation card recharger

승차권 판매기 seungchagwon panmaegi
교통 카드 충전기 gyotong kadeu chungjeon-gi

A Which machine should I use?

어떤 기계를 사용해야 해요?

eotteon gigyereul sayonghaeya haeyo

B Use this one.

이것을 사용하세요.

igeoseul sayonghaseyo

I can't read the Korean for the fare information. Could you help me?

한글을 몰라서 요금을 모르겠어요. 좀 도와주세요.

hangeureul mollaseo yogeumeul moreugesseoyo jom dowajuseyo

Would you mind showing me how to use this ticket machine?

자동 매표기 사용법을 가르쳐 주시겠어요?

jadong maepyogi sayongbeobeul gareuchyeo jusigesseoyo

I don't have any cash.

제가 현금이 없어요.

jega hyeongeumi eopseoyo

Can I buy a ticket with a credit card?

신용카드로 표를 살 수 있어요?

sinyongkadeuro pyoreul sal su isseoyo

You can add more money to a transportation card. There are machines at subway stations. The minimum amount you can add is 1,000 won and you can add more money in increments of 1,000 won. You can also add money to the card at certain convenience stores or supermarkets. When you use the transportation card, you can get a discount when you transfer to buses or the subway. If you don't have a transportation card, you can buy a single-use transportation card. You need to leave a deposit to buy one, but you can get it back at the destination.

## To Transfer

**A** Where do I transfer
to Line <u>3</u>?

<u>3</u>호선은 어디서 갈아타요?
<u>sam</u>-hoseoneun eodiseo garatayo

\* Refer to page 345 for numerals.

**B** You should transfer
at <u>Jongno-3ga
Station</u>.

<u>종로3가역</u>에서 갈아타세요.
<u>jongnosamgayeog</u>eseo garataseyo

\* Refer to page 366 for subway stations.

**A** I'm trying to get to
<u>Gangnam Station</u>,
which line should
I transfer to?

<u>강남역</u>으로 가려면 몇 호선으로
갈아타야 돼요?
<u>gangnamyeog</u>euro garyeomyeon
myeot hoseoneuro garataya dwaeyo

**B** You should transfer
to Line <u>2</u> at <u>City Hall
Station</u>.

<u>시청역</u>에서 <u>2</u>호선으로 갈아타야 돼요.
<u>sicheong-yeog</u>eseo <u>i</u>-hoseoneuro
garataya dwaeyo

**A** What's the next
station?

다음 정거장은 어디예요?
da-eum jeonggeojangeun eodiyeyo

**B** Next is <u>Yangjae
Station</u>.

다음은 <u>양재역</u>이에요.
da-eumeun <u>yangjaeyeog</u>ieyo

**A** Where is Exit <u>1</u>?

<u>1</u>번 출구가 어디에 있어요?
<u>il</u>-beon chulguga eodie isseoyo

**B** Exit <u>1</u> is at the top
of the stairs on the
<u>right</u>.

<u>1</u>번 출구는 <u>오른쪽</u> 계단 위에 있어요.
<u>il</u>-beon chulguneun <u>oreunjjok</u> gyedan
wie isseoyo

| | |
|---|---|
| right | 오른쪽 oreunjjok |
| left | 왼쪽 oenjjok |

| | |
|---|---|
| A Where is the exit to <u>Gyeongbokgung Palace</u>? | 경복궁 쪽 출구가 어디예요?<br>gyeongbokgung jjok chulguga eodieyo<br>* Refer to page 366 for areas. |
| B Follow the <u>purple line</u>. | <u>보라색 선을</u> 따라가세요.<br>borasaek seoneul ttaragaseyo |

| | |
|---|---|
| purple line | 보라색 선을 borasaek seoneul |
| arrow | 화살표를 hwasalpyoreul |
| sign | 표지판을 pyojipaneul |

## Others

| | |
|---|---|
| Do you know what time the <u>first train</u> is? | 첫차가 언제 있어요?<br><u>cheotchaga</u> eonje isseoyo |

| | |
|---|---|
| first train | 첫차 cheotcha |
| last train | 막차 makcha |

| | |
|---|---|
| A Where can I get a subway map in English? | 영어로 된 지하철 노선도를 어디서 구할 수 있어요?<br>yeong-eoro doen jihacheol noseondoreul eodiseo guhal su isseoyo |

| B You can get it at the information desk. | 안내소에 가면 받을 수 있어요.<br>annaeso-e gamyeon badeul su isseoyo |
| --- | --- |
| Where is the <u>restroom</u>? | 여기 화장실이 어디에 있어요?<br>yeogi <u>hwajangsiri</u> eodie isseoyo |
| restroom<br>Lost and Found | 화장실이 hwajangsiri<br>분실물 보관소가 bunsilmul bogwansoga |
| I've lost my <u>bag</u>. | <u>가방을</u> 잃어버렸어요.<br><u>gabang-eul</u> ireobeoryeosseoyo |
| bag<br>camera<br>wallet | 가방을 gabang-eul<br>카메라를 kamerareul<br>지갑을 jigabeul |

## MOVING AROUND

| Is there anything worth seeing around here? | 근처에 볼만한 것이 뭐가 있어요?<br>geuncheo-e bolmanhan geosi mwoga isseoyo |
| --- | --- |
| A Where is the tourist information center? | 여행 안내소가 어디에 있어요?<br>yeohaeng annaesoga eodie isseoyo |
| B It's around <u>Anguk Station</u>. | <u>안국역</u> 근처에 있어요.<br><u>angungnyeok</u> geuncheo-e iseoyo |

* Refer to page 366 for subway stations.

**B** There's no information desk around here.

이 근처에는 없어요.
i geuncheo-eneun eopseoyo

Are there English guidebooks for <u>Seoul</u>?

영어로 된 <u>서울</u> 관광 안내서가 있나요?
yeong-eoro doen <u>seoul</u> gwangwang annaeseoga innayo

* Refer to page 365 for cities.

I'd like to see the <u>downtown area</u>.

<u>시내</u>에 가 보고 싶어요.
<u>sinae</u>-e ga bogo sipeoyo

. . . . . . . . . . . . . . . . . . . . . . . . . . . . . . . . . . . . . . . . . . . . . .

| | |
|---|---|
| downtown | 시내 sinae |
| market | 시장 sijang |
| museum | 박물관 bangmulgwan |
| royal palace | 고궁 gogung |
| park | 공원 gong-won |
| Buddhist temple | 절 jeol |
| zoo | 동물원 dongmurwon |

. . . . . . . . . . . . . . . . . . . . . . . . . . . . . . . . . . . . . . . . . . . . . .

**A** Can I walk from <u>Gyeongbokgung Palace</u> to <u>Insa-dong</u>?

<u>경복궁</u>에서 <u>인사동</u>까지 걸어갈 수 있어요?
<u>gyeongbokgung</u>-eseo <u>insadong</u>kkaji georeogal su isseoyo

* Refer to page 366 for areas.

**B** It will take about <u>15 minutes</u> on foot.

걸어서 <u>15분</u>쯤 걸릴 거예요.
georeoseo <u>sibo-bun</u>jjeum geollil geoyeyo

* Refer to page 356 for times.

There are many Buddhist temples in Korea. The word "temple," or *jeol* in Korean, usually means Buddhist temple in this country.

# MOVING OUT OF TOWN

## GENERAL EXPRESSIONS

## Buying a Ticket

| | |
|---|---|
| Where can I take the <u>express bus</u> to <u>Busan</u>? | 부산 가는 고속버스는 어디서 타요?<br>busan ganeun gosokbeoseuneun eodiseo tayo |

| | |
|---|---|
| express bus<br>train<br>airplane<br>ferry | 고속버스는 gosokbeoseuneun<br>기차는 gichaneun<br>비행기는 bihaenggineun<br>여객선은 yeogaekseoneun |

\* Refer to page 365 for cities.

| | |
|---|---|
| Where can I buy a bus ticket for Gwangju? | 광주행 차표는 어디에서 살 수 있어요?<br>gwangjuhaeng chapyoneun eodieseo sal su isseoyo |

| | |
|---|---|
| Can I get the <u>express bus</u> timetable? | 고속버스 운행 시간표 좀 얻을 수 있을까요?<br><u>gosokbeoseu</u> unhaeng siganpyo jom eodeul su isseulkkayo |

\* Refer to page 154 for transportation.

| | |
|---|---|
| I'd like to buy a train ticket for Busan, please. | 부산행 기차표를 사고 싶은데요.<br>busanhaeng gichapyoreul sago sipeundeyo |

| Is there a bus to Daejeon leaving now? | 지금 출발하는 대전행 버스 있어요? |
| | jigeum chulbalhaneun daejeonhaeng beoseu isseoyo |
| A When does the next bus leave? | 다음 버스는 몇 시에 출발해요? |
| | da-eum beoseuneun myeot sie chulbalhaeyo |
| B It's going to depart in 10 minutes. | 10분 후에 출발합니다. |
| | sip-bun hue chulbalhamnida |
| | * Refer to page 356 for times. |
| A How often does the bus for Daejeon depart? | 대전행 버스는 얼마나 자주 있어요? |
| | daejeonhaeng beoseuneun eolmana jaju isseoyo |
| B There's a bus every 30 minutes. | 30분마다 있어요. |
| | samsip-bunmada isseoyo |
| Please give me a window seat. | 창문 쪽 자리로 주세요. |
| | changmun jjok jariro juseyo |

| window seat | 창문 쪽 자리 changmun jjok jari |
| aisle seat | 통로 쪽 자리 tongno jjok jari |

| A one-way ticket, please. | 편도로 한 장 주세요. |
| | pyeondoro han jang juseyo |

| one-way ticket | 편도로 pyeondoro |
| roundtrip ticket | 왕복으로 wangbogeuro |

A Do you have special rates for children?

아이는 요금 할인이 되나요?

aineun yogeum harini doenayo

B There is a 10% discount for children's tickets.

어린이는 10퍼센트 할인이 됩니다.

eorinineun sip-peosenteu harini doemnida

* Refer to page 345 for numerals.

What's the fare to Gangneung?

강릉까지 요금이 얼마예요?

gangneungkkaji yogeumi eolmayeyo

* Refer to page 365 for cities.

How much is the fare for the premium express bus to Gangneung?

강릉행 우등고속 요금이 얼마예요?

gangneunghaeng udeunggosok yogeumi eolmayeyo

| | |
|---|---|
| premium express bus | 우등고속 udeunggosok |
| regular express bus | 일반고속 ilbangosok |
| late-night express bus | 심야버스 simyabeoseu |
| KTX train | KTX 열차 keitiekseu yeolcha |
| Saemaul train | 새마을호 saema-eulho |
| Mugunghwa train | 무궁화호 mugunghwaho |
| airplane | 비행기 bihaenggi |
| ferry | 여객선 yeogaekseon |

How long does it take to Sokcho?

속초까지 얼마나 걸려요?

sokchokkaji eolmana geollyeoyo

## Booking a Ticket

I'd like to reserve a train ticket to Busan on the 10th of December.

<u>12월 10일</u>에 출발하는 <u>부산행 기차</u>를 예약하고 싶은데요.

<u>sibi-wol sib-ire</u> chulbalhaneun <u>busanhaeng gicha</u>reul yeyakago sipeundeyo

\* Refer to page 353 for dates.
\* Refer to page 365 for cities.
\* Refer to page 154 for transportation.

I'd like to book a train ticket for Busan.

부산행 기차표를 예매하고 싶은데요.

busanhaeng gichapyoreul yemaehago sipeundeyo

A Which date will you be leaving?

언제 출발하실 거예요?

eonje chulbalhasil geoyeyo

B I'd like to book a ticket for the KTX train leaving at <u>1:00 p.m.</u> tomorrow.

내일 <u>오후 1시</u>에 출발하는 KTX를 예약하고 싶어요.

naeil <u>ohu han-sie</u> chulbalhaneun keitiexeu-reul yeyakago sipeoyo

\* Refer to page 356 for times.


## Cancel & Refund

I would like to cancel the ticket that I booked a few days ago.

며칠 전에 예약한 표를 취소하고 싶은데요.

myeochil jeone yeyakan pyoreul chwisohago sipeundeyo

I'd like to get a refund on this ticket.

이 표를 환불하고 싶은데요.

i pyoreul hwanbulhago sipeundeyo

You can get a refund
when you cancel
at least a day before.

하루 전에 취소하셔야 환불 받으실 수
있습니다.

haru jeone chwisohasyeoya hwanbul
badeusil su isseumnida

I'm sorry. It's too late
for a refund.

죄송하지만 환불 기간이 지났습니다.

joesonghajiman hwanbul gigani
jinasseumnida

How much is the
refund charges?

환불 수수료가 얼마예요?

hwanbul susuryoga eolmayeyo

## Boarding

A How soon before
the departure
time do you allow
boarding?

출발 몇 분 전부터 승차할 수 있어요?

chulbal myeot bun jeonbuteo
seungchahal su isseoyo

B You can board <u>20
minutes</u> before.

<u>20분</u> 전부터 승차할 수 있습니다.

<u>isip-bun</u> jeonbuteo seungchahal su
isseumnida

* Refer to page 356 for times.

A Can you tell me
which platform
I need to be on
to catch the train
to <u>Jeonju</u>?

<u>전주</u>로 가는 기차를 타려면 어느
승강장으로 가야 해요?

<u>jeonju</u>ro ganeun gichareul
taryeomyeon eoneu
seunggangjang-euro gaya heayo

* Refer to page 365 for cities.

B Go to Platform <u>4</u>.

<u>4</u>번 홈으로 가세요.

<u>sa</u>-beon homeuro gaseyo

* Refer to page 345 for numerals.

| A Is this express bus going to Daegu? | 이 고속버스가 대구까지 가는 게 맞나요? |
| | i gosokbeoseuga daegukkaji ganeun ge mannayo |

| B Yes, that's right. | 네, 맞아요. |
| | ne majayo |

| B No, this bus is going to <u>Busan</u>. | 아니요, 이건 <u>부산</u> 가는 버스예요. |
| | aniyo igeon <u>busan</u> ganeun beoseuyeyo |

*\* Refer to page 365 for cities.*

## On board

| Could you help me find my seat on this ticket? | 이 좌석이 제 자리가 맞는지 확인 좀 해 주시겠어요? |
| | i jwaseogi je jariga manneunji hwagin jom hae jusigesseoyo |

| Excuse me, I think this is my seat. | 죄송하지만 여기가 제 자리인 것 같은데요. |
| | joesonghajiman yeogiga je jariin geot gateundeyo |

| A Can you tell me what time we are arriving? | 몇 시쯤에 도착해요? |
| | myeot sijjeume dochakaeyo |

| B Estimated time of arrival is <u>5:00 p.m.</u> | <u>5시</u> 도착 예정입니다. |
| | <u>daseot-si</u> dochak yejeongimnida |

*\* Refer to page 356 for times.*

| Could you <u>turn down</u> the <u>volume</u>? | <u>소리</u>를 좀 <u>줄여</u> 주시겠어요? |
| | <u>sorireul</u> jom <u>juryeo</u> jusigeseoyo |

| | |
|---|---|
| volume | 소리를 sorireul |
| air conditioner | 에어컨을 e-eokeoneul |
| heater | 히터를 hiteoreul |
| | |
| turn down | 줄여 juryeo |
| turn up | 높여 nopyeo |

**A** May I see your
ticket, please?

표 좀 보여주시겠어요?
pyo jom boyeojusigesseoyo

**B** Here it is.

여기 있어요.
yeogi isseoyo

## Lost & Found

I've lost my camera.

카메라를 잃어버렸어요.
kamerareul ireobeoryeosseoyo

| | |
|---|---|
| camera | 카메라를 kamerareul |
| wallet | 지갑을 jigabeul |
| traveler's checks | 여행자 수표를 yeohaengja supyoreul |

Where is the Lost and
Found office?

유실물 보관소가 어디에 있어요?
yusilmul bogwansoga eodie isseoyo

Please contact
me if you find my
belongings.

물건을 찾으시면 저에게 연락
부탁드려요.
mulgeoneul chajeusimyeon jeo-ege
yeollak butakdeuryeoyo

Please, find my bag.
I really need it back.

제 물건 좀 꼭 찾아주세요.
je mulgeon jom kkok chajajuseyo

---

When you are at Lost and Found after losing something,
you have to describe the item specifically. To do that, you
need vocabulary for color, size, and shape.

## Color

| white | 하얀색 | hayansaek |
| black | 까만색 | kkamansaek |
| red | 빨간색 | ppalgansaek |
| brown | 갈색 | galsaek |
| yellow | 노란색 | noransaek |
| blue | 파란색 | paransaek |
| purple | 보라색 | borasaek |
| orange | 주황색 | juhwangsaek |

## Size

| big | 큰 | keun |
| small | 작은 | jageun |

## Shape

| round | 둥근 | dunggeun |
| square | 네모난 | nemonan |
| triangle | 세모난 | semonan |
| short | 짧은 | jjalbeun |
| long | 긴 | gin |

## EXPRESS BUS

What's the fare for the
<u>regular express bus</u> to
<u>Gangneung</u>?

<u>강릉행 일반고속</u> 요금이 얼마예요?
<u>gangneunghaeng ilban-gosok</u>
yogeumi eolmayeyo

---

regular express bus
premium express bus
late-night express bus

일반고속 ilban-gosok
우등고속 udeunggosok
심야버스 simnyabeoseu

* Refer to page 365 for cities.

* Refer to page 365 for cities.

Where are the
buses for <u>Gyeongbu
Expressway</u>?

<u>경부선</u> 타는 곳이 어디예요?
<u>gyeongbuseon</u> taneun gosi eodiyeyo

---

Gyeongbu Expressway
Yeongdong Expressway
Honam Expressway

경부선 gyeongbuseon
영동선 yeongdongseon
호남선 honamseon

---

A How many times
does the bus stop
along the way?

도중에 몇 번이나 쉬어요?
dojung-e myeot beonina swieoyo

B We stop <u>twice</u> at the
rest areas.

두 번 휴게소에서 쉴 거예요.
<u>du beon</u> hyugeso-eseo swil geoyeyo

* Refer to page 345 for numerals.

* Refer to page 345 for numerals.

A When do we stop at
an expressway rest
area?

휴게소는 언제 들러요?
hyugesoneun eonje deulleoyo

**B** We are going to stop in 30 minutes.

30분 후에 들릴 예정이에요.
**samsip-bun** hue deullil yejeongieyo

\* Refer to page 356 for times.

**A** How long will we be at the expressway rest area?

휴게소에서 몇 분이나 쉬어요?
hyugesoeseo myeot bunina swieoyo

**B** We will be there for 15 minutes.

15분 정도 쉬어요.
sibo-bun jeongdo swieoyo

We depart after 15 minutes.

15분 후에 출발합니다.
sibo-bun hue chulbalhamnida

---

## Korean Transportation

Public transportation in Korea is very well developed and connected to help you travel using your favorite means of transportation. Buses and subways are transferrable within an hour for free, so you can save on transportations costs. But keep in mind that this is only possible when you use a transportation card.

| | |
|---|---|
| bus | 버스 beoseu |
| subway | 지하철 jihacheol |
| taxi | 택시 taeksi |
| express bus | 고속버스 gosokbeoseu |
| train | 기차 gicha |

**Bus:** Get the bus route map at the airport information center. You can get a discount with a transportation card.

- Airport Limousine: The bus that connects you from the airport to major areas in downtown.

## Subway:
The most convenient form of transportation without congestion and announcements at every stop. Refrain from boarding in rush hours (8:00-9:00 a.m. and 6:00-7:00 p.m.) to avoid packed passengers. You can buy a single-use transportation card and get a refund when you return it.

## Taxi:
If you want the most comfortable means possible, you should use a taxi. The basic fee is different from city to city but if you check whether the driver registers the basic fee on the meter, you won't get ripped off. Also, you don't have to tip the driver in Korea. But rates are increased between 12:00 a.m. and 4:00 a.m.

## Express Bus:
When you travel to other cities, you can take an express bus or highway bus from the Express Bus Terminal.

## Train:
Trains are also another convenient form of transportation. You can reserve a ticket online or at the train station. If you want a faster trip, you can use the KTX Express Train.

## Rental Car:
You must be over 21 years old and have more than one year's driving experience. You must also possess either an international driver's license or a national driver's license to rent a car. If possible, you should get an extra key and study the gas information beforehand.

## Transportation Card

It is convenient to use the T-money transportation card when using public transportation in Korea. You can buy and recharge one at a convenience store. You can use it on buses, the subway, and even in taxis. You can pay in cash for a bus but you have to buy a ticket for the subway, so it's more convenient to use the transportation card.

For taxis, you can use the transportation card for most taxis in Seoul, but be careful because you can not use the card in some cities. Starting from 12:00 a.m. and continuing until 4:00 a.m., there is a higher taxi fare. They charge up to extra 20% according to duration and distance. The basic fare for a taxi is 2,400 won and it shows on the meter when your ride begins.

You can get a transfer discount on a bus and the subway using the transportation card, and the fares are usually 1,000-1,200 won.

## Express Bus

There are express bus terminals in major cities in Korea. Seoul Express Bus Terminal in Gangnam and Dong Seoul Terminal in Gangdong are two major bus terminals in Seoul. Between the two, Seoul Express Bus Terminal is the larger one, and you can catch buses to most of the cities there. Routes differ with three expressways—Gyeongbu, Yeongdong, and Honam—according to the province, and ticketing windows at the bus terminals are divided according to destinations. On their websites, you can search timetables and buy tickets. They also contain other useful travel information.

**Seoul Express Bus Terminal:** http://www.exterminal.co.kr
**Dong Seoul Terminal:** https://www.ti21.co.kr/
**KOBUS Express Bus Lines Association:** http://www.kobus.co.kr/web/eng/index.jsp

## TRAIN

| | |
|---|---|
| Where can I catch the KTX on the <u>Gyeongbu Railway</u>? | **경부선 타는 곳이 어디예요?**<br><u>gyeongbuseon</u> keitiekseu taneun gosi eodiyeyo |

| | | |
|---|---|---|
| Gyeongbu Railway | **경부선** | gyeongbuseon |
| Yeongdong Railway | **영동선** | yeongdongseon |
| Honam Railway | **호남선** | honamseon |

| Which platform does the KTX for Busan leave from? | 부산행 KTX는 어느 홈에서 출발해요? busanhaeng keitiekseuneun eoneu homeseo chulbalhaeyo |
|---|---|

. . . . . . . . . . . . . . . . . . . . . . . . . . . . . . . . . . . . . . . . . . . . . . . . . . . . . . . . . . . .

| KTX Saemaul Mugunghwa | KTX keitiekseu 새마을호 saemaeulho 무궁화호 mugunghwaho |
|---|---|

. . . . . . . . . . . . . . . . . . . . . . . . . . . . . . . . . . . . . . . . . . . . . . . . . . . . . . . . . . . .

* Refer to page 365 for cities.

| A Is this the platform for the train to Gyeongju? | 여기가 경주행 홈이에요? yeogiga gyeongjuhaeng homieyo |
|---|---|

| B No, go to platform 5. | 아니요, 5번 홈으로 가세요. aniyo o-beon homeuro gaseyo |
|---|---|

* Refer to page 345 for numerals.

| A Is there a dining car on this train? | 이 열차에 식당차가 있어요? i yeolchae sikdangchaga isseoyo |
|---|---|

| B This train doesn't have a dining car. | 이 열차에는 식당차가 없어요. i yeolchaeneun sikdangchaga eopseoyo |
|---|---|

| A Is there a place I can get something to eat or drink? | 이 열차에 음식이나 음료수를 살 수 있는 데가 있어요? i yeolcha-e eumsigina eumnyosureul sal su inneun dega isseoyo |
|---|---|

| B Two cars ahead. | 두 칸 앞에 있어요. du kan ape isseoyo |
|---|---|

| Where is the restroom? | 화장실이 어디에 있어요?<br>hwajangsiri eodie isseoyo |

---

## Trains in Korea

Trains have many different seats and cars. On KTX, there is a movie car and a special car for children. You can choose them when you reserve a ticket. Also, there is a dining car where you can eat snacks and drinks. It also offers free Internet access. There is a tour train which a lot of people take to travel around the nation. If you are a tourist, we recommend you get on board Haerang, a train with hotel rooms.

## Vendors

| What kind of <u>juice</u> do you have? | 어떤 <u>주스가</u> 있어요?<br>eotteon <u>juseuga</u> isseoyo |

---

| juice | 주스가 juseuga |
| drinks | 음료수가 eumnyosuga |
| lunch box | 도시락이 dosiragi |
| snacks | 과자가 gwajaga |

---

* Refer to page 233 for food.

| Excuse me, do you have <u>beer</u>? | 저기요, 맥주 있어요?<br>jeogiyo <u>maekju</u> isseoyo |

| juice | 주스 juseu |
| water | 물 mul |
| coffee | 커피 keopi |
| black tea | 홍차 hongcha |
| green tea | 녹차 nokcha |
| lunch box | 도시락 dosirak |
| candy | 사탕 satang |
| gum | 껌 kkeom |
| ice cream | 아이스크림 aiseukeurim |
| clementine | 귤 gyul |
| peanuts | 땅콩 ttangkong |
| cookies | 과자 gwaja |
| sandwich | 샌드위치 saendeuwichi |

| What is that? | 그건 뭐예요?<br>geugeon mwoyeyo |

| Give me a orange juice and a sandwich, please. | 오렌지 주스하고 샌드위치 하나 주세요.<br>orenji juseuhago seandeuwichi hana juseyo |

| Do you have a straw? | 빨대 있어요?<br>ppaldae isseoyo |

| How much is it? | 얼마예요?<br>eolmayeyo |

# AIRPLANE

## To the Airport

A How should I get to the airport?

여기서 공항까지 뭘 타고 가는 게 좋을까요?
yeogiseo gonghangkkaji mwol tago ganeun ge joeulkkayo

B Take the <u>Airport Limousine</u>.

<u>공항 리무진을</u> 타세요.
<u>gonghang rimujineul</u> taseyo

---

Airport Limousine
Airport Railroad
taxi

공항 리무진을 gonghang rimujineul
공항철도를 gonghangcheoldoreul
택시를 taeksireul

---

Where is the Airport Limousine stop?

공항 리무진 타는 곳이 어디예요?
gonghang rimujin taneun gosi eodiyeyo?

Is the Airport Limousine stop around here?

근처에 공항 리무진 타는 곳이 있어요?
geuncheo-e gonghang rimujin taneun gosi isseoyo

---

### Airport Train

When you go to Incheon Airport from downtown Seoul, you can take the Airport Railroad from Seoul Station. You can also check your luggage there, which will save your time at the airport.

## Buying a Ticket

| | |
|---|---|
| 1 ticket for Daegu, <u>business class</u> on Korean Air, please. | 대구행 대한항공 <u>비지니스석</u>으로 1장 주세요.<br>daeguhaeng daehanhanggong <u>bijiniseuseo</u>geuro han-jang juseyo |

| | |
|---|---|
| economy class | 일반석 ilbanseok |
| business class | 비지니스석 bijiniseuseok |
| first class | 일등석 ildeungseok |

| | |
|---|---|
| **A** How many kilograms is the baggage allowance? | 수하물은 몇 킬로그램까지 무료예요?<br>suhamureun myeot killogeuraemkkaji muryoyeyo |
| **B** The free baggage allowence is <u>10</u> kg. | <u>10</u>킬로그램까지 무료입니다.<br><u>sip</u>-killogeuraemkkaji muryoimnida<br><br>* Refer to page 345 for numerals. |

| | |
|---|---|
| I'd like to check this suitcase. | 이 가방 좀 맡기고 싶은데요.<br>i gabang jom matgigo sipeundeyo |
| My luggage is <u>one</u> bag and <u>two</u> boxes. | 수하물은 이 가방 <u>한</u> 개하고 박스 <u>두</u> 개가 있어요.<br>suhamureun i gabang <u>han</u> gaehago bakseu <u>du</u> gaega isseoyo<br><br>* Refer to page 345 for numerals. |

| | |
|---|---|
| I'll carry this on. | 이건 들고 탈 거예요.<br>igeon deulgo tal geoyeyo |

**A** What is the boarding gate?

탑승 게이트는 몇 번이에요?

tapseung geiteuneun myeot beonieyo

**B** Go to Gate 8.

8번 게이트로 가세요.

pal-beon geiteuro gaseyo

## Boarding

Can you please place this bag up in the overhead compartment?

이 가방 좀 위에 있는 짐칸에 넣어 주시겠어요?

i gabang jom wie inneun jimkane neo-eo jusigesseoyo

May I have <u>a glass of water</u>, please?

<u>물 한 잔</u> 좀 부탁합니다.

<u>mul han jan</u> jom butakamnida

| | |
|---|---|
| a glass of water | 물 한 잔 mul han jan |
| a glass of juice | 주스 한 잔 juseu han jan |
| a glass of Coke | 콜라 한 잔 kolla han jan |
| a blanket | 담요 한 장 damnyo han jang |
| a newspaper | 신문 한 부 sinmun han bu |

# DRIVING

## RENTING A CAR

Where can I rent
a car?

차를 어디서 빌릴 수 있어요?
chareul eodiseo billil su isseoyo

I want to rent a car.

차를 한 대 빌리고 싶어요.
chareul han dae billigo sipeoyo

I'd like to rent a car for
a day.

차를 하루 빌리려고 해요.
chareul haru billiryeogo haeyo

Here is my international
driver's license.

여기 제 국제 면허증이 있어요.
yeogi je gukje myeonheojeung-i
isseoyo

How old do I have to
be to rent a car?

렌트할 수 있는 나이는 몇 살부터예요?
renteuhal su inneun naineun myeot
salbuteoyeyo

What documents do
I need?

준비해야 할 서류는 무엇이 있어요?
junbihaeya hal seoryuneun mueosi
isseoyo

How many years of
driving experience
should I have?

운전 경력은 몇 년 이상이어야 해요?
unjeon gyeongnyeogeun myeot
nyeon isang-ieoya haeyo

Can you show me the
list of available cars?

렌터카 목록을 좀 보여 주시겠어요?
renteoka mongnogeul jom boyeo
jusigesseoyo

| What kinds of cars can I rent? | 렌트할 수 있는 차의 종류는 무엇이 있어요? |
| | renteuhal su inneun chaui jongnyuneun mueosi isseoyo |

| Do you have <u>compact cars</u>? | <u>소형차</u> 있어요? |
| | <u>sohyeongcha</u> isseoyo |

| compact cars | 소형차 sohyeongcha |
| medium-sized cars | 중형차 junghyeongcha |
| large cars | 대형차 daehyeongcha |

| Can you show me the fees plan? | 요금표 좀 보여 주시겠어요? |
| | yogeumpyo jom boyeo jusigesseoyo |

| How much is the daily rate? | 하루 대여하는 데 요금이 얼마예요? |
| | haru daeyeohaneun de yogeumi eolmayeyo |

| Are the prices different during the peak season and the off-season? | 성수기와 비수기 때 요금이 달라요? |
| | seongsugiwa bisugi ttae yogeumi dallayo |

| Does the rental fee include gas? | 요금에 기름값이 포함되어 있어요? |
| | yogeume gireumgapsi pohamdoe-eo isseoyo |

| Is cost of insurance included in the rental fee? | 이 요금에 보험료도 포함되어 있어요? |
| | i yogeume boheomnyodo pohamdoe-eo isseoyo |

| I'll buy comprehensive insurance. | 종합 보험으로 들게요. |
| | jonghap boheomeuro deulgeyo |

| comprehensive insurance | 종합 보험 jonghap boheom |
| basic insurance | 기본 보험 gibon boheom |

| How much is the premium? | 보험료는 얼마예요? |
| | boheomnyoneun eolmayeyo |

| How much is the deposit? | 보증금이 얼마예요? |
| | bojeunggeumi eolmayeyo |

| Should I pay in advance? | 선불로 드려야 해요? |
| | seonbullo deuryeoya haeyo |

| Can I pay by credit card? | 신용카드로 계산해도 될까요? |
| | sinyongkadeuro gyesanhaedo doelkkayo |

| The car is in good running order, right? | 차에는 아무런 이상이 없지요? |
| | cha-eneun amureon isang-i eopjiyo |

| Should I return the car with a full tank of gas? | 차를 반납할 때 기름도 채워 넣어야 해요? |
| | chareul bannapal ttae gireumdo chaewo neoeoya haeyo |

| Where should I return the car? | 차를 어디에 반납하면 돼요? |
| | chareul eodie bannapamyeon dwaeyo |

| I want to keep it longer. How much extra is that? | 반납 시간을 연장하고 싶은데 추가요금이 얼마예요? |
| | bannap siganeul yeonjanghago sipeunde chugayogeumi eolmayeyo |

| Tell me the emergency contact numbers. | 비상 전화번호 좀 가르쳐 주세요. |
| | bisang jeonhwabeonho jom gareuchyeo juseyo |

---

## Using a Rental Car in Korea

Rental car prices depend on the type of car and rental time. If you rent a car for a day, it costs anywhere from at least 90,000 won to 170,000 won. You have to be over 21 years old and have more than one year's worth of driving experience to rent a car. You also have to have either an international driver's license or a national driver's license. If possible, you should get an extra key and keep in separate, and study the gas information beforehand.

## DEALING WITH AN ACCIDENT

| Did you report it to the police? | 경찰서에 연락했어요? |
| | gyeongchalseo-e yeollakaesseoyo |

| Call 119 immediately if someone's been hurt. | 다친 사람이 있으면 지금 즉시 119에 전화하세요. |
| | dachin sarami isseumyeon jigeum jeuksi ililgu-e jeonhwahaseyo |

| Are you OK? I'll call an ambulance. | 괜찮으세요? 구급차를 불러 드릴게요. |
| | gwaenchaneuseyo gugeupchareul bulleo deurilkkeyo |

Don't go anywhere. Just stay where you are.

다른 곳으로 이동하지 말고 그 자리에 그대로 계세요.

dareun goseuro idonghaji malgo geu jarie geudaero gyeseyo

It wasn't my fault.

저에게는 과실이 없어요.

jeo-egeneun gwasiri eopseoyo

I wasn't speeding.

저는 과속을 하지 않았어요.

jeoneun gwasogeul haji anasseoyo

Are you a witness?

사고를 목격하셨나요?

sagoreul mokgyeokasyeonnayo

He / She crossed the street without looking at the traffic light.

그 사람이 교통신호를 보지 않고 길을 건넜어요.

geu sarami gyotongsinhoreul boji anko gireul geonneosseoyo

My car is totaled.

제 차가 완전히 찌그러졌어요.

je chaga wanjeonhi jjigeureojyeosseoyo

Will you be reporting this to your insurance company or taking care of it yourself?

보험 처리를 하시겠어요, 아니면 본인이 부담하시겠어요?

boheom cheorireul hasigesseoyo animyeon bonini budamhasigesseoyo

Do you have insurance?

보험에 드셨어요?

boheome deusyeosseoyo

Call the insurance company if the car was badly damaged.

차가 많이 파손되었으면 보험 회사에 전화하세요.

chaga mani pasondoe-eosseumyeon boheom hoesa-e jeonhwahaseyo

| | |
|---|---|
| Could you take pictures of the scene of the accident? | 사고 현장 사진을 찍어 주시겠어요?<br>sago hyeonjang sajineul jjigeo jusigesseoyo |
| Please get the contact information of any witnesses. | 혹시 주변에 목격자가 있으면 연락처를 받아 두세요.<br>hoksi jubyeone mokgyeokjaga isseumyeon yeollakcheoreul bada duseyo |
| Give me your business card with your contact numbers on, please. | 연락처가 적힌 명함이 있으면 한 장 주세요.<br>yeollakcheoga jeokin myeonghami isseumyeon han jang juseyo |

## GAS STATION

| | |
|---|---|
| How much gas is there left in the car now? | 차 안에 지금 기름이 얼마나 있어요?<br>cha ane jigeum gireumi eolmana isseoyo |
| <u>Gasoline</u>, please. | <u>휘발유로</u> 부탁해요.<br><u>hwibalyuro</u> butakaeyo |

| | |
|---|---|
| gasoline | 휘발유로 hwibalyuro |
| disel | 경유로 gyeongyuro |
| LPG | LPG로 elpijiro |

| | |
|---|---|
| Which pump should I pull up to? | 몇 번 주유기에 차를 세울까요?<br>myeot beon juyugie chareul se-ulkkayo |

| | |
|---|---|
| 30 liters, please. | 30리터 넣어 주세요.<br>**samsip**-riteo neoeo juseyo<br><br>* Refer to page 345 for numerals. |
| Put in as much as worth of 50,000 won, please. | 50,000원어치 넣어 주세요.<br>**oman**-woneochi neoeo juseyo<br><br>* Refer to page 95 for money. |
| Fill it up, please. | 가득 채워 주세요.<br>gadeuk chaewo juseyo |
| Can you do the wash as well, please? | 세차도 해 주시겠어요?<br>sechado hae jusigesseoyo |
| May I have a receipt, please? | 영수증 좀 끊어 주시겠어요?<br>yeongsujeung jom kkeuneo jusigesseoyo |
| Can I pay with a credit card? | 카드로 계산해도 될까요?<br>kadeuro gyesanhaedo doelkkayo |
| Should I turn off the engine? | 차 시동을 끌까요?<br>cha sidongeul kkeulkkayo |
| Should I open the gas tank? | 주유구를 열까요?<br>juyugureul yeolkkayo |

## AUTO REPAIR

| | |
|---|---|
| There is something wrong with the steering wheel. | 핸들에 문제가 생겼어요.<br>haendeure munjega saenggyeosseoyo |

| steering wheel | 핸들 haendeul |
| brakes | 브레이크 beureikeu |
| accelerator | 액셀 aeksel |
| wipers | 와이퍼 waipeo |
| wheel | 바퀴 bakwi |
| brake lights | 브레이크 등 beureikeu deung |
| tail lights | 미 등 mi deung |
| headlights | 헤드라이트 hedeuraiteu |
| back up light | 후진 등 hujin deung |
| blinkers | 점멸 등 jeommyeol deung |

| I don't know exactly what the problem is. | 차의 어느 부분에 이상이 있는지 모르겠어요.<br>chaui eoneu bubune isang-i inneunji moreugesseoyo |
| I'm not quite sure, but there seems to be something wrong with the battery. | 잘은 모르겠지만 배터리에 이상이 있는 것 같아요.<br>jareun moreugetjiman baeteorie isang-i inneun geot gatayo |
| Please charge the battery. | 배터리 충전 좀 부탁합니다.<br>baeteori chungjeon jom butakamnida |
| Change this tire, please. | 이 타이어 좀 갈아 주세요.<br>i taieo jom gara juseyo |
| It seems like it's leaking oil. Check the oil, please. | 오일이 새는 것 같은데 오일을 좀 점검해 주세요.<br>oiri saeneun geot gateunde oireul jom jeomgeomhae juseyo |
| Is there anything wrong with the car? | 뭐가 잘못 되었어요?<br>mwoga jalmot doe-eoseoyo |

| Do you think you can repair it? | 수리 가능할까요? |
| | suri ganeunghalkkayo |
| Do you have the necessary parts for the repairs? | 수리에 필요한 부속품은 있어요? |
| | surie piryohan busokpumeun isseoyo |
| Could you repair it right now? | 지금 바로 고칠 수 있을까요? |
| | jigeum baro gochil su isseulkkayo |
| How long do you need to repair it? | 수리하는 데 얼마나 걸려요? |
| | surihaneun de eolmana geollyeoyo |
| My car suddenly stalled. | 시동이 갑자기 꺼졌어요. |
| | sidong-i gapjagi kkeojyeosseoyo |
| Could you check the engine? | 차의 엔진 상태 좀 점검해 주시겠어요? |
| | chaui enjin sangtae jom jeomgeomhae jusigesseoyo |
| There seems to be something wrong with the brakes. | 브레이크에 뭔가 문제가 있는 것 같아요. |
| | beureikeue mwonga munjega inneun geot gatayo |
| Would you put some air in the tires? | 타이어에 공기 좀 가득 넣어 주시겠어요? |
| | taieo-e gonggi jom gadeuk neoeo jusigesseoyo |
| One of the blinkers is burned out. | 점멸 등이 하나 나갔어요. |
| | jeommyeol deung-i hana nagasseoyo |
| Would you check the tire pressure? | 타이어 공기압을 점검해 주시겠어요? |
| | taieo gonggiabeul jeomgeomhae jusigesseoyo |

The engine is making a strange noise. Could you check it?

엔진에서 이상한 소리가 나는데 좀 봐 주시겠어요?

enjineseo isanghan soriga naneunde jom bwa jusigesseoyo

The engine is overheated.

엔진이 과열되었어요.

enjini gwayeoldoe-eosseoyo

There's no air in one of the tires.

타이어에 바람이 빠졌어요.

taieoe barami ppajyeosseoyo

Is everything done?

수리 다 끝났어요?

suri da kkeunnasseoyo

Now, the car starts.

이제 시동이 걸리네요.

ije sidong-i geollineyo

Thank you for repairing my car.

고쳐주셔서 감사합니다.

gochyeojusyeoseo gamsahamnida

Can you give me the bill?

수리비 견적 좀 뽑아 주세요.

suribi gyeonjeok jom ppoba juseyo

Do you want me to pay in advance or later?

선불로 드려야 해요? 아니면 후불로 드려야 해요?

seonbullo deuryeoya haeyo animyeon hubullo deuryeoya haeyo

## PARKING

What time does the parking lot open?

주차장은 몇 시에 문을 열어요?

juchajang-eun myeot sie muneul yeoreoyo

173

| How much is it for one hour? | 한 시간에 주차료가 얼마예요?<br>hansigane jucharyoga eolmayeyo |
| I'd like to park for two hours. | 두 시간 주차하려고 해요.<br>dusigan juchaharyeogo haeyo |
| Excuse me, can I park here? | 실례합니다만, 여기에 주차 가능해요?<br>sillyehamnidaman yeogie jucha ganeunghaeyo |
| Is this a no-parking zone? | 여기가 주차 금지 구역이에요?<br>yeogiga jucha geumji guyeogieyo |
| Aren't there any free parking lots around here? | 이 주변에 무료 주차장은 없어요?<br>i jubyeone muryo juchajang-eun eopseoyo |
| Are there any open spots where I can park? | 지금 제 차를 주차할 공간이 있나요?<br>jigeum je chareul juchahal gonggani innayo |
| It's difficult to find a parking space. | 주차할 곳을 찾기가 어렵네요.<br>juchahal goseul chatgiga eoryeomneyo |
| Where is the customer parking? | 고객 전용 주차장은 어디에 있어요?<br>gogaek jeonyong juchajang-eun eodie isseoyo |
| The parking lot is full. | 주차장이 꽉 찼네요.<br>juchajang-i kkwak channeyo |
| Is this a towaway zone? | 여기는 견인지역이에요?<br>yeogineun gyeoninjiyeogieyo |

Could you back up a little, please?

차를 뒤로 좀 빼 주실래요?

chareul dwiro jom ppae jusillaeyo

I'd like a valet parking, please?

대신 주차 좀 해 주시겠어요?

daesin jucha jom hae jusigesseoyo

## ROAD SIGNS

| 통행금지 | 자동차통행금지표시 | 자전거통행금지표시 | 정차 · 주차금지표시 |
|---|---|---|---|
| No Trespassing | No Cars | No Bicycles | No Stopping or Parking |

| 앞지르기금지 | 최고속도제한 | 최저속도제한 | 진입금지 |
|---|---|---|---|
| No Passing | Speed Limit | Minimum Speed | Do Not Enter |

| 자동차전용도로 | 자전거전용차로 | 주차장 | 어린이보호(어린이보호구역안) |
|---|---|---|---|
| Cars Only | Bicycles Only | Parking | Children Zone |

175

## Position of Driver's Seat in Korea

In Korea, LHD (left-hand drive) is a standard policy. Driver's seats are on the left side of the cars and the drivers control steering wheels using left hand whereas change gears using right hand.

## ASKING DIRECTIONS

| | |
|---|---|
| Can you tell me where I am on this map? | 이 지도에서 지금 제가 있는 곳이 어디인지 말씀해 주시겠어요?<br>i jido-eseo jigeum jega inneun gosi eodiinji malsseumhae jusigesseoyo |
| Can you tell me where Hanguk Hospital is on this map? | 이 지도에서 한국병원이 어디에 있는지 좀 알려주세요.<br>i jidoeseo hangukbyeongwoni eodie inneunji jom allyeojuseyo |
| Should I go straight? | 곧장 가야 해요?<br>gotjang gaya haeyo |
| Should I turn right? | 오른쪽으로 돌아야 해요?<br>oreunjjogeuro doraya haeyo |
| Where is the ramp for the expressway? | 고속도로 진입로가 어디에 있어요?<br>gosokdoro jinimnoga eodie isseoyo |
| What is the best way to go there? | 거기에 가려면 어떻게 가는 게 좋아요?<br>geogie garyeomyeon eotteoke ganeun ge joayo |

| | |
|---|---|
| Should I make a <u>right turn</u> here? | 여기서 <u>우회전</u>하면 돼요?<br>yeogiseo uhoejeonhamyeon dwaeyo |

| | |
|---|---|
| right turn | 우회전 uhoejeon |
| left turn | 좌회전 jwahoejeon |
| U-turn | 유턴 yuteon |

| | |
|---|---|
| You will see the detour if you go a little more. | 조금만 더 가면 우회로가 나올 거예요.<br>jogeumman deo gamyeon uhoeroga naol geoyeyo |
| There is heavy traffic. Can you find the side streets? | 차가 많이 막히네요. 이면 도로를 찾아 봐 주시겠어요?<br>chaga mani makineyo imyeon dororeul chaja bwa jusigesseoyo |
| Which way is the fastest? | 어느 길로 가는 게 가장 빠를까요?<br>eoneu gillo ganeun ge gajang ppareulkkayo |
| Where is the nearest intersection? | 여기에서 가장 가까운 교차로가 어디예요?<br>yeogieseo gajang gakkaun gyocharoga eodiyeyo |
| Which road should I take to go there? | 거기에 가려면 어느 길로 가야 해요?<br>geogie garyeomyeon eoneu gillo gaya haeyo |
| Take a left turn at the next intersection. | 다음 교차로에서 좌회전을 하세요.<br>da-eum gyocharo-eseo jwahoejeoneul haseyo |

# COMMUNICATIONS

## TELEPHONE

Hello.

여보세요.
yeoboseyo

Would you get the
phone, please?

전화 좀 대신 받아 주시겠어요?
jeonhwa jom daesin bada
jusigesseoyo

Is this _____'s cell
phone?

_____ 씨 휴대 전화인가요?
_____ ssi hyudae jeonhwaingayo

Is _____ there? Can
I speak to _____?

_____ 씨 계세요? _____ 씨 좀
바꿔주세요.
_____ ssi gyeseyo _____ ssi jom
bakkwojuseyo

May I ask who's
calling, please?

실례지만 누구십니까?
sillyejiman nugusimnikka

Hold on, please.
I'll put you through.

잠깐만 기다려 주세요. 바로 연결해
드리겠습니다.
jamkkanman gidaryeo juseyo baro
yeongyeolhae deurigesseumnida

He / She is not in.
Would you like to
leave a message?

지금 자리에 안 계세요. 메모 남겨
드릴까요?
jigeum jarie an gyeseyo memo
namgyeo deurilkkayo

| Could you tell him / her that I called? | 제가 전화했었다고 전해 주시겠어요? |
| | jega jeonhwahaesseotdago jeonhae jusigesseoyo |

| I'll call back later. | 제가 나중에 다시 전화 드리겠습니다. |
| | jega najunge dasi jeonhwa deurigesseumnida |

| What time are you expecting him / her? | 몇 시쯤 들어오실까요? |
| | myeot sijjeum deureoosilkkayo |

| Could you call back? He / She will be back soon. | 다시 전화 주시겠어요? 금방 돌아오실 거예요. |
| | dasi jeonhwa jusigesseoyo geumbang doraosil geoyeyo |

| Who was that on the phone? | 누구에게서 온 전화였어요? |
| | nuguegeseo on jeonhwayeosseoyo |

| I heard that you called me. What's going on? | 제게 전화하셨다고 하던데 무슨 일이에요? |
| | jege jeonhwahasyeotdago hadeonde museun irieyo |

| A Mr. / Ms. _____, there's a call for you. Pick it up please. | _____ 씨, 전화 왔어요. 전화 받으세요. |
| | _____ ssi jeonhwa wasseoyo jeonhwa badeuseyo |

| B I am not available now. Tell him / her that I'll call back later. | 지금은 전화 받기가 곤란해요. 제가 나중에 다시 전화한다고 전해 주세요. |
| | jigeumeun jeonhwa batgiga gollanhaeyo jega najung-e dasi jeonhwahandago jeonhae juseyo |

Were there any phone calls for me?

저한테 전화 온 것 없었어요?

jeohante jeonhwa on geot eopseosseoyo

Take a message if anyone calls for me, please.

저한테 전화 오면 메모 좀 받아 주세요.

jeohante jeonhwa omyeon memo jom bada juseyo

Could you call me back in ten minutes?

10분 뒤에 다시 전화 주시겠어요?

sip-bun dwie dasi jeonhwa jusigesseoyo

You must have call the wrong number. What number did you dial?

전화 잘못 거신 것 같은데 몇 번으로 거셨어요?

jeonhwa jalmot geosin geot gateunde myeot beoneuro geosyeosseoyo

I'm sorry. I must have call the wrong number.

죄송합니다. 전화 잘못 걸었습니다.

joesonghamnida jeonhwa jalmot georeosseumnida

This is regarding an urgent matter, could you give me _____'s cell phone number?

조금 급해서 그런데 _____ 씨 휴대전화 번호 좀 알 수 있을까요?

jogeum geupaeseo geureonde _____ ssi hyudaejeonhwa beonho jom al su isseulkkayo

I'm sorry to call you so early.

이른 시간에 전화 드려서 죄송해요.

ireun sigane jeonhwa deuryeoseo joesonghaeyo

I haven't called you for a long time. How have you been?

정말 오랜만에 연락 드려요. 그동안 잘 지내셨어요?

jeongmal oraenmane yeollak deuryeoyo geudongan jal jinaesyeosseoyo

| We have a bad connection. I'll call you back. | 전화 상태가 안 좋은데 제가 다시 걸게요. |
| | jeonhwa sangtaega an jo-eunde jega dasi geolgeyo |

## MAKING INTERNATIONAL CALLS

| Where can I buy <u>international calling cards</u>? | <u>국제전화카드는</u> 어디서 구입할 수 있나요? |
| | gukjejeonhwakadeuneun eodiseo guipal su innayo |

| international calling cards | 국제전화카드는 gukjejeonhwakadeuneun |
| prepaid international calling cards | 선불국제전화카드는 seonbulgukjejeonhwakadeuneun |
| disposable phones | 일회용 휴대폰은 ilhoeyong hyudaeponeun |
| SIM cards | 유심카드는 yusimkadeuneun |

| Do you have prepaid international calling cards? | 선불국제전화카드를 판매하시나요? |
| | seonbulgukjejeonhwakadeureul panmaehasinayo |

| How can I make an international phone call? | 국제전화는 어떻게 하나요? |
| | gukjejeonhwaneun eotteoke hanayo |

| What's the rate for international phone calls? | 국제전화 비용은 얼마예요? |
| | gukjejeonhwa biyongeun eolmayeyo |

| Is the card rechargeable? | 카드는 충전 가능해요?<br>kadeuneun chungjeon ganeunghaeyo |
| Would I be able to use this SIM card on my phone? | 제 휴대폰에서 이 유심카드를 사용할 수 있을까요?<br>je hyudaeponeseo i yusimkadeureul sayonghal su isseulkkayo |
| Give me one with instructions in English. | 영어 사용 설명이 있는 카드로 주세요.<br>yeong-eo sayong seolmyeong-i inneun kadeuro juseyo |
| I would like to make a collect call to the <u>USA</u>. | 미국으로 수신자 요금 부담 전화를 걸고 싶어요.<br>migugeuro susinja budam jeonhwareul geolgo sipeoyo |

\* Refer to page 362 for countries.

| How long can I use this card to call Canada? | 이 카드로 캐나다에 몇 분이나 통화할 수 있어요?<br>i kadeuro kaenada-e myeot bunina tonghwahal su isseoyo |
| What's the country code for Austrailia? | 호주 국가 번호가 뭐죠?<br>hoju gukga beonhoga mwojyo |
| Where are the pay phones? | 공중전화는 어디에 있어요?<br>gongjungjeonhwaneun eodie isseoyo |

## AT THE POST OFFICE

| I'd like to send it by <u>regular mail</u>. | 보통우편으로 보내고 싶어요.<br>botong-upyeoneuro bonaego sipeoyo |

| regular mail = first (class) mail | 보통우편으로 botong-upyeoneuro |
| one day express | 당일특급으로 dang-ilteukgeubeuro |
| next morning express | 익일오전특급으로 igilojeonteukgeubeuro |
| next day express | 익일특급으로 igilteukgeubeuro |

Give me three stamps, please.

우표 세 장 주세요.
upyo se jang juseyo

When is the commemorative stamp released?

기념우표는 언제부터 발매해요?
ginyeomupyoneun eonjebuteo balmaehaeyo

Is the commemorative stamp still available ?

기념우표가 아직 남아 있어요?
ginyeomupyoga ajik nama isseoyo

I'd like a delievery service. How much would that be?

택배로 보내려고 하는데 요금이 얼마예요?
taekbaero bonaeryeogo haneunde yogeumi eolmayeyo

How much does it cost for international parcel?

국제소포는 우편요금이 얼마예요?
gukjesoponeun upyeonyogeumi eolmayeyo

Are there banned items that I can't mail overseas?

외국으로 소포를 부치지 못 하는 물품들이 있어요?
oegugeuro soporeul buchiji mot haneun mulpumdeuri isseoyo

I want to check the delivery status.

수신 조회를 하고 싶어요.
susin johoereul hago sipeoyo

|  |  |
|---|---|
| I'd like to mail it by EMS scheduled service. | EMS 정기특급우편으로 보내고 싶어요.<br>iemeseu jeonggiteukgeubupyeoneuro bonaego sipeoyo |
| scheduled service | 정기특급우편<br>jeonggiteukgeubupyeon |
| on demand service | 부정기특급우편<br>bujeonggiteukgeubupyeon |
| on demand casual service | 수시특급우편<br>susiteukgeubupyeon |
| I'd like to have this card registered. | 이 카드를 등기로 부쳐 주세요.<br>i kadeureul deunggiro buchyeo juseyo |
| card | 카드 kadeu |
| postcard | 엽서 yeopseo |
| letter | 편지 pyeonji |
| How long does it take to get there? | 그곳까지 도착하는 데 얼마나 걸려요?<br>geugotkkaji dochakaneun de eolmana geollyeoyo |
| What is the postal code? | 우편번호가 몇 번이에요?<br>upyeonbeonhoga myeot beonieyo |
| How much does this parcel weigh? | 이 소포 무게가 얼마나 나가요?<br>i sopo mugega eolmana nagayo |
| Where should I write the sender's name and address? | 보내는 사람 주소와 이름을 어디에 쓰면 돼요?<br>bonaeneun saram jusowa ireumeul eodie sseumyeon dwaeyo |

| | |
|---|---|
| sender | 보내는 사람 bonaeneun saram |
| recipient | 받는 사람 banneun saram |

| | |
|---|---|
| How much does it cost to send this letter to the USA? | 이 편지를 미국에 보내는 데 비용이 얼마나 들어요?<br>i pyeonjireul miguge bonaeneun de biyong-i eolmana deureoyo<br>* Refer to page 362 for countries. |
| Which window should I go to buy stamps? | 우표를 사려면 몇 번 창구로 가야 해요?<br>upyoreul saryeomyeon myeot beon changguro gaya haeyo |
| When will this letter arrive? | 이 편지는 언제쯤 그곳에 도착해요?<br>i pyeonjineun eonjejjeum geugose dochakaeyo |
| The item is fragile. Please mark on it. | 내용물이 깨지기 쉬운 것이어서 별도로 표시 부탁합니다.<br>naeyongmuri kkaejigi swiun geosieoseo byeoldoro pyosi butakamnida |
| Which service should I use to send this parcel quickly? | 이 소포를 빨리 보내려면 어떤 우편으로 보내야 하나요?<br>i soporeul ppalli bonaeryeomyeon eotteon upyeoneuro bonaeya hanayo |
| Please send this to me by wire. | 이것을 전보로 보내 주세요.<br>igeoseul jeonboro bonae juseyo |

## USING THE INTERNET

Internet processing is too slow.

인터넷 속도가 너무 느려요.
inteonet sokdoga neomu neuryeoyo

Please tell me any interesting websites.

재미있는 인터넷 사이트가 있으면 좀 알려 주세요.
jaemiinneun inteonet saiteuga isseumyeon jom allyeo juseyo

I made my own homepage on the Internet.

인터넷에 제 홈페이지를 만들었어요.
inteonese je hompeijireul mandeureosseoyo

I made my own homepage recently.

최근에 제 홈페이지를 만들었어요.
choegeune je hompeijireul mandeureosseoyo

Click here.

여기를 클릭해 보세요.
yeogireul keullikae boseyo

Let me search for it on the Internet.

인터넷으로 검색해볼게요.
inteoneseuro geomsaekaebolgeyo

Is there any website you visit frequently?

자주 이용하는 인터넷 사이트가 있어요?
jaju iyonghaneun inteonet saiteuga isseoyo

I can't get on the Internet right now.

인터넷이 지금 안 돼요.
inteonesi jigeum an dwaeyo

When you get on the Internet, send me an e-Mail.

인터넷이 되면 이메일로 보내 주세요.
inteonesi doemyeon imeillo bonae juseyo

| Do you have an Internet line here? | 여기에 인터넷 전용선이 깔려 있어요?<br>yeogie inteonet jeonyongseoni kkallyeo isseoyo |
| --- | --- |
| These days many people use the shopping malls on the Internet. | 요즘 사람들은 인터넷 쇼핑몰을 많이 이용해요.<br>yojeum saramdeureun inteonet syopingmoreul mani iyonghaeyo |
| I contact my friends through e-Mail. | 이메일로 친구와 연락해요.<br>imeillo chinguwa yeollakaeyo |
| I chat with my friend on the Internet. | 인터넷에서 친구와 채팅을 해요.<br>inteoneseseo chinguwa chaeting-eul haeyo |
| My cellphone has wireless Web access. | 제 휴대폰으로 무선 인터넷을 사용할 수 있어요.<br>je hyudaeponeuro museon inteoneseul sayonghal su isseoyo |
| It's great that I can search for the information on the Internet these days. | 요즘은 인터넷으로 정보를 검색할 수 있어서 좋아요.<br>yojeumeun inteoneseuro jeongboreul geomsaekal su isseoseo joayo |
| Can I download movies on the Internet for free? | 인터넷에서 무료로 영화를 다운 받을 수 있나요?<br>inteoneseseo muryoro yeonghwareul daun badeul su innayo |
| The Internet stops working often and it is inconvenient. | 인터넷 접속이 자주 끊겨서 불편해요.<br>inteonet jeopsogi jaju kkeungyeoseo bulpyeonhaeyo |

Can I use the WiFi
here?

여기에서 와이파이를 사용할 수 있어요?

yeogieseo waipaireul sayonghal su
isseoyo

Could you recommend
a cheap wireless
router?

저렴한 무선 공유기 좀 추천해주세요.

jeoryeomhan museon gongyugi jom
chucheonhaejuseyo

# MEETING PEOPLE

## MEETING FOR THE FIRST TIME

| How are you? | 안녕하세요.<br>annyeonghaseyo |
| --- | --- |
| A Nice to meet you. | 만나서 반가워요.<br>mannaseo bangawoyo |
| B Nice to meet you, too. | 저도 반갑습니다.<br>jeodo bangapsseumnida |
| I'm glad to meet you. | 만나서 기뻐요.<br>mannaseo gippeoyo |
| A What shall I call you? | 성함을 어떻게 불러야 할까요?<br>seonghameul eotteoke bulleoya halkkayo |
| B Call me _____. | _____ 라고 부르세요.<br>_____ rago bureuseyo |
| Allow me to introduce myself. | 제 소개를 하겠습니다.<br>je sogaereul hagesseumnida |
| My name is _____. | 제 이름은 _____ 입니다.<br>je ireumeun _____ imnida |
| A Where are you from? | 어디에서 오셨어요?<br>eodieseo osyeosseoyo |

**B** I'm from New
Zealand.

저는 뉴질랜드에서 왔어요.
jeoneun nyujilaendeueseo wasseoyo

* Refer to page 362 for countries.

**A** Have you been in
Korea long?

한국에 계신지 오래 되셨나요?
hanguge gyesinji orae doesyeonnayo

**B** No, I just got here
today.

아니요, 오늘 막 왔어요.
aniyo oneul mak wasseoyo

Where do you live?

어디에 사세요?
eodie saseyo

**A** What do you do?

무슨 일을 하세요?
museun ireul haseyo

**B** I work in business.

사업을 하고 있어요.
saeobeul hago isseoyo

**A** Where are you
headed?

어디로 가세요?
eodiro gaseyo

**B** I'm going to Daegu.

대구로 가요.
daeguro gayo

* Refer to page 365 for cities.

**A** How long do you
plan to stay there?

거기에 얼마나 계실 거예요?
geogie eolmana gyesil geoyeyo

**B** About a week.

일주일 정도 있을 거예요.
iljuil jeongdo isseul geoyeyo

* Refer to page 356 for times.

## AFTER A LONG TIME

| Long time, no see. | 오랜만입니다.<br>oraenmanimnida |
| It's been a long time. | 오래간만이에요.<br>oraeganmanieyo |
| A How are you doing? | 어떻게 지내세요?<br>eotteoke jinaeseyo |
| B I'm doing well. | 전 잘 지내요.<br>jeon jal jinaeyo |
| B I'm very well. | 아주 좋아요.<br>aju joayo |
| B Nothing much. | 별일 없어요.<br>byeolil eopseoyo |

## WITH LOCALS

| I'm planning to go to Busan, Gyeongju, and Ulsan. | 부산, 경주, 울산에 들릴 예정이에요.<br>busan gyeongju ulsane deullil yejeongieyo |

\* Refer to page 365 for cities.

| What do you think of my itinerary? | 제 여행 일정이 어때요?<br>je yeohaeng iljeong-i eottaeyo |

| Is there anything not on my itinerary that you would recommend? | 이 외에 어디 갈 만한 곳 없어요? |
| | i oe-e eodi gal manhan got eopseoyo |
| | |
| Could you recommend a good place to eat? | 어디 좋은 식당 하나 소개해 주시겠어요? |
| | eodi jo-eun sikdang hana sogaehae jusigesseoyo |
| | |
| Where's a good place to buy souvenirs? | 기념품을 사려고 하는데 어디가 좋아요? |
| | ginyeompumeul saryeogo haneunde eodiga joayo |
| | |
| Do you live <u>here</u>? | <u>여기에</u> 사세요? |
| | <u>yeogie</u> saseyo |

- - -

| here | 여기에 yeogie |
| in Seoul | 서울에 seoure |
| in Busan | 부산에 busane |

- - -

| I've always wanted to come here. | 여길 꼭 한 번 오고 싶었어요. |
| | yeogil kkok han beon ogo sipeosseoyo |
| | |
| It's a wonderful place. | 정말 좋은 곳이네요. |
| | jeongmal jo-eun gosineyo |
| | |
| I've really been enjoying my time here. | 여기 있는 동안 정말 즐거웠어요. |
| | yeogi inneun dongan jeongmal jeulgeowosseoyo |
| | |
| I've been to Busan, Gyeongju, and Ulsan so far. | 지금까지 부산, 경주, 울산을 다녀왔어요. |
| | jigeumkkaji busan gyeongju ulsaneul danyeowasseoyo |

| Are you with a tour group? | 단체 관광하는 사람들과 함께 오셨어요? |
| | danche gwangwanghaneun saramdeulgwa hamkke osyeosseoyo |

| a tour group | 단체 관광하는 사람들과 |
| | danche gwangwanghaneun saramdeulgwa |
| your family | 가족과 gajokgwa |
| your friend | 친구와 chinguwa |

| A Are you on your own? | 혼자 오셨어요? |
| | honja osyeosseoyo |
| B I'm here alone. | 혼자 왔어요. |
| | honja wasseoyo |

| alone | 혼자 honja |
| with my wife | 아내와 같이 anaewa gachi |
| with my husband | 남편과 같이 nampyeongwa gachi |
| with my colleague | 동료와 같이 dongnyowa gachi |

| How long will you be staying here? | 여기서 얼마나 계실 거예요? |
| | yeogiseo eolmana gyesil geoyeyo |
| Where are you staying? | 어디에 머물고 계세요? |
| | eodie meomulgo gyeseyo |
| Where are you from? | 어디서 오셨어요? |
| | eodiseo osyeosseoyo |
| I hear it's nice there. | 거기가 좋다면서요? |
| | geogiga jotamyeonseoyo |

| What's Jejudo famous for? | 제주도는 무엇으로 유명해요?<br>jejudoneun mueoseuro<br>yumyeonghaeyo |
|---|---|

* Refer to page 365 for cities.

| What dish is Jeonju famous for? | 전주에는 어떤 특별한 음식이 있어요?<br>jeonjueneun eotteon teukbyeolhan<br>eumsigi isseoyo |
|---|---|
| What's a good hotel to stay in Gyeongju? | 경주에서는 어떤 호텔이 좋아요?<br>gyeongjueseoneun eotteon hoteri joayo |
| A Are you here for sightseeing, or on business? | 관광차 오셨어요, 사업차 오셨어요?<br>gwangwangcha osyeosseoyo sa-<br>eopcha osyeosseoyo |
| B I'm here for sightseeing. | 여기에 관광차 왔어요.<br>yeogie gwangwangcha wasseoyo |

---

| sightseeing<br>business | 관광차 gwangwangcha<br>사업차 sa-eopcha |
|---|---|

---

| A When did you come here? | 여기 언제 오셨어요?<br>yeogi eonje osyeosseoyo |
|---|---|
| B I've been in Korea for two days. | 한국에 온 지 이틀 됐어요.<br>hanguge on ji iteul dwaesseoyo |

---

| two days<br>three days<br>four days<br>one week | 이틀 iteul<br>사흘 saheul<br>나흘 naheul<br>일주일 iljuil |
|---|---|

* Refer to page 352-354 for times.

| I came here <u>today</u>. | 전 <u>오늘</u> 왔어요. |
| | jeon <u>oneul</u> wasseoyo |

| today | 오늘 oneul |
| yesterday | 어제 eoje |
| two days ago | 이틀 전에 iteul jeone |
| three days ago | 사흘 전에 saheul jeone |

* Refer to page 355 for times.

| How do you like it here? | 여기 어때요? |
| | yeogi eottaeyo |

| What have you seen here? | 여기서 어떤 것들을 보셨어요? |
| | yeogiseo eotteon geotdeureul |
| | bosyeosseoyo |

| Have you been to Nami Island ? | 남이섬에 가 보셨어요? |
| | namiseome ga bosyeosseoyo |

| I recommend that you go to Busan. | 부산 한 번 가 보세요. |
| | busan han beon ga boseyo |

| What do you think of this palce? | 여기 어때요? |
| | yeogi eottaeyo |

| I think it is very <u>beautiful</u>. | 정말 <u>아름답네요</u>. |
| | jeongmal <u>areumdamneyo</u> |

| beautiful | 아름답네요 areumdamneyo |
| interesting | 재미있네요 jaemiinneyo |
| magnificent | 웅장하네요 ungjanghaneyo |
| wonderful | 훌륭하네요 hullyunghaneyo |

195

As you travel around seeing the sights, you'll have many opportunities to meet Koreans. Although Koreans prefer formal introductions, sightseeing does provide various situations where you can strike up a casual conversation. You may have questions about the places you're visiting, and Koreans are by nature hospitable; most would try to assist you. This section will help you get the conversation started—and to continue it if it seems appropriate! You can use these phrases with local Korean people, and with those from out of town, too. Koreans enjoy sightseeing, you'll probably meet a lot of Korean tourists. For more information on Korean customs in social situations, see "Korea and Its People."

## MAKING NEW FRIENDS

| | |
|---|---|
| Excuse me. | **실례합니다.**<br>sillyehamnida |
| My name is _____. | **제 이름은 _____ 입니다.**<br>je ireumeun _____ imnida |
| I'm from the <u>USA</u>. | **저는 <u>미국</u>에서 왔어요.**<br>jeoneun <u>migugeseo</u> wasseoyo<br>* Refer to page 362 for countries. |
| Do you have a minute? | **시간 좀 내 주시겠어요?**<br>sigan jom nae jusigesseoyo |
| Do you mind if I sit here? | **여기에 앉아도 될까요?**<br>yeogie anjado doelkkayo |

| Would you like dinner with me? | 저랑 같이 식사하실래요? |
| | jeorang gachi siksahasillaeyo |

| I would like to have good memories of this place. | 여기에서 좋은 추억을 만들고 싶어요. |
| | yeogieseo jo-eun chueogeul mandeulgo sipeoyo |

| It will be a good experience. | 제겐 좋은 경험이 될 거예요. |
| | jegen jo-eun gyeongheomi doel geoyeyo |

| A Are you a student? | 학생이에요? |
| | haksaeng-ieyo |

| B Yes, I'm a student. | 네, 학생이에요. |
| | ne haksaeng-ieyo |

| a student | 학생이에요 haksaeng-ieyo |
| an office worker | 회사원이에요 hoesawonieyo |
| an artist | 예술가예요 yesulgayeyo |
| a doctor | 의사예요 uisayeyo |
| a journalist | 기자예요 gijayeyo |
| a salesperson | 판매원이에요 panmaewonieyo |
| an engineer | 기술자예요 gisuljayeyo |
| a teacher | 교사예요 gyosayeyo |
| a lawyer | 변호사예요 byeonhosayeyo |

| A What are you studying? | 지금 뭘 공부하고 있어요? |
| | jigeum mwol gongbuhago isseoyo |

| B I'm studying business. | 경영학을 공부하고 있어요. |
| | gyeongyeonghageul gongbuhago isseoyo |

197

| business | 경영학을 gyeongyeonghageul |
| Korean literature | 국문학을 gungmunhageul |
| English literature | 영문학을 yeongmunhageul |
| hotel management | 호텔경영학을 hotelgyeongyeonghageul |
| mass communications | 신문방송학을 sinmunbangsonghageul |
| fashion design | 의상학을 uisanghageul |
| biology | 생물학을 saengmulhageul |
| electrical engineering | 전자공학을 jeonjagonghageul |
| chemical engineering | 화학공학을 hwahakgonghageul |

**A** What do you do?

지금 무슨 일을 하세요?
jigeum museun ireul haseyo

**B** I run my own business.

사업하고 있어요.
sa-eopago isseoyo

**B** I'm working in the clothing field.

의류 분야에서 일하고 있어요.
uiryu bunnyaeseo ilhago isseoyo

I'm retired.

전 은퇴했어요.
jeon euntoehaesseoyo

**A** Are you married?

결혼 하셨어요?
gyeoron hasyeosseoyo

**B** No, I'm single. / Yes, I'm married.

아뇨, 미혼입니다. / 네, 결혼했어요.
anyo mihonimnida / ne gyeoronhaesseoyo

**A** Do you have children?

애들이 있으세요?
aedeuri isseuseyo

**B** I have no children.

애들은 없어요.
aedeureun eopseoyo

| A How many children do you have? | 애들은 몇이나 돼요?<br>aedeureun myeochina dwaeyo |
| B I have <u>one</u> child(ren). | 애가 <u>하나</u> 있어요.<br>aega <u>hana</u> isseoyo |

| one<br>two<br>three | 하나 hana<br>둘 dul<br>셋 set |

*Refer to page 345 for numerals.

| How old are they? | 애들은 몇 살이나 됐어요?<br>aedeureun myeot sarina dwaesseoyo |
| Is your <u>family</u> here? | <u>가족은</u> 여기에 있어요?<br><u>gajogeun</u> yeogie isseoyo |

| family<br>wife<br>husband | 가족은 gajogeun<br>부인은 buineun<br>남편은 nampyeoneun |

| Do you have any pictures of your <u>family</u>? | <u>가족</u> 사진 갖고 있어요?<br><u>gajok</u> sajin gatgo isseoyo |

| family<br>children<br>parents | 가족 gajok<br>애들 aedeul<br>부모님 bumonim |

| These are pictures of my family. | 이게 제 가족사진이에요. |
| | ige je gajok sajinieyo |
| | |
| What do you like to do? | 당신은 뭐 하는 걸 좋아하세요? |
| | dangsineun mwo haneun geol joahaseyo |
| | |
| A What do you do when you have free time? | 당신은 시간이 나면 뭘 하세요? |
| | dangsineun sigani namyeon mwol haseyo |
| | |
| B I like to read books. | 전 책 읽는 걸 좋아해요. |
| | jeon chaek ingneun geol joahaeyo |

---

| to read books | 책 읽는 걸 chaek ingneun geol |
| to workout | 운동하는 걸 undonghaneun geol |
| to watch movies | 영화보는 걸 yeonghwaboneun geol |
| to play football | 축구하는 걸 chukguhaneun geol |
| to travel | 여행하는 걸 yeohaenghaneun geol |
| to walk | 걷는 걸 geonneun geol |

---

| I don't like to drink. | 전 술 마시는 걸 좋아하지 않아요. |
| | jeon sul masineun geol joahaji anayo |

---

| to drink | 술 마시는 걸 sul masineun geol |
| to eat out | 외식하는 걸 oesikaneun geol |

---

| A What are you good at? | 당신은 뭘 잘해요? |
| | dangsineun mwol jalhaeyo |
| | |
| B I'm good at singing. | 노래를 잘 해요. |
| | noraereul jal haeyo |

| | |
|---|---|
| singing | 노래를 noraereul |
| sports | 운동을 undong-eul |

| | |
|---|---|
| Wow, you are so cool! | 와, 정말 멋져요!<br>wa jeongmal meotjyeoyo |
| **A** Do you often go overseas? | 해외 여행을 자주 다녀요?<br>hae-oe yeohaeng-eul jaju danyeoyo |
| **B** This is my first time. | 이번이 처음이에요.<br>ibeoni cheo-eumieyo |
| It's my first time in <u>Korea</u>. | <u>한국엔</u> 처음이에요.<br><u>hangugen</u> cheo-eumieyo |

| | |
|---|---|
| Korea | 한국 han-guk |
| Jejudo | 제주도 jejudo |
| Busan | 부산 busan |

| | |
|---|---|
| I'll stay here overnight. | 여기서 하루 묵을 거예요.<br>yeogiseo haru mugeul geoyeyo |
| I'm staying at the Hanguk Hotel. | 전 한국 호텔에서 머물 거예요.<br>jeon hanguk hotereseo meomul geoyeyo |
| Do you like to travel alone? | 혼자 여행하는 것을 좋아해요?<br>honja yeohaenghaneun geoseul joahaeyo |

I like making new friends.

새로운 사람 사귀는 것을 좋아해요.
saeroun saram sagwineun geoseul joahaeyo

I enjoyed talking with you.

얘기 재미있었어요.
yaegi jaemiisseosseoyo

Can we meet again?

다시 만날 수 있겠죠?
dasi mannal su itgetjyo

Let's keep in touch.

우리 연락하고 지내요.
uri yeollakago jinaeyo

Do you have e-Mail address?

이메일 사용해요?
imeil sayonghaeyo

Can I get your e-Mail address?

이메일 주소를 알 수 있을까요?
imeil jusoreul al su isseulkkayo

I'll give you my e-Mail address.

제 이메일 주소를 알려 드릴게요.
je imeil jusoreul allyeo deurilgeyo

Can I have your phone number?

전화번호 좀 가르쳐 주시겠어요?
jeonhwabeonho jom gareuchyeo jusigesseoyo

Do you mind if I call you?

제가 전화 걸어도 괜찮아요?
jega jeonhwa georeodo gwaenchanayo

Don't forget to call me.

전화하는 거 잊지 마세요.
jeonhwahaneun geo itji maseyo

## MAKING APPOINTMENTS

| | |
|---|---|
| Would it be possible to meet with you today? | 오늘 만나는 것 괜찮으세요?<br>oneul mannaneun geot gwaenchaneuseyo |
| Could you meet me sometime next week? | 다음 주 중에 저와 만나실 수 있어요?<br>da-eum ju jung-e jeowa mannasil su isseoyo |
| Do you have plans for <u>tomorrow</u>? | <u>내일</u> 할 일 있어요?<br><u>naeil</u> hal il isseoyo |

| | |
|---|---|
| tomorrow | 내일 naeil |
| this afternoon | 오늘 오후에 oneul ohue |
| this evening | 오늘 저녁에 oneul jeonyeoge |

| | |
|---|---|
| If you don't mind, I'd like to set up an appointment for tomorrow. | 괜찮으시다면, 내일 만날 시간을 정하고 싶어요.<br>gwaenchaneusidamyeon naeil mannal siganeul jeonghago sipeoyo |
| I'd like to meet with you today. Would that be possible? | 오늘 뵙고 싶어요. 가능할까요?<br>oneul boepgo sipeoyo ganeunghalkkayo |
| I'd like to meet with you at your earliest convenience. | 가능한 한 빨리 만나고 싶어요.<br>ganeunghan han ppalli mannago sipeoyo |
| In the meantime, shall I just pencil you in for coming Monday? | 그러면, 일단 다음 월요일로 정할까요?<br>geureomyeon ildan da-eum woryoillo jeonghalkkayo |

| What time would be best for you? | 몇 시가 제일 좋으세요?<br>myeot siga jeil jo-euseyo |
| What time shall we meet? | 몇 시에 만날까요?<br>myeot sie mannalkkayo |
| Is <u>6 o'clock</u> OK with you? | <u>6시</u> 어때요?<br><u>yeoseot-si</u> eottaeyo<br><small>* Refer to page 356 for times.</small> |
| I'm free <u>tomorrow</u>. | <u>내일</u> 시간 돼요.<br><u>naeil</u> sigan dwaeyo |

| tomorrow<br>in the afternoon<br>tonight | 내일 naeil<br>오늘 오후에 oneul ohue<br>오늘 저녁에 oneul jeonyeoge |

| My schedule is pretty open. | 전 언제든지 괜찮아요.<br>jeon eonjedeunji gwaenchanayo |
| Where would you like to meet? | 어디서 만나는 것이 좋을까요?<br>eodiseo mannaneun geosi jo-eulkkayo |
| Shall I meet you at the <u>hotel lobby</u>? | <u>호텔 로비</u>에서 만날까요?<br><u>hotel lobi</u>eseo mannalkkayo |

| hotel lobby<br>restaurant<br>cocktail lounge | 호텔 로비 hotel lobi<br>레스토랑 reseutorang<br>칵테일 라운지 kakteil launji |

| How about a dinner together? | 저녁이나 함께 해요. |
| | jeonyeogina hamkke haeyo |

| dinner | 저녁이나 jeonyeogina |
| drinks | 술이나 surina |
| sightseeing | 관광이나 gwangwangina |

| Let me have a look at my schedule. | 제 일정을 확인해 볼게요. |
| | je iljeong-eul hwaginhae bolgeyo |

| Shall I come and pick you up? | 차로 모시러 갈까요? |
| | charo mosireo galkkayo |

| See you then. | 그럼 그 때 뵐게요. |
| | geureom geu ttae boelgeyo |

| I'm sorry, something's come up. Can we reschedule the plans we had for tomorrow? | 죄송하지만 일이 좀 생겼어요. 내일로 잡았던 약속을 변경할 수 있을까요? |
| | joesonghajiman iri jom saenggyeosseoyo naeillo jabatdeon yaksogeul byeongyeonghal su isseulkkayo |

| I'm sorry, but I have to go. Can I call you back a little later? | 죄송하지만, 지금 가 봐야 해요. 제가 조금 후에 다시 전화를 드려도 될까요? |
| | joesonghajiman jigeum ga bwaya haeyo jega jogeum hue dasi jeonhwareul deuryeodo doelkkayo |

| I look forward to hearing from you soon. | 곧 연락주시길 기다리고 있겠습니다. |
| | got yeollakjusigil gidarigo itgesseumnida |

## INVITING

Do you have any plans
for tonight?

오늘 밤에 특별한 계획 있어요?
oneul bame teukbyeolhan gyehoek
isseoyo

I have plans for
tomorrow evening.

내일 밤은 약속이 있어요.
naeil bameun yaksogi isseoyo

I'd like to invite you to
my <u>party</u>.

당신을 <u>파티</u>에 초대하고 싶어요.
dangsineul <u>patie</u> chodaehago
sipeoyo

party
my home
for dinner

파티 pati
우리 집 urijip
저녁 식사 jeonyeok siksa

Do you want to come
to my party?

파티에 올래요?
patie ollaeyo

I hope you can come.

오셨으면 해요.
osyeosseumyeon haeyo

I'm really looking
forward to seeing you.

오시길 무척 기다리고 있어요.
osigil mucheok gidarigo isseoyo

A Do you think you
can make it or not?

올 거예요? 안 올 거예요?
ol geoyeyo an ol geoyeyo

B Sure. I'd love to.

알았어요. 갈게요.
arasseoyo galgeyo

Should I dress up?

옷을 갖춰 입고 가야 해요?
oseul gatchwo ipgo gaya haeyo

| Where and when? | 시간하고 장소는요?<br>siganhago jangsoneunyo |
| Can I bring my friend? | 친구를 데려가도 돼요?<br>chingureul deryeogado dwaeyo |
| Do you want me to bring anything? | 뭐 가져가야 할 것 있어요?<br>mwo gajyeogaya hal geot isseoyo |
| You don't have to bring anything. | 아무것도 가져올 필요 없어요.<br>amugeotdo gajyeool piryo eopseoyo |
| Welcome! | 어서 오세요!<br>eoseo oseyo |
| Thank you for inviting me. | 초대해 주셔서 감사합니다.<br>chodaehae jusyeoseo gamsahamnida |
| Thank you for inviting me to the <u>dinner</u>. | <u>저녁 식사</u>에 초대해 주셔서 감사해요.<br><u>jeonyeok siksa</u>-e chodaehae jusyeoseo gamsahaeyo |

| dinner | 저녁 식사 jeonyeok siksa |
| banquet | 연회 yeonhoe |
| party | 파티 pati |

| I brought some wine. | 와인 좀 가져왔어요.<br>wain jom gajyeowasseoyo |
| Please have a seat here. | 여기 앉으세요.<br>yeogi anjeuseyo |

| Please help yourself. | 마음껏 많이 드세요. |
| | ma-eumkkeot mani deuseyo |
| | |
| Thank you for a | 맛있는 저녁 식사 감사합니다. |
| delicious dinner. | masinneun jeonyeok siksa |
| | gamsahamnida |

## When Visiting a Korean Family

You must take off your shoes when entering a Korean house. There are still many Koeans who sit on the floor when having a meal or a conversation. You're not supposed to step on the cushions on the floor. Also, you should not step on the threshold of the door because it means bad luck in Korea.

When you have a meal, the older people at the table start the meal by picking up their spoon and then the younger people can start. Even after the meal, younger people try not to finish before the older people have. Also, you are not supposed to have a spoon and chopsticks in one hand and use both hands. Don't make any sound when you eat, and cover your mouth with your hand if there is food in your mouth but you have to say something.

There are rules of etiquette even for drinking. You have to hold the bottle using both hands when you pour for someone older than you, and vise versa. When taking a drink, you're not supposed to look at someone who is older than you are. You have to turn your head a little bit to the side.

## TURNING DOWN REQUESTS

**A** What are you going to do tonight?

오늘 밤에 뭐하세요?
oneul bame mwohaseyo

**B** Sorry, I have plans for tonight.

미안해요, 오늘 밤엔 약속이 있어요.
mianhaeyo oneul bamen yaksogi isseoyo

I'm afraid I won't be able to attend, because I'm leaving earlier than expected.

아쉽게도 예정보다 일찍 떠나게 되어 참석할 수 없어요.
aswipgedo yejeongboda iljjik tteonage doe-eo chamseokal su eopseoyo

Unfortunately, the timing doesn't work for me.

죄송하지만, 그 시간엔 제가 안 될 것 같아요.
joesonghajiman geu siganen jega an doel geot gatayo

Sorry to disappoint you.

실망시켜 드려서 죄송해요.
silmangsikyeo deuryeoseo joesonghaeyo

I'm sorry, but I'm busy.

죄송하지만, 제가 좀 바빠요.
joesonghajiman jega jom bappayo

I wish you'd asked me just a day earlier.

하루만 더 일찍 말씀해 주셨으면 좋았을 텐데요.
haruman deo iljjik malsseumhae jusyeosseumyeon joasseul tendeyo

I'm sorry, I have to go.

죄송하지만, 가야 해요.
joesonghajiman gaya haeyo

## SAYING GOOD-BYE

Good-bye.

안녕히 가세요.
annyeonghi gaseyo

Take care.

잘 지내세요.
jal jinaeseyo

Bye for now.

잘 가요.
jal gayo

See you again.

다시 만나요.
dasi mannayo

I am sorry, I have to leave.

먼저 실례하겠습니다.
meonjeo sillyehagesseumnida

Nice talking to you.

이야기 재미있었어요.
iyagi jaemiisseosseoyo

Thanks, I had a good time.

고마워요, 즐거웠어요.
gomawoyo jeulgeowosseoyo

I owe you big time.

신세를 많이 졌습니다.
sinsereul mani jyeosseumnida

I will miss you.

보고 싶을 거예요.
bogo sipeul geoyeyo

When can we see each other again?

언제 또 볼 수 있을까요?
eonje tto bol su isseulkkayo

See you soon.

곧 만나요.
got mannayo

| | |
|---|---|
| Have a good trip. | 여행 잘 하세요.<br>yeohaeng jal haseyo |
| Drop me a line. | 편지 주세요.<br>pyeonji juseyo |
| Good luck. | 행운을 빌어요.<br>haenguneul bireoyo |
| Looking forward to seeing you again. | 다시 만나길 기대할게요.<br>dasi mannagil gidaehalgeyo |
| Hope I can see you again. | 또 뵙겠습니다.<br>tto boepgesseumnida |
| Please call me later. | 나중에 전화 주세요.<br>najung-e jeonhwa juseyo |
| I will call you later. | 나중에 전화 할게요.<br>najung-e jeonhwa halgeyo |
| Give me a call if you ever come to England. | 영국에 오시게 되면 저한테 연락해 주세요.<br>yeongguge osige doemyeon jeohante yeollakae juseyo |

\* Refer to page 362 for the countries.

# SIGHTSEEING

## ASKING ABOUT THE SIGHTS

Please recommend
a good tourist spot if
there is one.

좋은 관광지가 있으면 추천해 주세요.
jo-eun gwangwangjiga isseumyeon
chucheonhae juseyo

Where is the most
famous place in
Korea?

한국에서 가장 유명한 곳이 어디예요?
hangugeseo gajang yumyeonghan
gosi eodiyeyo

Where is the most
popular place for
foreigners?

외국인들에게 가장 인기 있는 곳이
어디예요?
oegugindeurege gajang in-gi inneun
gosi eodiyeyo

Where is a good city
for an overnight-trip?

1박 2일로 관광하기에 좋은 곳이
어디예요?
il-bak i-illo gwangwanghagie jo-eun
gosi eodiyeyo

Can you tell me the
way there?

거기로 가는 길 좀 알려 주시겠어요?
geogiro ganeun gil jom allyeo
jusigesseoyo

How can I get there?

그곳에 가려면 어떻게 가야 해요?
geugose garyeomyeon eotteoke gaya
haeyo

How long does it take
to get there?

그곳까지 가는데 몇 시간 걸려요?
geugotkkaji ganeunde myeot sigan
geollyeoyo

| How much would it cost to take a trip there? | 그곳을 관광하는 데 드는 비용은 얼마 정도예요? |
| | geugoseul gwangwanghaneunde deuneun biyong-eun eolma jeongdoyeyo |
| What is it famous for? | 그곳은 무엇으로 유명해요? |
| | geugoseun mueoseuro yumyeonghaeyo |
| Where in <u>Gyeonggi-do</u> is famous? | <u>경기도</u>에서는 어디가 유명해요? |
| | <u>gyeonggido</u>eseoneun eodiga yumyeonghaeyo |

---

| Gyeonggi-do | 경기도 gyeonggido |
| Gangwon-do | 강원도 gangwondo |
| Chungcheongbuk-do | 충청북도 chungcheongbukdo |
| Chungcheongnam-do | 충청남도 chungcheongnamdo |
| Gyeongsangbuk-do | 경상북도 gyeongsangbukdo |
| Gyeongsangnam-do | 경상남도 gyeongsangnamdo |
| Jeollabuk-do | 전라북도 jeollabukdo |
| Jeollanam-do | 전라남도 jeollanamdo |
| Jeju-do | 제주도 jejudo |

* Refer to page 365 for cities.

| What kind of food is popular there? | 무슨 음식이 유명해요? |
| | museun eumsigi yumyeonghaeyo |
| Is there accommodations near the tourist spot? | 관광지 근처에 숙박 시설이 있어요? |
| | gwangwangji geuncheo-e sukbak siseori isseoyo |
| Are there many sightseeing spots near the destination? | 관광지 주변에 볼거리가 많아요? |
| | gwangwangji jubyeone bolgeoriga manayo |

| I would like to have a good trip on a small budget. Where would be good? | 적은 비용으로 알차게 여행하고 싶은데 어디가 좋을까요?<br>jeogeun biyong-euro alchage yeohaenghago sipeunde eodiga jo-eulkkayo |
| Please recommend a package program if there is one. | 관광 패키지 상품이 있으면 추천해 주세요.<br>gwangwang paekiji sangpumi isseumyeon chucheonhae juseyo |
| Let me know an efficient tour course. | 효율적으로 여행할 수 있는 관광 코스를 알려 주세요.<br>hyoyuljeogeuro yeohaenghal su inneun gwangwang koseureul allyeo juseyo |
| Where is the place that young people go these days? | 요즘 젊은 사람들이 많이 가는 곳은 어디예요?<br>yojeum jeolmeun saramdeuri mani ganeun goseun eodiyeoyo |
| Where is the place with good views? | 경치가 좋은 곳으로는 어디가 있어요?<br>gyeongchiga jo-eun goseuroneun eodiga isseoyo |
| Where can I experience traditional Korean culture? | 한국 전통 문화를 체험할 수 있는 곳이 어디에 있어요?<br>hanguk jeontong munhwareul cheheomhal su inneun gosi eodie isseoyo |
| Where is a famous tourist attraction? | 관광 명소가 어디예요?<br>gwangwang myeongsoga eodiyeyo |

## FINDING A TOURIST INFORMATION CENTER

| | |
|---|---|
| Where is the tourist information center? | 관광 안내소가 어디에 있어요?<br>gwangwang annaesoga eodie isseoyo |
| Is there a tourist information center around here? | 이 주변에 관광 안내소가 있나요?<br>i jubyeone gwangwang annaesoga innayo |
| Could you tell me the way to the tourist information center? | 관광 안내소로 가는 길 좀 알려 주시겠어요?<br>gwangwang annaesoro ganeun gil jom allyeo jusigesseoyo |
| How can I get to the tourist information center? | 관광 안내소에 어떻게 가야 하나요?<br>gwangwang annaesoe eotteoke gaya hanayo |
| How long does it take to get to the tourist information center? | 관광 안내소까지 얼마나 걸리나요?<br>gwangwang annaesokkaji eolmana geollinayo |
| What time does the tourist information center <u>open</u>? | 관광 안내소는 몇 시에 <u>문을 열어요</u>?<br>gwangwang annaesoneun myeot sie <u>muneul yeoreoyo</u> |

. . . . . . . . . . . . . . . . . . . . . . . . . . . . . . . . . . . .

| | |
|---|---|
| open | 문을 열어요  muneul yeoreoyo |
| close | 문을 닫아요  muneul dadayo |

. . . . . . . . . . . . . . . . . . . . . . . . . . . . . . . . . . . .

| | |
|---|---|
| Where is the nearest tourist information center from here? | 여기에서 가장 가까운 관광 안내소는 어디인가요?<br>yeogieseo gajang gakkaun gwangwang annaesoneun eodiingayo |

| What is the fastest way to the tourist information center? | 관광 안내소로 가는 빠른 길이 어디인가요? |
| | gwangwang annaesoro ganeun ppareun giri eodiingayo |
| Can I get a <u>travel guide</u>? | <u>관광 안내 책자</u> 하나 주세요. |
| | <u>gwangwang annae chaekja</u> hana juseyo |

| travel guide | 관광 안내 책자 |
| | gwangwang annae chaekja |
| city map | 시내 지도 sinae jido |
| bus route map | 버스 노선도 beoseu noseondo |
| subway lines map | 지하철 노선도 jihacheol noseondo |

| Will I be able to see all of this huge area in one day? | 아주 넓은데 하루에 다 볼 수 있을까요? |
| | aju neolbeunde harue da bol su isseulkkayo |
| Could you recommend a good place for souvenirs around here? | 이 주변에 기념품을 살 만한 곳이 있나요? |
| | i jubyeone ginyeompumeul sal manhan gosi innayo |

## TICKET PURCHASE

| What is the admission for <u>adults</u>? | 어른 입장료는 얼마예요? |
| | <u>eoreun</u> ipjangnyoneun eolmayeyo |

| | |
|---|---|
| adults | 어른 eoreun |
| teens | 청소년 cheongsonyeon |
| children | 어린이 eorini |

| | |
|---|---|
| How many should there be to get a group discount? | 단체 할인은 몇 명부터 적용돼요?<br>danche harineun myeot myeongbuteo jeogyongdwaeyo |
| One adult, please. | 어른 한 장 주세요.<br>eoreun han jang juseyo |
| One tourist pamphlet, please. | 관람 팸플릿 한 장 주세요.<br>gwallam paempeullit han jang juseyo |
| Can I quickly leave and come back in? | 잠시 나갔다가 다시 들어올 수 있을까요?<br>jamsi nagatdaga dasi deureool su isseulkkayo |
| I'd like to park; what's the parking fee? | 주차를 하고 싶은데 주차 요금은 얼마예요?<br>juchareul hago sipeunde jucha yogeumeun eolmayeyo |
| May I pay by credit card? | 카드로 계산해도 돼요?<br>kadeuro gyesanhaedo dwaeyo |
| Aren't there any discounts? | 할인 혜택은 없어요?<br>harin hyetaegeun eopseoyo |
| I'm sorry, but can I get my money back? | 죄송합니다만 환불을 해도 될까요?<br>joesonghamnidaman hwanbureul haedo doelkkayo |

## ASKING ABOUT SCHEDULE

| When does it <u>open</u>? | 입장 시간은 몇 시부터예요? |
| | ipjang siganeun myeot sibuteoyeyo |

| open | 입장 ipjang |
| close | 폐장 pyejang |

| From when to when are the opening hours? | 관람 시간은 몇 시부터 몇 시까지예요? |
| | gwallam siganeun myeot sibuteo myeot sikkajiyeyo |

| Tell me the general itinerary. | 전반적인 관광 일정을 알려 주세요. |
| | jeonbanjeogin gwangwang iljeong-eul allyeo juseyo |

| Tell me how long it will take at each course. | 각 코스에서 소요되는 시간을 알려 주세요. |
| | gak koseueseo soyodoeneun siganeul allyeo juseyo |

| How long will it take to the next spot by car? | 차를 타고 다음 장소까지 몇 분 걸리나요? |
| | chareul tago da-eum jangsokkaji myeot bun geollinayo |

| What time do we leave? | 몇 시에 출발해요? |
| | myeot sie chulbalhaeyo |

| What time do we arrive there? | 몇 시에 도착해요? |
| | myeot sie dochakaeyo |

| By what time do we have to be back here? | 몇 시까지 이곳으로 돌아오면 돼요? |
| | myeot sikkaji igoseuro doraomyeon dwaeyo |

| What is next on the schedule? | 다음 관광 일정은 어떻게 돼요?<br>da-eum gwangwang iljeong-eun eotteoke dwaeyo |
|---|---|

## TAKING PICTURES

| Can I take a picture here? | 여기에서 사진을 찍어도 되나요?<br>yeogieseo sajineul jjigeodo doenayo |
|---|---|
| Could you take a picture for me? | 사진 좀 찍어 주시겠어요?<br>sajin jom jjigeo jusigesseoyo |
| Just press the shutter button. | 이 셔터를 누르면 돼요.<br>i syeoteoreul nureumyeon dwaeyo |
| Won't you take a picture with me? | 저하고 같이 사진 한 장 찍지 않을래요?<br>jeohago gachi sajin han jang jjikji aneullaeyo |
| Look over here. | 여기 보세요.<br>yeogi boseyo |
| Are you ready?<br>All right. Smile. | 자, 준비됐어요? 그럼, 웃으세요.<br>ja junbidwaesseoyo geureom useuseyo |
| Do you want me to take a picture of you? | 사진 한 장 찍어 드릴까요?<br>sajin han jang jjigeo deurilkkayo |
| Send me a copy later, please. | 나중에 저에게도 사진 한 장 보내주세요.<br>najung-e jeo-egedo sajin han jang bonaejuseyo |

| | |
|---|---|
| I'm sorry, the camera was shaking. | 미안해요, 사진기가 흔들렸어요.<br>mianhaeyo sajingiga<br>heundeullyeosseoyo |
| The picture came out a litte dark. | 사진이 조금 어둡게 나왔네요.<br>sajini jogeum eodupge nawanneyo |
| I'll take one more. | 한 번 더 찍을게요.<br>han beon deo jjigeulgeyo |
| You take great pictures. | 사진을 정말 잘 찍으시는군요.<br>sajineul jeongmal jal<br>jjigeusineungunnyo |

## General Tips for Tourist Spots in Korea

Some etiquette is universal except for some differences caused by cultural differences. When traveling in Korea, don't spit or litter. Wait in line at public places, and you must not take pictures or touch items at museums and exhibitions where you are not allowed to take pictures. Bringing in food or pets unless it's a seeingeye dog is also prohibited. Smoking is also not allowed at no smoking areas or on the street. Korean people usually yield their seats to the elderly or pregnant women on the buses and the subway.

## TOURIST SERVICE

Can I ask for
interpretation service?

통역 안내 서비스를 받을 수 있나요?
tongyeok annae seobiseureul badeul
su innayo

I lost my stuff.
Could you make an
announcement?

물건을 분실했는데 안내 방송 좀 해
주시겠어요?
mulgeoneul bunsilhaenneunde
annae bangsong jom hae
jusigesseoyo

I lost my child. Where
is the place for lost
children?

아이를 잃어버렸는데 미아보호소가
어디에 있나요?
aireul ireobeoryeonneunde
miabohosoga eodie innayo

Where can I change
my baby's diaper?

기저귀 교환대는 어디에 있나요?
gijeogwi gyohwandaeneun eodie
innayo

I hurt my hand. Can
I get first aid?

손을 다쳤는데 응급 치료를 받을 수
있을까요?
soneul dachyeonneunde eunggeup
chiryoreul badeul su isseulkkayo

Can you rent
a stroller?

유모차를 대여해 주실 수 있어요?
yumochareul daeyeohae jusil su
isseoyo

stroller
wheelchair
bicycle

유모차 yumocha
휠체어 hwilche-eo
자전거 jajeon-geo

| I want to hear the explanations in a foreign language; which languages can you provide? | 외국어로 해설을 듣고 싶은데, 지원 가능한 언어는 어떤게 있나요?<br>oegugeoro haeseoreul deutgo sipeunde jiwon ganeunghan eoneoneun eotteonge innayo |
| I want to check some things. Where can I check them? | 물품을 보관하고 싶은데, 물품 보관소가 어디에 있어요?<br>mulpumeul bogwanhago sipeunde mulpum bogwansoga eodie isseoyo |
| Can I check my valuables? | 제 귀중품을 좀 맡아 주실 수 있을까요?<br>je gwijungpumeul jom mata jusil su isseulkkayo |
| Is there a nursery for children here? | 이 안에 어린이 놀이방 있어요?<br>i ane eorini noribang isseoyo |

## FINDING LOCATION

| Where is the entrance? | 입구가 어디에 있어요?<br>ipguga eodie isseoyo |
| entrance<br>exit | 입구 ipgu<br>출구 chulgu |
| Where is the nearest restroom? | 제일 가까운 화장실이 어디죠?<br>jeil gakkaun hwajangsiri eodijyo |

| I want a pamphlet. Where is the information desk? | 소책자를 구하고 싶은데 안내소가 어디에 있어요? |
| | sochaekjareul guhago sipeunde annaesoga eodie isseoyo |

| It's so crowded on the weekend. | 주말이라 많이 혼잡하네요. |
| | jumarira mani honjapaneyo |

| Aren't there any places nearby to rest for a moment? | 이 근처에 잠시 앉아서 쉴만한 곳은 없어요? |
| | i geuncheo-e jamsi anjaseo swilmanhan goseun eopseoyo |

| To get there, should I go <u>to the right</u> from here? | 그곳에 가려면 여기에서 <u>오른쪽으로</u> 가야 해요? |
| | geugose garyeomyeon yeogieseo <u>oreunjjogeuro</u> gaya haeyo |

| to the right | 오른쪽으로 oreunjjogeuro |
| to the left | 왼쪽으로 oenjjogeuro |
| up | 위로 wiro |
| down | 아래로 araero |
| straight | 똑바로 ttokbaro |
| sideways | 옆으로 yeopeuro |
| backward | 뒤로 dwiro |
| to the east | 동쪽으로 dongjjogeuro |
| to the west | 서쪽으로 seojjogeuro |
| to the south | 남쪽으로 namjjogeuro |
| to the north | 북쪽으로 bukjjogeuro |

| Excuse me, where am I? | 실례합니다만, 여기가 어디예요? |
| | sillyehamnidaman yeogiga eodiyeyo |

| | |
|---|---|
| Where is a souvenir shop? | 기념품 가게는 어디에 있어요?<br>ginyeompum gageneun eodie isseoyo |
| I'm looking for a restaurant. Where is one? | 식당을 찾고 있는데 어디에 있어요?<br>sikdang-eul chatgo inneunde eodie isseoyo |
| Isn't there a convenience store nearby? | 편의점은 이 근처에 없어요?<br>pyeonuijeomeun i geuncheo-e eopseoyo |
| Where is the smoking area? | 흡연 구역이 어디예요?<br>heubyeon guyeogi eodiyeyo |

# EATING & DRINKING OUT

## LOCATING RESTAURANTS

Can you recommend
a nice restaurant?

좋은 레스토랑 하나 소개해 주시겠어요?
jo-eun reseutorang hana sogaehae
jusigesseoyo

Where's the most
popular restaurant?

가장 인기 있는 식당은 어디인가요?
gajang in-gi inneun sikdang-eun
eodiingayo

Is there a restaurant
nearby?

이 근처에 식당이 있어요?
i geuncheo-e sikdang-i isseoyo

I'd like to have Korean
food.

한국 음식을 먹고 싶습니다.
hanguk eumsigeul meokgo
sipseumnida

* Refer to page 362 for countries.

What are their hours?

영업 시간이 어떻게 돼요?
yeongeop sigani eotteoke dwaeyo

## Booking

Do you take
reservation?

예약 받으시나요?
yeyak badeusinayo

I'd like to make
a reservation for
dinner tomorrow.

내일 저녁으로 예약을 하려고 하는데요.
naeil jeonyeogeuro yeyageul
haryeogo haneundeyo

| dinner tomorrow | 내일 저녁으로 naeil jeonyeogeuro |
| lunch today | 오늘 점심으로 oneul jeomsimeuro |

Three people at <u>6:00</u>
p.m. please.

저녁 <u>6시</u>에 세 명입니다.
jeonyeok <u>yeoseot-sie</u> se
myeong-imnida

* Refer to page 357 for hours.

I would like to reserve
a room.

방으로 예약하고 싶은데요.
bang-euro yeyakago sipeundeyo

Can I pre-order?

식사를 미리 주문해도 될까요?
siksareul miri jumunhaedo
doelkkayo

Do you have a brunch
menu?

브런치 메뉴가 있나요?
beureonchi menyuga innayo

Can I change the
reservation time?

예약 시간을 바꿔도 될까요?
yeyak siganeul bakkwodo doelkkayo

Can I have a table
with a good view?

전망이 좋은 자리로 주세요.
jeonmang-i jo-eun jariro juseyo

## Seating

A Welcome. Do you
have a reservation?

어서 오십시오. 예약 하셨어요?
eoseo osipsio yeyak hasyeosseoyo

B I haven't made
a reservation.
Is there a table
available?

예약을 하지 않았는데, 자리 있어요?
yeyageul haji ananneunde jari
isseoyo

| Will I have to wait long? | 오래 기다려야 해요? |
| | orae gidaryeoya haeyo |

| How long will I have to wait? | 얼마나 기다려야 해요? |
| | eolmana gidaryeoya haeyo |

| A How many are in your party? | 몇 분이세요? |
| | myeot buniseyo |

| B A table for <u>four</u>, please. | <u>네 명</u> 앉을 자리 부탁해요. |
| | <u>ne myeong</u> anjeul jari butakaeyo |

<sup>*</sup> Refer to page 349 for countings.

| <u>Smoking section</u>, please. | <u>흡연석으로</u> 부탁해요. |
| | <u>heubyeonseogeuro</u> butakaeyo |

| smoking section | 흡연석 heubyeonseok |
| non-smoking section | 금연석 geumyeonseok |

| A table <u>by the window</u>, please. | <u>창가</u> 자리로 부탁해요. |
| | <u>changga</u> jariro butakaeyo |

| by the window | 창가 changga |
| in the corner | 구석 guseok |

| A quiet table, please. | 조용한 자리로 부탁해요. |
| | joyonghan jariro butakaeyo |

| This way, please. | 이쪽으로 오세요. |
| | ijjogeuro oseyo |

## Ordering & Eating

Can I have some
water, please?

물 좀 주세요.
mul jom juseyo

May I have a glass of
<u>cold</u> water?

<u>시원한</u> 물 좀 주세요.
<u>siwonhan</u> mul jom juseyo

cold
hot

시원한 siwonhan
따뜻한 ttatteutan

May I see the menu,
please?

메뉴판 좀 주세요.
menyupan jom juseyo

Is there an English
menu?

영어로 된 메뉴가 있어요?
yeong-eoro doen menyuga isseoyo

I'd like to order now.

주문 할게요.
jumun halgeyo

A What would you
like?

무엇을 드시겠습니까?
mueoseul deusigesseumnikka

B *Bulgogi* for <u>two</u>,
please.

불고기 <u>2인분</u> 주세요.
bulgogi <u>i-inbun</u> juseyo

* Refer to page 349 for countings.

I'll have the same.

같은 걸로 주세요.
gateun geollo juseyo

Same here.

저도 그걸로 주세요.
jeodo geugeollo juseyo

| May I change my order? | 제 주문을 바꿔도 될까요? |
| | je jumuneul bakkwodo doelkkayo |

| What is the house specialty? | 이 식당에서 가장 잘하는 요리가 뭐예요? |
| | i sikdang-eseo gajang jalhaneun yoriga mwoyeyo |

| What is the most popular item on the menu? | 가장 인기 있는 음식은 뭐예요? |
| | gajang in-gi inneun eumsigeun mwoyeyo |

| Can I have the local specialty? | 이 지방의 특별한 요리가 있어요? |
| | i jibangui teukbyeolhan yoriga isseoyo |

| What's today's special? | 오늘의 특별 메뉴는 뭐죠? |
| | oneurui teukbyeol menyuneun mwojyo |

| Will it take long to prepare? | 준비하는 데 시간이 오래 걸려요? |
| | junbihaneun de sigani orae geollyeoyo |

| Could you bring it as soon as possible? | 최대한 빨리 갖다 주시겠어요? |
| | choedaehan ppalli gatda jusigesseoyo |

| Please don't make it too spicy. | 너무 맵게 하지 마세요. |
| | neomu maepge haji maseyo |

---

| spicy | 맵게 maepge |
| salty | 짜게 jjage |
| sweet | 달게 dalge |
| oily | 기름지게 gireumjige |

| | |
|---|---|
| Extra vegetables to my dish, please. | 야채를 많이 넣어 주세요.<br>yachaereul mani neoeo juseyo |
| My food hasn't come yet. | 주문한 요리가 아직 안 나왔어요.<br>jumunhan yoriga ajik an nawasseoyo |
| How long will it take? | 앞으로 얼마 정도 걸려요?<br>apeuro eolma jeongdo geollyeoyo |
| Can I have some more rice? | 밥 좀 더 주세요.<br>bap jom deo juseyo |
| rice<br>kimchi<br>side dishes | 밥 bap<br>김치 gimchi<br>반찬 banchan |
| Could you give me another set of chopsticks, please. | 젓가락 한 벌 더 갖다 주세요.<br>jeotgarak han beol deo gatda juseyo |
| set of chopsticks<br>spoon | 젓가락 한 벌 jeotgarak han beol<br>숟가락 한 개 sutgarak han gae |
| I am allergic to eggs. | 저는 계란 알레르기가 있어요.<br>jeoneun gyeran allereugiga isseoyo |

| eggs | 계란 gyeran |
| honey | 꿀 kkul |
| peaches | 복숭아 boksunga |
| nuts | 땅콩 ttangkong |
| prawns | 새우 saeu |
| crabs | 게 ge |

| Can I have that without <u>eggs</u>? | <u>계란</u>을 빼고 요리해 주시겠어요?<br>gyeraneul ppaego yorihae jusigesseoyo |

| egg | 계란을 gyeraneul |
| meat | 고기를 gogireul |
| fish | 생선을 saengseoneul |

| Are there any sugar-free dishes? | 설탕이 들어있지 않은 요리는 뭐예요?<br>seoltang-i deureoitji aneun yorineun mwoyeyo |
| Are there any low-fat dishes? | 저지방 요리는 뭐예요?<br>jeojibang yorineun mwoyeyo |
| Are there any dishes suitable for a low-salt diet? | 소금이 적게 든 요리는 뭐예요?<br>sogeumi jeokge deun yorineun mwoyeyo |
| Excuse me, could you bring me the menu again? | 여기요, 메뉴를 다시 갖다 주시겠어요?<br>yeogiyo menyureul dasi gatda jusigesseoyo |

| Can I get you anything else? | 더 필요한 거 있으세요? |
| | deo piryohan geo isseuseyo |
| | |
| Could you bring some extra napkins? | 냅킨 좀 더 갖다 주실래요? |
| | naepkin jom deo gatda jusillaeyo |
| | |
| This is not what I ordered. | 이건 제가 주문한 게 아니에요. |
| | igeon jega jumunhan ge anieyo |
| | |
| I ordered *gimbap*. | 저는 김밥을 시켰어요. |
| | jeoneun gimbabeul sikyeosseoyo |

| *gimbap* | 김밥을 gimbabeul |
| *bibimbap* | 비빔밥을 bibimbabeul |
| *bulgogi* | 불고기를 bulgogireul |
| *galbi* | 갈비를 galbireul |
| *kimchijjigae* | 김치찌개를 gimchijjigaereul |
| *doenjangjjigae* | 된장찌개를 doenjangjjigaereul |
| *sundubujjigae* | 순두부찌개를 sundubujjigaereul |
| *galbitang* | 갈비탕을 galbitang-eul |
| *samgyetang* | 삼계탕을 samgyetang-eul |
| *naengmyeon* | 냉면을 naengmyeoneul |
| *mandutguk* | 만둣국을 mandutgugeul |
| *jjajangmyeon* | 자장면을 jajangmyeoneul |
| *bokkeumbap* | 볶음밥을 bokkeumbabeul |

* Refer to page 233 for food.

| Give me a doggy bag, please. | 남은 음식은 싸 주세요. |
| | nameun eumsigeun ssa juseyo |

# Korean Food

In Korea, a meal is composed of rice, soup or casserole, and side dishes. The basic element of Korean food is rice. Soup is a dish eaten with rice. There are *yukgaejang, seolleongtang, doenjangguk,* and *kimchijjigae.* Side dishes are usually made with *namul* (vegetables from mountains), vegetables, fish, meat, and eggs. Kimchi and *bulgogi* which are well-known to foreigners are also Koreans' favorites. Especially, kimchi is a dish enjoyed every day. These days, Koreans eat not only Korean food but also Western, Chinese, and Japanese foods. But still Koreans' main food is rice and soup and side dishes.

Koreans also make seasonal dishes with fresh seasonal ingredients. In the spring, people eat *jindallae hwajeon* made with Korean rosebay and mugwort rice cake. In the summer, *samgyetang* made with chicken, spicy *yukgaejang,* cool noodles made with bean soup, and *naengmyeon* are eaten to beat the heat. In the fall, *gukhwajeon* is made with chrysanthemum and *hwachae* with autumn fruits. In the winter, warm food like *jeongol* or cold *naengmyeon* is eaten to fight with winter cold.

| | |
|---|---|
| rice | 밥 bap |
| kimchi | 김치 gimchi |
| side dishes | 반찬 banchan |
| rice with mixed vegetables | 비빔밥 bibimbap |
| grilled beef | 불고기 bulgogi |
| grilled beef ribs | 갈비 galbi |
| grilled pork belly | 삼겹살 samgyeopsal |
| chicken and ginseng soup | 삼계탕 samgyetang |
| beef soup | 설렁탕 seolleongtang |
| spicy beef and egg soup | 육개장 yukgaejang |

| | |
|---|---|
| kimchi stew | 김치찌개 gimchijjigae |
| bean paste stew | 된장찌개 doenjangjjigae |
| soft tofu stew | 순두부찌개 sundubujjigae |
| noodles | 국수 guksu |
| cold noodles | 냉면 naengmyeon |
| stir-fried rice | 볶음밥 bokkeumbap |
| spicy rice cake | 떡볶이 tteokbokki |
| rice-filled sausage | 순대 sundae |
| battered deep fries | 튀김 twigim |
| seafood and scallion pancake | 해물파전 haemulpajeon |
| kimchi pancake | 김치전 gimchijeon |

## Paying the Bill

| | |
|---|---|
| How much is it? | 모두 얼마예요?<br>modu eolmayeyo |
| Do you take credit cards? | 신용카드로 계산할 수 있어요?<br>sinyongkadeuro gyesanhal su isseoyo |
| We only take Visa and Master Card. | 비자와 마스터 카드만 받습니다.<br>bijawa maseuteo kadeuman batseumnida |
| We only accept cash. | 현금만 받습니다.<br>hyeongeumman batseumnida |
| I don't have any cash right now. | 제가 지금 현금이 없는데요.<br>jega jigeum hyeongeumi eomneundeyo |

| You can pay with any international credit card. | 국제적으로 사용 가능한 신용카드는 다 사용하실 수 있어요.<br>gukjejeogeuro sayong ganeunghan sinyongkadeuneun da sayonghasil su isseoyo |
| --- | --- |
| There appears to be a problem with the bill. | 계산이 잘못 된 것 같아요.<br>gyesani jalmot doen geot gatayo |
| May I have the receipt? | 영수증 좀 주시겠어요?<br>yeongsujeung jom jusigesseoyo |
| My treat. | 제가 낼게요.<br>jega naelgeyo |
| I have a coupon that I'd like to use. | 여기 쿠폰을 사용하고 싶은데요.<br>yeogi kuponeul sayonghago sipeundeyo |
| The food was excellent! | 음식이 정말 맛있었어요!<br>eumsigi jeongmal masisseosseoyo |
| Let's go Dutch. | 계산은 각자 해요.<br>gyesaneun gakja haeyo |

## DRINKING COFFEE AND TEA

## Ordering Tea

| Can I take your order? | 주문하시겠어요?<br>jumunhasigesseoyo |
| --- | --- |
| What would you like? | 뭐 드시겠어요?<br>mwo deusigesseoyo |

| What kind of <u>coffee</u> do you have? | <u>커피</u>는 뭐가 있어요? |
|---|---|
| | <u>keopi</u>neun mwoga isseoyo |

| coffee | 커피 keopi |
|---|---|
| soft drinks | 음료수 eumnyosu |
| tea | 차 cha |

| A What is <u>ginseng tea</u> good for? | <u>인삼차</u>는 어디에 좋아요? |
|---|---|
| | <u>insamcha</u>neun eodie joayo |

| ginseng tea | 인삼차 insamcha |
|---|---|
| ginger tea | 생강차 saenggangcha |
| solomon's seal tea | 둥굴레차 dunggullecha |
| jujube tea | 대추차 daechucha |
| cinnamon tea | 계피차 gyepicha |
| japanese apricot tea | 매실차 maesilcha |
| citron tea | 유자차 yujacha |
| quince tea | 모과차 mogwacha |
| ssanghwa tea | 쌍화차 ssanghwacha |
| rubus coreanus tea | 복분자차 bokbunjacha |

| B This tea is good for <u>relieving fatigue</u>. | 이 차는 <u>피로회복</u>에 좋아요. |
|---|---|
| | i chaneun <u>pirohoeboge</u> joayo |

| relieving fatigue | 피로회복 pirohoebok |
|---|---|
| calming nerves | 신경 안정 singyeong anjeong |
| high blood pressure | 고혈압 gohyeorap |
| cold | 감기 gamgi |
| cough | 기침 gichim |
| headache | 두통 dutong |
| rejuvenation | 원기회복 wongihoebok |

| | |
|---|---|
| Give me a cup of iced coffee. | 아이스 커피 한 잔 주세요.<br>aiseu keopi han jan juseyo<br><br>* Refer to page 349 for countings. |
| A Do you take syrup? | 시럽을 넣어 드릴까요?<br>sireobeul neo-eo deurilkkayo |
| B Without syrup, please. | 시럽은 빼 주세요.<br>sireobeun ppae juseyo |

. . . . . . . . . . . . . . . . . . . . . . . . . . . . . . . . . . . . . . . . . . . . . . . . . . . . . .

| | |
|---|---|
| syrup<br>whipped cream | 시럽 sireop<br>생크림 saengkeurim |

. . . . . . . . . . . . . . . . . . . . . . . . . . . . . . . . . . . . . . . . . . . . . . . . . . . . . .

| | |
|---|---|
| Please add syrup. | 시럽을 넣어 주세요.<br>sireobeul neo-eo juseyo |
| Please add whipped cream. | 생크림을 올려 주세요.<br>saengkeurimeul ollyeo juseyo |
| Pick up your drink on the right, please. | 음료는 오른쪽에서 받으세요.<br>eumnyoneun oreunjjogeseo badeuseyo |

. . . . . . . . . . . . . . . . . . . . . . . . . . . . . . . . . . . . . . . . . . . . . . . . . . . . . .

| | |
|---|---|
| the right<br>the left<br>the side | 오른쪽 oreunjjok<br>왼쪽 oenjjok<br>옆 yeop |

. . . . . . . . . . . . . . . . . . . . . . . . . . . . . . . . . . . . . . . . . . . . . . . . . . . . . .

| | |
|---|---|
| Syrup and sugar are available on the right. | 시럽과 설탕은 오른쪽에 준비되어 있습니다.<br>sireopgwa seoltang-eun oreunjjoge junbidoe-eo isseumnida |

## To Go or Eat-in

**A** Are you taking this to go?

가지고 가실 거예요?
gajigo gasil geoyeyo

**B** Yes, to go please.

네, 가지고 갈게요.
ne gajigo galgeyo

**A** Is this for eat-in?

여기에서 드실 거예요?
yeogieseo deusil geoyeyo

**B** Yes, I'm going to eat here.

네, 먹고 갈 거예요.
ne meokgo gal geoyeyo

**A** Do you want a mug?

머그컵에 드릴까요?
meogeukeobe deurilkkayo

**B** Give me a <u>mug</u>, please.

<u>머그컵에</u> 주세요.
<u>meogeukeobe</u> juseyo

- - - - - - - - - - - - - - - - - - - - - - - -

a mug
a disposable cup

머그컵 meogeukeop
일회용 컵 ilhoeyong keop

- - - - - - - - - - - - - - - - - - - - - - - -

**A** Is there anything else you need?

더 필요한 것 있으세요?
deo piryohan geot isseuseyo

**B** No, thank you.

아니요, 없어요.
aniyo eopseoyo

## STREET FOOD

Can I help you?

뭐 드릴까요?
mwo deurilkkayo

**A** What is the most delicious thing here?

여기 뭐가 제일 맛있어요?
yeogi mwoga jeil masisseoyo

**B** *Tteokbokki* is the most delicious. Try it.

떡볶이가 제일 맛있어요. 한 번 드셔 보세요.
tteokbokkiga jeil masisseoyo han beon deusyeo boseyo

. . . . . . . . . . . . . . . . . . . . . . . . . . . . . . . . . . . . . . . . . . . .

| | |
|---|---|
| *tteokbokki* | 떡볶이가 tteokbokkiga |
| *sundae* | 순대가 sundaega |
| fishcakes | 어묵이 eomugi |
| fries | 튀김이 twigimi |
| skewered chicken | 닭꼬치가 dak-kkochiga |
| *gimbap* | 김밥이 gimbabi |

. . . . . . . . . . . . . . . . . . . . . . . . . . . . . . . . . . . . . . . . . . . .

**B** Everything here is delicious.

다 맛있어요.
da masisseoyo

Give me one portion of *gimbap*.

김밥 1인분 주세요.
gimbap il-inbun juseyo

Give me 2,000 won worth of *sundae*.

순대 2,000원 어치 주세요.
sundae icheon-won eochi juseyo

Can I have some more soup?

국물 좀 더 주세요.
gungmul jom deo juseyo

Hope you sell a lot.

많이 파세요.
mani paseyo

# SHOPPING

## IN GENERAL

| I'm going for shopping <u>this evening</u>. | 저는 <u>오늘 저녁에</u> 쇼핑을 할 거예요.<br>jeoneun <u>oneul jeonyeoge</u><br>syopingeul hal geoyeyo<br>* Refer to page 356 for times. |
|---|---|
| Where is a good place for shopping? | 쇼핑하기에 좋은 곳이 어디예요?<br>syopinghagie jo-eun gosi eodiyeyo |
| Shall we go shopping tomorrow? | 내일 같이 쇼핑 갈까요?<br>naeil gachi syoping galkkayo |
| Where is the nearest <u>department store</u> from here? | 여기에서 가장 가까운 <u>백화점이</u> 어디예요?<br>yeogieseo gajang gakkaun <u>baekwajeomi</u> eodiyeyo |

| duty-free store | 면세점이 myeonsejeomi |
|---|---|
| jewellery store | 보석가게가 boseokgagega |
| souvenir shop | 기념품 가게가 ginyeompum gagega |
| cosmetics store | 화장품 가게가 hwajangpum gagega |
| music store | 음반 가게가 eumban gagega |
| clothing store | 옷가게가 otgagega |
| bookstore | 서점이 seojeomi |
| newsstand | 신문 가판대가 sinmun gapandaega |
| stationery store | 문구점이 mungujeomi |
| shoe store | 신발 가게가 sinbal gagega |
| photo studio | 사진관이 sajingwani |

| supermarket | 슈퍼마켓이 syupeomakesi |
|---|---|
| local products store | 토산품 가게가 tosanpum gagega |
| antique shop | 골동품점이 goldongpumjeomi |
| flower shop | 꽃집이 kkotjibi |

| Is it far from here? | 여기에서 멀어요? |
|---|---|
| | yeogieseo meoreoyo |

| How do I get there? | 거기까지 어떻게 가요? |
|---|---|
| | geogikkaji eotteoke gayo |

| Where is good for window-shopping? | 윈도쇼핑 하려면 어디로 가는 게 좋아요? |
|---|---|
| | windosyoping haryeomyeon eodiro ganeun ge joayo |

| What are you looking for? | 뭘 찾으세요? |
|---|---|
| | mwol chajeuseyo |

| May I help you? | 뭘 도와 드릴까요? |
|---|---|
| | mwol dowa deurilkkayo |

| Do you need anything? | 뭐 드릴까요? |
|---|---|
| | mwo deurilkkayo |

## Contracted Forms

They are usually used in a spoken language rather than in a written language.

무엇을 mueoseul ⇨ 뭘 mwol ⇨ 뭐 mwo

| Is there anything you need? | 필요한 거 있으세요?<br>piryohan geo isseuseyo |
| I'm just looking around. | 그냥 둘러보는 중이에요.<br>geunyang dulleoboneun jung-ieyo |
| Please show me your passport and airplane ticket. | 여권하고 항공권 좀 보여 주세요.<br>yeogwonhago hanggonggwon jom boyeo juseyo |
| We are sorry, but we don't have that in our store. | 죄송합니다. 지금 저희 매장에는 없네요.<br>joesonghamnida jigeum jeohui maejang-eneun eomneyo |
| What do you think? | 어떠세요?<br>eotteoseyo |
| A Do you like it? | 마음에 드세요?<br>ma-eume deuseyo |
| B Yes, I like it. | 네, 마음에 들어요.<br>ne ma-eume deureoyo |
| B It doesn't match me. | 저랑은 좀 안 어울리는 것 같아요.<br>jeorangeun jom an eoullineun geot gatayo |
| I'll come back after looking around. | 다른 곳도 보고 다시 올게요.<br>dareun gotdo bogo dasi olgeyo |
| How much is it? | 이거 얼마예요?<br>igeo eolmayeyo |
| I'll take it. | 이걸로 주세요.<br>igeollo juseyo |

| Do you accept credit cards? | 카드 받아요? |
| | kadeu badayo |

| Please give me the receipt. | 영수증 좀 주세요. |
| | yeongsujeung jom juseyo |

| I'll pay with cash. Please give me a discount. | 현금이니까 좀 깎아 주세요. |
| | hyeongeuminikka jom kkakka juseyo |

| Do you need a <u>plastic bag</u>? | <u>비닐봉지</u> 필요하세요? |
| | <u>binilbongji</u> piryohaseyo |

- - - - - - - - - - - - - - - - - - - - - - - - - - - - - - - - - - - -

| plastic bag | 비닐봉지 binilbongji |
| paper bag | 종이봉투 jongibongtu |

- - - - - - - - - - - - - - - - - - - - - - - - - - - - - - - - - - - -

| The bag is <u>100</u> won. | 봉투 값은 <u>100</u>원입니다. |
| | bongtu gapseun <u>baeg</u>-wonimnida |
| | * Refer to page 95 for money. |

| Purchased items can be exchanged or refunded within a week from the purchase date. | 교환이나 환불은 구매한 날로부터 일주일 이내에만 가능합니다. |
| | gyohwanina hwanbureun gumaehan nallobuteo iljuil inaeeman ganeunghamnida |

| All sales final. | 이 상품은 교환 및 환불이 안 됩니다. |
| | i sangpumeun gyohwan mit hwanburi an doemnida |

# Shopping Spots in Seoul

**Myeong-dong:** Myeong-dong is in the heat of downtown Seoul. Shopping malls are in between skyscrapers and there are big department stores in Myeong-dong. The department stores usually open at 10:30 and close at 20:00. There is also a duty free store in the department store, so it's easy for foreigners to shop around. You can easily get to Myeong-dong from the subway stations Myeong-dong or Euljiro Ipgu.

**Dongdaemun Market:** Dongdeamun Market is always crowded with people until dawn. It starts from Jongno-4ga and Chunggae-4ga up to Dongdaemun. There are many shopping malls which sell clothes, shoes, and accessories. There are also many food stalls that will make your shopping enjoyable. It is close to the subway stations Dongdaemun or Deongdaemun History and Culture Park.

**Itaewon:** This is the "representative" area for foreigners in Seoul. There are stores selling both imported products and Korean products for export. It also boasts the highest number of international restaurants and bars.

**Yongsan Electronic Market:** Yongsan Electronic Market sells various kinds of electronic goods such as computers and cell phones. All the electronic goods are all in one place so it is convenient to look around and even more, they are cheap. A department store and a movie theater are also in the neighborhood.

**Insa-dong:** This is a "cultural street" that stretches from Jongno 2-ga street to Anguk-dong. There are plenty of cultural, artistic, and culinary delights to be enjoyed here (http://www.insadong.info).

**Hongdae:** "Hongdae" is short for Hongik Daehakgyo, or Hongik University. In front of this university are many cute stores and upscale coffee houses. At night it is a prime spot for clubs and other forms of entertainment.

**Apgujeong:** Apgujeong is popular among tourists for its many exotic cafes and stores selling expensive imported goods. If you are lucky, you may also see many famous Korean entertainers walking its streets and back alleys.

**Gangnam Coex Mall:** Coex Mall is the biggest basement shopping area in Asia where you can enjoy various facilities such as clothes, shoes, bags, and cosmetics stores and restaurants, convenience stores, movie theaters, and an aquarium. Many people visit Coex for the events and performances.

## DEPARTMENT STORE

| | |
|---|---|
| Which floor are <u>shoes</u> on? | 신발 매장이 몇 층에 있어요?<br><u>sinbal maejang-i</u> myeot cheung-e isseoyo |

| shoes | 신발 매장이 sinbal maejang-i |
| bags | 가방 매장이 gabang maejang-i |
| cosmetics | 화장품 매장이 hwajangpum maejang-i |
| casual wear | 영캐주얼 매장이 yeongkaejueol maejang-i |
| ladies' wear | 부인복 매장이 bu-inbok maejang-i |
| underwear | 속옷 매장이 sogot maejang-i |
| men's wear | 신사복 매장이 sinsabok maejang-i |
| sporting goods | 스포츠 용품 매장이 seupocheu yongpum maejang-i |
| home appliances | 가전 매장이 gajeon maejang-i |
| furniture | 가구 매장이 gagu maejang-i |
| living goods | 생활용품 매장이 saenghwaryongpum maejang-i |
| duty-free shops | 면세점이 myeonsejeomi |
| the restaurants | 식당가가 sikdanggaga |
| the coffee shop | 커피숍이 keopisyobi |
| after-sales repairs | A/S실이 eieseu-siri |
| the information desk | 안내데스크가 annaedeseukeuga |
| the bathrooms | 화장실이 hwajangsiri |

Now it's on sale.

지금 세일기간이에요.
jigeum seilgiganieyo

Are you currently having a sale?

지금 세일 중이에요?
jigeum seil jung-ieyo

**A** How much of a discount can I get?

얼마나 세일해요?
eolmana seilhaeyo

**B** It's on sale for <u>20%</u> off.

<u>20</u>퍼센트 세일하고 있습니다.
isip-peosenteu seilhago isseumnida

* Refer to page 345 for numerals.

We provide giveaways to customers who spend more than 100,000 won.

100,000원 이상 구입하시면 사은품을 드립니다.

simman-won isang gu-ipasimyeon sa-eunpumeul deurimnida

* Refer to page 95 for money.

Do you provide after-sales service?

A/S 받을 수 있어요?

eieseu badeul su isseoyo

## DUTY-FREE STORE

Please show me your passport.

여권 좀 보여 주세요.

yeogwon jom boyeo juseyo

Departure date, please.

출국 날짜 좀 알려 주세요.

chulguk naljja jom allyeo juseyo

Would you give me your departure date?

출국 날짜 좀 알려 주시겠어요?

chulguk naljja jom allyeo jusigesseoyo

departure date
the flight number

출국 날짜 chulguk naljja
비행기편 bihaenggipyeon

You can find your purchases at the airport.

공항에서 구입하신 물건을 찾으실 수 있어요.

gonghang-eseo gu-ipasin mulgeoneul chajeusil su isseoyo

# JEWELERY

| | |
|---|---|
| Please show me this (that). | 이것(저것/그것) 좀 보여 주세요. igeot(jeogeot/geugeot) jom boyeo juseyo |

| | |
|---|---|
| this ring | 이 반지 i banji |
| this necklace | 이 목걸이 i mokgeori |
| this bracelet | 이 팔찌 i paljji |

| | |
|---|---|
| that earring | 저(그) 귀걸이 jeo(geu) gwigeori |
| that pin | 저(그) 핀 jeo(geu) pin |
| that brooch | 저(그) 브로치 jeo(geu) beurochi |

---

이것 *igeot*, "this thing," is a pronoun used to refer to a noun near the speaker. 저것 *jeogeot*, "that thing," is used to refer to a noun near to neither the speaker nor the listener. 그것 *geugeot*, "that thing" or "the thing," is used to refer to a noun near the listener, or to a noun already mentioned in a given conversation, i.e. a noun known to both speaker and listener.

---

| | |
|---|---|
| **A** Is this(that) 14-Karat gold? | 이(저/그)거 금 14K예요? i(jeo/geu)geo geum sipsa-keiyeyo |
| **B** This(that) is 18-Karat gold. | 이(저/그)건 금 18K예요. i(jeo/geu)geon geum sippal-keiyeyo |

| 14-Karat gold | 금 14K geum sipsa-kei |
| 18-Karat gold | 금 18K geum sippal-kei |
| 24-Karat gold | 금 24K geum isipsa-kei |
| platinum | 백금 baekgeum |
| pure gold | 순금 sungeum |
| gilding | 도금 dogeum |
| silver | 은 eun |

## 이/저/그 + Noun

"이/저/그" (this, that, that/the) are indicative pre-nominals modifying the nouns they precede. "이" is used to indicate a noun near the speaker. "저" is used to indicate a noun near to neither the speaker nor the listener. "그" is used to indicate a noun near the listener, or a noun already mentioned in a given conversation, i.e. a noun known to both speaker and listener.

| May I try it on? | 한번 해 봐도 돼요?<br>hanbeon hae bwado dwaeyo |
| Try it on. | 한번 해 보세요.<br>hanbeon hae boseyo |
| Here's a mirror. | 여기 거울이 있어요.<br>yeogi geouri isseoyo |
| Please show me a diamond. | 다이아몬드 좀 보여 주세요.<br>daiamondeu jom boyeo juseyo |

| | | |
|---|---|---|
| a diamond | 다이아몬드 | daiamondeu |
| a pearl | 진주 | jinju |
| a garnet | 가넷 | ganet |
| an amethyst | 자수정 | jasujeong |
| an aquamarine | 아쿠아마린 | akuamarin |
| an emerald | 에메랄드 | emeraldeu |
| a ruby | 루비 | rubi |
| a peridot | 페리도트 | peridoteu |
| a sapphire | 사파이어 | sapaieo |
| an opal | 오팔 | opal |
| a topaz | 토파즈 | topajeu |
| a turquoise | 터키석 | teokiseok |
| a jade | 비취 | bichwi |
| an amber | 호박 | hobak |

| | |
|---|---|
| Do you have a pearl? | 진주 있어요? |
| | jinju isseoyo |
| Are there any other shapes? | 다른 모양도 있나요? |
| | dareun moyangdo innayo |
| Is there anything special I have to do to look after it? | 보관할 때 주의할 점이 있나요? |
| | bogwanhal ttae juuihal jeomi innayo |
| Where is it from? | 원산지가 어디예요? |
| | wonsanjiga eodiyeyo |
| It comes with a warranty. | 품질 보증서가 있습니다. |
| | pumjil bojeungseoga isseumnida |

## CLOCKS & WATCHES

| Please show me <br> a wristwatch. | 손목 시계 좀 보여 주세요. <br> sonmok sigye jom boyeo juseyo |
|---|---|

| a wristwatch | 손목 시계 sonmok sigye |
|---|---|
| an alarm clock | 알람 시계 allam sigye |
| a wall clock | 벽 시계 byeok sigye |
| an electronic watch | 전자 시계 jeonja sigye |
| the men's watches | 남자 시계 namja sigye |
| the women's watches | 여자 시계 yeoja sigye |
| a calendar watch | 달력 시계 dallyeok sigye |

| The watch strap is <br> replaceable. | 시계 줄은 교체하실 수 있어요. <br> sigye jureun gyochehasil su isseoyo |
|---|---|
| Is it a leather strap? | 그건 가죽 줄인가요? <br> geugeon gajuk juringayo |
| I'm looking for <br> waterproof watches. | 방수 시계를 좀 보려구요. <br> bangsu sigyereul jom boryeoguyo |
| Do you have lighter <br> ones? | 좀더 가벼운 것 있어요? <br> jomdeo gabyeoun geot isseoyo |

## COSMETICS STORE

| Do you have a toner? | 스킨 있어요? |
| | seukin isseoyo |

| a toner | 스킨 seukin |
| an emulsion | 로션 rosyeon |
| a sunscreen | 선크림 seonkeurim |
| a moisture cream | 수분크림 subunkeurim |
| a rich cream | 영양크림 yeongyangkeurim |
| a wrinkle cream | 주름개선크림 jureumgaeseonkeurim |
| an eye cream | 아이크림 aikeurim |
| a BB cream | 비비크림 bibikeurim |
| a lipstick | 립스틱 ripseutik |
| a lipgloss | 립글로스 ripgeulloseu |
| an eyeshadow | 아이섀도 aisyaedo |
| an eyeliner | 아이라이너 airaineo |

| What is your skin type? | 피부가 어떤 타입이세요? |
| | pibuga eotteon taibiseyo |

| I would like to have a skin test. | 피부테스트 좀 해 주세요. |
| | pibuteseuteu jom hae juseyo |

| A Do you have oily or dry skin? | 피부가 지성이에요, 건성이에요? |
| | pibuga jiseongieyo geonseongieyo |

| B I have oily skin. | 저는 지성 피부예요. |
| | jeoneun jiseong pibuyeyo |

| oily | 지성 jiseong |
| dry | 건성 geonseong |
| normal | 중건성 junggeonseong |
| combination | 복합성 bokapseong |

| This product is for dry skin. | 이 제품은 건성 피부에 맞는 제품이에요. |
| | i jepumeun geonseong pibue manneun jepumieyo |

## MUSIC STORE

| Where is Classical? | 클래식은 어디에 있어요? |
| | keullaesigeun eodie isseoyo |

| Classical | 클래식은 keullaesigeun |
| K-pop | 케이팝은 keipabeun |
| Jazz | 재즈는 jaejeuneun |
| Bestselling | 인기곡은 ingigogeun |
| Opera | 오페라는 operaneun |
| Pop | 팝송은 papsong-eun |

| Do you have the Wonder Girls' albums? | 원더걸스 앨범 있어요? |
| | wondeogeolseu aelbeom isseoyo |

| Which album is popular these days? | 요즘 어떤 앨범이 제일 인기가 있어요? |
| | yojeum eotteon aelbeomi jeil ingiga isseoyo |

## CLOTHING STORE

| Please show me some <u>pants</u>. | <u>바지</u> 좀 보여 주세요.<br><u>baji</u> jom boyeo juseyo |
|---|---|

| pants | 바지 baji |
|---|---|
| shorts | 반바지 banbaji |
| skirts | 치마 chima |
| T-shirt | 티셔츠 tisyeocheu |
| blouse | 블라우스 beullauseu |
| dress | 원피스 wonpiseu |
| jeans | 청바지 cheongbaji |
| jacket | 재킷 jaekit |
| cardigan | 카디건 kadigeon |
| suit | 양복 yangbok |
| dress shirt | 와이셔츠 waisyeocheu |
| sweater | 스웨터 seuweteo |
| underwear | 속옷 sogot |
| panties | 팬티 paenti |
| bra | 브래지어 beuraejieo |
| socks | 양말 yangmal |
| stockings | 스타킹 seutaking |
| scarf | 목도리 mokdori |
| swimsuit | 수영복 suyeongbok |
| bikini | 비키니 bikini |

| Please try it on. | 한번 입어 보세요.<br>hanbeon ibeo boseyo |
|---|---|
| There's a fitting room over there. | 탈의실은 저쪽이에요.<br>taruisireun jeojjogieyo |

A What size do you take?

어떤 치수로 드릴까요?
eotteon chisuro deurilkkayo

B I wear size 55.

제 치수는 55예요.
je chisuneun o-oyeyo

\* Refer to page 256 for sizes.

Do you have other sizes?

다른 사이즈 있어요?
dareun saijeu isseoyo

.....................................................

| sizes | 사이즈 saijeu |
| colors | 색깔 saegkkal |
| designs | 디자인 dijain |

.....................................................

It's a little short.

좀 짧네요.
jom jjamneyo

.....................................................

| short | 짧네요 jjamneyo |
| long | 기네요 gineyo |

| small | 작네요 jangneyo |
| big | 크네요 keuneyo |

.....................................................

Would you shorten these pants?

바지 길이 좀 줄일 수 있어요?
baji giri jom juril su isseoyo

It has a flaw here.

여기 좀 불량인데요.
yeogi jom bullyang-indeyo

## Sizes for Women

|  | HS | S | M | L | HL |
|---|---|---|---|---|---|
| ADK | 44 | 55 | 66 | 77 | 88 |
|  | 85 | 90 | 95 | 100 | 105 |
| USA | 2 | 4  6 | 8  10 | 12  14 | 16  18 |
| EU | 36 | 38-40 | 42-44 | 46-48 | 50-52 |
| UK | 6 | 8 | 10 | 12 | 14 |

## Sizes for Men

|  | HS | S | M | L | HL | HHL |
|---|---|---|---|---|---|---|
| ADK | 85 | 90 | 95 | 100 | 105 | 110 |
| USA | 85-90 | 90-95 | 95-100 | 100-105 | 105-110 | 110- |
|  | 14 | 15 | 15.5-16 | 16.5 | 17.5 | - |
| EU | 44-46 | 46 | 48 | 50 | 52 | 54 |
| UK | 0 | 1 | 2 | 3 | 4 | 5 |

## SOUVENIR SHOP

| Do you have <u>postcards</u>? | <u>우편 엽서</u> 있어요?<br>upyeon yeopseo isseoyo |
|---|---|

postcards     우편 엽서 upyeon yeopseo
keychains     열쇠고리 yeolsoegori
lighters     라이터 raiteo
traditional goods     전통 물건 jeontong mulgeon

| I'm looking for something for my <u>friend</u>. What would you recommend? | <u>친구에게</u> 주려고 하는데요, 좀 추천해 주세요. <br> chingu-ege juryeogo haneundeyo jom chucheonhae juseyo |
|---|---|

| husband | 남편 nampyeon |
|---|---|
| wife | 아내 anae |
| family | 가족 gajok |

## BOOKSTORE & STATIONERY STORE

| Where are the <u>foreign books</u>? | <u>외국 서적이</u> 어디에 있어요? <br> oeguk seojeogi eodie isseoyo |
|---|---|

| foreign books | 외국 서적이 oeguk seojeogi |
|---|---|
| new arrivals | 새로 나온 책이 saero naon chaegi |
| best sellers | 베스트셀러가 beseuteuselleoga |
| novels | 소설책이 soseolchaegi |
| dictionaries | 사전이 sajeoni |
| magazines | 잡지가 japjiga |
| cook books | 요리책이 yorichaegi |
| travel books | 여행책이 yeohaengchaegi |
| comics | 만화책이 manhwachaegi |
| arts and culture books | 예술 문화책이 yesul munhwachaegi |
| politics and social sciences | 정치 사회과학책이 jeongchi sahoegwahakchaegi |
| textbooks | 교재가 gyojaega |
| books on religion | 종교책이 jonggyochaegi |

| | |
|---|---|
| Do you have books by _____? | _____ 작가의 책 있어요?<br>_____ jakgaui chaek isseoyo |
| Do you have an <u>English newspapers</u>? | <u>영자신문</u> 있어요?<br><u>yeongjasinmun</u> isseoyo |

| | |
|---|---|
| English newspapers | 영자신문 yeongjasinmun |
| international phone cards | 국제전화카드 gukjejeonhwakadeu |

| | |
|---|---|
| Where can I find <u>a pen</u>? | <u>볼펜이</u> 어디에 있어요?<br><u>bolpeni</u> eodie isseoyo |

| | |
|---|---|
| a pen | 볼펜이 bolpeni |
| a pencil | 연필이 yeonpiri |
| an eraser | 지우개가 jiugaega |
| a notebook | 공책이 gongchaegi |
| a ruler | 자가 jaga |
| an envelope | 봉투가 bongtuga |
| a paper clip | 클립이 keullibi |
| a pair of scissors | 가위가 gawiga |

## SHOE STORE

| | |
|---|---|
| Do you have <u>high heels</u>? | <u>하이힐</u> 있어요?<br><u>haihil</u> isseoyo |
| Can you show me some <u>sneakers</u>? | <u>운동화</u> 좀 보여 주세요.<br><u>undonghwa</u> jom boyeo juseyo |

| high heels | 하이힐 haihil |
| sneakers | 운동화 undonghwa |
| flats | 단화 danhwa |
| sandals | 샌들 saendeul |
| slippers | 슬리퍼 seullipeo |
| dress shoes | 정장 구두 jeongjang gudu |

| Try them on. | 한번 신어 보세요.<br>hanbeon sineo boseyo |

| Can I try these on? | 신어 봐도 돼요?<br>sineo bwado dwaeyo |

| **A** What size are you looking for? | 발 치수가 몇이세요?<br>bal chisuga myeosiseyo |

| **B** I take <u>240</u> mm. | 제 치수는 <u>240</u>밀리미터예요.<br>je chisuneun <u>ibaeksasip-</u><br><u>millimiteoyeyo</u> |

\* Refer to page 261 for shoe sizes.

| I have <u>wide</u> feet. | 제 발볼이 좀 <u>넓어요</u>.<br>je balbori jom <u>neolbeoyo</u> |

| wide | 넓어요 neolbeoyo |
| narrow | 좁아요 jobayo |

| Walk around and see how they feel. | 한번 걸어 보세요.<br>hanbeon georeo boseyo |

A What do you think?
어떠세요?
eotteoseyo

B They're a little uncomfortable.
좀 불편해요.
jom bulpyeonhaeyo

B They are comfy.
편하네요.
pyeonhaneyo

Do you have any <u>higher</u> ones than this?
이것보다 <u>높은 굽</u> 있어요?
igeotboda <u>nopeun gup</u> isseoyo

higher
높은 굽 nopeun gup
lower
낮은 굽 najeun gup

How many centimeters is this heel?
굽이 몇 센티미터예요?
gubi myeot sentimiteoyeyo

Please get them stretched a little.
좀 늘여 주세요.
jom neuryeo juseyo

A Do you need insoles?
깔창이 필요하세요?
kkalchang-i piryohaseyo

B Yes, would you put in the insoles?
네, 깔창 좀 깔아주세요.
ne kkalchang jom kkarajuseyo

We will put in the insoles.
깔창 깔아 드릴게요.
kkalchang kkara deurilgeyo

Do you replace heels?
여기에서 굽을 갈 수 있어요?
yeogieseo gubeul gal su isseoyo

## Shoe Sizes

| KOREA | | 210 | 220 | 230 | 240 | 250 | 260 | 270 | 280 | 290 |
|---|---|---|---|---|---|---|---|---|---|---|
| USA | | 3.5 | 4.5 | 5.5 | 6.5 | 7.5 | 8.5 | 9.5 | 10.5 | 11.5 |
| JAPAN | | 21 | 22 | 23 | 24 | 25 | 26 | 27 | 28 | 29 |
| EU | M | 35 | 36 | 37.5 | 38.5 | 40 | 41 | 42.5 | 44.5 | 45.5 |
| | W | 34.5 | 35.5 | 36.5 | 38 | 39 | 40.5 | 42 | 43 | 44.5 |

## PHOTO STUDIO

**A** Who is going to have a picture taken?

어느 분이 찍으실 거예요?
eoneu buni jjigeusil geoyeyo

**B** I will have my picture taken.

제가 찍을 건데요.
jega jjigeul geondeyo

**A** When can I pick up my photos?

언제 찾을 수 있을까요?
eonje chajeul su isseulkkayo

**B** You can come pick up at <u>3:00</u>.

<u>3시</u>에 찾으러 오세요.
<u>se-si</u>e chajeureo oseyo

* Refer to page 356 for times.

The photos are <u>500</u> won each.

사진 한 장에 <u>500</u>원입니다.
sajin han jang-e <u>obaeg</u>-wonimnida

* Refer to page 95 for money.

| A | Which size of photos do you want? | 사진 크기는 어떻게 하시겠어요? |
|---|---|---|
| | | sajin keugineun eotteoke hasigesseoyo |
| B | I'll have them in this size. | 이 크기로 할게요. |
| | | i keugiro halgeyo |

## SUPERMARKET

| Where are the <u>vegetables</u>? | <u>채소가</u> 어디에 있어요? |
|---|---|
| | chaesoga eodie isseoyo |

| vegetables | 채소가 chaesoga |
|---|---|
| fruits | 과일이 gwairi |
| dairy products | 유제품이 yujepumi |
| fish | 생선이 saengseoni |
| meat | 육류가 yungnyuga |
| commodities | 생필품이 saengpilpumi |

| Please weigh this. | 이거 무게 좀 달아 주세요. |
|---|---|
| | igeo muge jom dara juseyo |

| There's no price tag on this. | 가격표가 안 붙어 있어요. |
|---|---|
| | gagyeokpyoga an buteo isseoyo |

| Put the price tag here, please. | 가격표 좀 붙여 주세요. |
|---|---|
| | gagyeokpyo jom buchyeo juseyo |

| Is this fresh? | 이거 신선해요? |
|---|---|
| | igeo sinseonhaeyo |

| Is this organic food? | 이거 유기농 식품이에요? |
| | igeo yuginong sikpumieyo |

| It's 5,000 won for three apples. | 사과 세 개에 5,000원이에요. |
| | sagwa se gae-e ocheon-wonieyo |

| apples | 사과 sagwa |
| bananas | 바나나 banana |
| strawberries | 딸기 ttalgi |
| melons | 멜론 mellon |
| oranges | 오렌지 orenji |

* Refer to page 349 for countings.
* Refer to page 95 for money.

| Where is the expiration date written? | 유통기한이 어디에 적혀 있어요? |
| | yutonggihani eodie jeokyeo isseoyo |

| Can I have a lighter? | 라이터 하나 주세요. |
| | raiteo hana juseyo |

| Is this cigarette mild? | 이 담배는 부드러워요? |
| | i dambaeneun budeureowoyo |

| mild | 부드러워요 budeureowoyo |
| strong | 독해요 dokaeyo |

| Do you need a bag? | 봉투 드릴까요? |
| | bongtu deurilkkayo |

## LOCAL PRODUCTS

What are the most
famous specialties in
this area?

이 지역에서 가장 유명한 특산품이
뭐예요?

i jiyeogeseo gajang yumyeonghan
teuksanpumi mwoyeyo

What is this good for?

이건 어디에 좋아요?

igeon eodie joayo

What is it made of?

그건 뭘로 만든 거예요?

geugeon mwollo mandeun geoyeyo

## GIFT WRAPPING

Please gift wrap this.

이거 포장 좀 해 주세요.

igeo pojang jom hae juseyo

Please put it in a bag.

가방에 좀 넣어 주세요.

gabang-e jom neoeo juseyo

This is a gift, so please
wrap it really pretty.

선물할 거니까 예쁘게 포장해 주세요.

seonmulhal geonikka yeppeuge
pojanghae juseyo

This is fragile, so
please use plenty of
wrapping.

깨지지 않게 잘 포장해 주세요.

kkaejiji anke jal pojanghae juseyo

Please tie a ribbon
around it.

리본 좀 달아 주세요.

ribon jom dara juseyo

## EXCHANGE & REFUND

**A** I'd like to <u>return</u> this.

환불하고 싶은데요.
hwanbulhago sipeundeyo

**B** You can't <u>return</u> discounted items.

세일 상품은 <u>환불</u>이 안 됩니다.
seil sangpumeun <u>hwanburi</u> an doemnida

---

return
exchange

환불 hwanbul
교환 gyohwan

---

Did you bring the receipt?

영수증 가지고 오셨어요?
yeongsujeung gajigo osyeosseoyo

Can you show me the receipt?

영수증 좀 주시겠어요?
yeongsujeung jom jusigesseoyo

I'd like to exchange this item for different <u>size</u>.

다른 <u>사이즈로</u> 바꾸고 싶어요.
dareun <u>saijeuro</u> bakkugo sipeoyo

---

size
color
product

사이즈로 saijeuro
색깔로 saegkkallo
제품으로 jepumeuro

---

**A** Is something the matter?

무슨 문제가 있으세요?
museun munjega isseuseyo

**B** This product is defective.

물건이 불량이에요.
mulgeoni bullyang-ieyo

I picked wrong size.

사이즈가 안 맞아서요.

saijeuga an majaseoyo

There's a scratch here.

여기에 흠이 있어요.

yeogie heumi isseoyo

It was stained.

뭐가 묻어 있어요.

mwoga mudeo isseoyo

# ENTERTAINMENT

## EXHIBITION

| | |
|---|---|
| I'd like to go to <u>a photo</u> exhibition. | <u>사진</u> 전시회에 가고 싶은데요.<br><u>sajin</u> jeonsihoe-e gago sipeundeyo |

| | | |
|---|---|---|
| a photo | 사진 | sajin |
| an art | 미술 | misul |
| an oil painting | 유화 | yuhwa |
| a traditional Korean art | 한국화 | hangukwa |
| a watercolor | 수채화 | suchaehwa |
| a sculpture | 조각 / 조소 | jogak / joso |
| a print | 판화 | panhwa |
| a craft | 공예 | gong-ye |
| a wood craft | 목공예 | mokgong-ye |
| a metal craft | 금속공예 | geumsokgong-ye |
| a glass craft | 유리공예 | yurigong-ye |
| a textile crafts | 섬유공예 | seomyugong-ye |
| a design | 디자인 | dijain |
| a visual design | 시각디자인 | sigakdijain |
| a product design | 제품디자인 | jepumdijain |
| a packaging design | 포장디자인 | pojangdijain |
| a video art | 비디오아트 | bidioateu |

| | |
|---|---|
| What kind of exhibitions open these days? | 요즘 어떤 전시회가 열려요?<br>yojeum eotteon jeonsihoega yeollyeoyo |

| Could you recommend a fine exhibition? | 좋은 전시회 좀 추천해 주시겠어요?<br>jo-eun jeonsihoe jom chucheonhae jusigesseoyo |
|---|---|
| These days there's a photo exhibition at the <u>museum</u>. | 요즘 박물관에서 사진 전시회를 하고 있어요.<br>yojeum <u>bangmulgwaneseo</u> sajin jeonsihoereul hago isseoyo |

| museum<br>art museum / gallery | 박물관 bangmulgwan<br>미술관 misulgwan |
|---|---|

| In this exhibition, <u>paintings</u> are on display. | 이 전시회에는 <u>그림</u>이 전시되어 있습니다.<br>i jeonsihoe-eneun <u>geurimi</u> jeonsidoe-eo isseumnida |
|---|---|

| paintings<br>photos<br>traditional crafts | 그림이 geurimi<br>사진이 sajini<br>전통 공예가 jeontong gong-yega |
|---|---|

| This exhibition will open for a month from <u>April 11</u> to <u>May 11</u>. | 이 전시회는 <u>4월 11일</u>부터 <u>5월 11일</u>까지 한 달 동안 열립니다.<br>i jeonsihoeneun <u>sa-wol sibil-il</u>buteo <u>o-wol sibil-il</u>kkaji han dal dong-an yeollimnida<br><br>* Refer to page 353 for dates. |
|---|---|
| A How much is the admission? | 입장료가 얼마예요?<br>ipjangnyoga eolmayeyo |

**B** <u>Adults</u> should pay <u>10,000</u> won for the ticket.

<u>성인은</u> 관람료가 <u>10,000원</u>입니다.
seongin-eun gwallamnyoga <u>man-wonimnida</u>

---

adults
students
children

성인은 seongin-eun
학생은 haksaeng-eun
어린이는 eorini-neun

* Refer to page 95 for money.

---

**A** Is there a discount for students?

학생인데 할인이 돼요?
haksaeng-inde harini dwaeyo

**B** Yes, show your <u>student card</u>, please.

네, <u>학생증을</u> 제시해 주세요.
ne <u>haksaengjeung-eul</u> jesihae juseyo

---

student card
international student card
identification card

학생증 haksaeng-jeung
국제학생증 gukjehaksaeng-jeung
신분증 sinbunjeung

---

**A** Is there a group discount?

단체할인 돼요?
dancheharin dwaeyo

**B** Groups of <u>30</u> or more can receive a discount.

<u>30명</u> 이상부터 단체할인을 받으실 수 있습니다.
<u>samsip-myeong</u> isangbuteo danchearineul badeusil su isseumnida

* Refer to page 345 for numerals.

When does the guided tour begin?

가이드 투어는 언제 시작해요?
gaideu tueoneun eonje sijakaeyo

ENTERTAINMENT

269

A Is there an
interpreter?

통역 서비스가 있어요?

tongyeok seobiseuga isseoyo

B Yes, we are providing
interpreters.

네, 저희는 통역 서비스를 제공하고
있습니다.

ne jeohui-neun tongyeok
seobiseureul jegonghago
isseumnida

Where do I ask for
interpretation service?

통역 서비스는 어디에서 신청해요?

tongyeok seobiseu-neun eodieseo
sincheonghaeyo

---

## Opening Hours and Interpretation Service

Each museum has its own policies on operation hours and
closing days. Check before you visit museums either online
or by phone. It will be also useful if you can check with
interpretation services and English speaking guide services
before you visit.

---

## CINEMA

Shall we go to the
movies?

같이 영화를 보러 갈래요?

gachi yeonghwareul boreo gallaeyo

Let's go to the movies.

같이 영화를 보러 가요.

gachi yeonghwareul boreo gayo

| | |
|---|---|
| What kinds of movies are showing these days? | 요즘 상영하는 영화가 뭐예요?<br>yojeum sang-yeonghaneun yeonghwaga mwoyeyo |
| What kinds of movies have opened recently? | 최근에 개봉한 영화가 뭐예요?<br>choegeune gaebonghan yeonghwaga mwoyeyo |
| What kinds of movies are popular these days? | 요즘에 인기가 있는 영화가 뭐예요?<br>yojeume ingiga inneun yeonghwaga mwoyeyo |
| Do I need to buy tickets in advance? | 미리 예매해야 해요?<br>miri yemaehaeya haeyo |
| Is it a Korean movie? | 한국 영화예요?<br>hanguk yeonghwayeyo |

| | |
|---|---|
| a Korean | 한국 hanguk |
| a foreign | 외국 oeguk |
| a Hollywood | 할리우드 halliudeu |

| | |
|---|---|
| Do they have English subtitles? | 영어 자막이 있어요?<br>yeong-eo jamagi isseoyo |
| Is that movie dubbed? | 이거 더빙이에요?<br>igeo deobing-ieyo |
| What is the title of the movie? | 영화 제목이 뭐예요?<br>yeonghwa jemogi mwoyeyo |

| Who is <u>starring</u>? | <u>주연 배우가</u> 누구예요? |
| | <u>juyeon bae-uga</u> nuguyeyo |

| starring | 주연 배우 juyeon bae-u |
| the actor | 남자 배우 namja bae-u |
| the actress | 여자 배우 yeoja bae-u |

**A** Who is the director of this film?
이 영화의 감독이 누구예요?
i yeonghwaui gamdogi nuguyeyo

**B** The director of this film is Park Chan-wook.
이 영화의 감독은 박찬욱이에요.
i yeonghwaui gamdogeun bakchanugieyo

**A** For how long does this movie run?
이 영화는 몇 분짜리 영화예요?
i yeonghwaneun myeot bunjjari yeonghwayeyo

**B** The movie runs <u>for an hour and a half</u>.
이 영화의 상영시간은 <u>1시간 30분</u>이에요.
i yeonghwaui sangyeongsiganeun <u>han-sigan samsip-bun</u>ieyo

\* Refer to page 356 for times.

When is the film opening?
이 영화는 언제 개봉해요?
i yeonghwaneun eonje gaebonghaeyo

**A** What genre is the movie?
그 영화는 장르가 뭐예요?
geu yeonghwaneun jangneuga mwoyeyo

**B** The movie is <u>a horror</u>.
<u>공포</u> 영화예요.
<u>gongpo</u> yeonghwayeyo

| a horror | 공포 gongpo |
| a drama | 드라마 deurama |
| a comedy | 코미디 komidi |
| a romance | 로맨스 romaenseu |
| an action | 액션 aeksyeon |
| a fantasy | 판타지 pantaji |
| science fiction | 공상과학 gongsanggwahak |

---

| What movie would you like to see? | 무슨 영화를 보시겠어요?<br>museun yeonghwareul bosigesseoyo |
| 2 tickets to *Romeo and Juliet* for 10:30, please. | 로미오와 줄리엣, <u>10시 30분</u>, <u>2</u>장 주세요.<br>romiowa julliet <u>yeol-si samsip-bun</u> <u>du</u>-jang juseyo |

* Refer to page 345 for numerals.
* Refer to page 349 for countings.
* Refer to page 356 for times.

| The movie is sold out. | 매진입니다.<br>maejinimnida |
| Please choose your seat. | 자리를 선택해 주세요.<br>jarireul seontaekae juseyo |
| A Where would you like to sit? | 어디에 앉으시겠어요?<br>eodie anjeusigesseoyo |
| B I prefer seats in the <u>center</u>. | <u>가운데</u> 자리로 주세요.<br><u>gaunde</u> jariro juseyo |

| center | 가운데 gaunde |
| aisle | 통로쪽 tongnojjok |
| front | 앞쪽 apjjok |
| rear | 뒤쪽 dwijjok |

**B** We'll take these seats.

여기 앉을게요.
yeogi anjeulgeyo

Let me check again. 2 tickets to Romeo and Juliet, 10:30.

확인해 드리겠습니다. 로미오와 줄리엣, 10시 30분, 2장입니다.
hwaginhae deurigesseumnida romiowa julliet yeol-si samsip-bun du-jang-imnida

* Refer to page 345 for numerals.
* Refer to page 349 for countings.
* Refer to page 356 for times.

Should we get some snacks for the movie?

영화 보면서 뭐 좀 먹을까요?
yeonghwa bomyeonseo mwo jom meogeulkkayo

Should we buy popcorn and drinks before going into the theater?

들어가기 전에 팝콘이랑 음료수 좀 살까요?
deureogagi jeone papkonirang eumnyosu jom salkkayo

Please enter now.

지금 입장하시기 바랍니다.
jigeum ipjanghasigi baramnida

You can not enter yet.

아직 입장하실 수 없습니다.
ajik ipjanghasil su eopseumnida

Please show me your ticket.

표 좀 보여 주세요.
pyo jom boyeo juseyo

A Did the movie start already?

영화 시작했어요?
yeonghwa sijakaesseoyo

B It has just started.

지금 막 시작했습니다.
jigeum mak sijakaesseumnida

B <u>10 minutes</u> left to start.

아직 <u>10분</u> 남았습니다.
ajik <u>sip-bun</u> namasseumnida

* Refer to page 356 for times.

The emergency exit is on your <u>left</u>.

비상구는 <u>왼쪽</u>에 있습니다.
bisangguneun <u>oenjjoge</u> isseumnida

---

left
right

왼쪽 oenjjok
오른쪽 oreunjjok

---

The movie is starting. Please turn off your cellphones.

곧 영화가 시작되오니 휴대폰을 꺼 주십시오.
got yeonghwaga sijakdoeoni hyudaeponeul kkeo jusipsio

Do not kick the seat in front of you.

앞 좌석을 발로 차지 마세요.
ap jwaseogeul ballo chaji maseyo

## THEATER & CONCERT HALL

What is the famous performance in Korea?

한국에서 유명한 공연이 뭐예요?
hangugeseo yumyeonghan gong-yeoni mwoyeyo

| What performances are running these days? | 요즘 하는 공연이 뭐예요?<br>yojeum haneun gong-yeoni mwoyeyo |
| Until when the <u>performance</u> lasts? | 그 <u>공연</u>은 언제까지 해요?<br>geu <u>gong-yeon</u>eun eonjekkaji haeyo |

---

| concert / show / performance<br>musical<br>opera<br>play | 공연은 gong-yeoneun<br><br>뮤지컬은 myujikeoreun<br>오페라는 operaneun<br>연극은 yeongeugeun |

---

| A Do I need to book in advance? | 미리 예약해야 돼요?<br>miri yeyakaeya dwaeyo |
| B Popular shows are selling out fast, so you should book your ticket in advance. | 인기가 있는 공연은 빨리 매진되기 때문에 미리 표를 예약해야 돼요.<br>ingiga inneun gong-yeoneun ppalli maejindoegi ttaemune miri pyoreul yeyakaeya dwaeyo |
| I booked over the <u>Internet</u>. | <u>인터넷으로</u> 예약했는데요.<br><u>inteoneseuro</u> yeyakaenneundeyo |

---

| Internet<br>phone | 인터넷으로 inteoneseuro<br>전화로 jeonhwaro |

---

| When does the show start? | 공연은 몇 시부터 시작해요?<br>gong-yeoneun myeot sibuteo sijakaeyo |

| I want to see the performance at 6:00 tonight. | 오늘 저녁 6시 공연을 보려고 하는데요. |
| --- | --- |
| | oneul jeonyeok yeoseot-si gong-yeoneul boryeogo haneundeyo |
| | * Refer to page 356 for times. |

| Are there any seats left? | 좌석이 남아 있어요? |
| --- | --- |
| | jwaseogi nama isseoyo |

| Are there any balcony seats? | 발코니 좌석 있어요? |
| --- | --- |
| | balkoni jwaseok isseoyo |

| balcony | 발코니 balkoni |
| --- | --- |
| front-row | 앞쪽 apjjok |
| back-row | 뒤쪽 dwijjok |
| aisle | 통로쪽 tongnojjok |

| Two tickets for 6:00 tonight, please. | 오늘 저녁 6시 표 두 장 주세요. |
| --- | --- |
| | oneul jeonyeok yeoseotsi pyo du jang juseyo |
| | * Refer to page 345 for numerals. |
| | * Refer to page 349 for countings. |

| Is there an intermission? | 중간에 휴식시간이 있어요? |
| --- | --- |
| | junggane hyusiksigani isseoyo |

| What is the show time? | 공연 시간이 어떻게 돼요? |
| --- | --- |
| | gong-yeon sigani eotteoke dwaeyo |

| performance, show | 공연 gong-yeon |
| --- | --- |
| rest | 휴식 hyusik |

| Use of <u>photographic</u> equipment is prohibited during the performance. | 공연 중에 <u>사진</u> 촬영은 금지입니다.<br>gong-yeon jung-e <u>sajin</u> chwaryeong-eun geumjiimnida |
|---|---|

| photographic<br>video | 사진 sajin<br>동영상 dong-yeongsang |
|---|---|

| The performance is about to begin. Please take your seats. | 곧 공연을 시작하오니 로비에 계신 분들은 입장하여 주시기 바랍니다.<br>got gong-yeoneul sijakaoni robie gyesin bundeureun ipjanghayeo jusigi baramnida |
|---|---|
| Is this a(an) <u>Korean</u> <u>singer</u>? | 한국 가수예요?<br><u>hanguk</u> <u>gasuyeyo</u> |

| singer | 가수 gasu |
|---|---|
| actor | 배우 bae-u |
| conductor | 지휘자 jihwija |
| composer | 작곡가 jakgokga |
| violinist | 바이올리니스트 baiolliniseuteu |
| pianist | 피아니스트 pianiseuteu |
| cellist | 첼리스트 chelliseuteu |
| violist | 비올리스트 biolliseuteu |

<sup>*</sup> Refer to page 362 for countries.

| Is there a singer giving a concert? | 요즘에 콘서트하는 가수 있어요?<br>yojeume konseoteuhaneun gasu isseoyo |
|---|---|

| A | What genre of music do you like? | 어떤 장르의 음악을 좋아하세요? |
|---|---|---|
| | | eotteon jangneu-ui eumageul joahaseyo |
| B | I am very interested in <u>pop</u>. | 저는 <u>팝송</u>에 관심이 많아요. |
| | | jeoneun <u>papsong</u>-e gwansimi manayo |

| pop | 팝송 papsong |
|---|---|
| K-pop | 케이팝 keipap |
| rock | 록 rok |
| hip-hop | 힙합 hipap |
| jazz | 재즈 jaejeu |
| ballad | 발라드 balladeu |
| classical | 클래식 keullaesik |
| R&B | 알앤비 araenbi |

| A | Who's your favorite singer? | 가수 중에 누구를 좋아하세요? |
|---|---|---|
| | | gasu jung-e nugureul joahaseyo |
| B | Wonder Girls is my favorite. | 저는 원더걸스를 제일 좋아해요. |
| | | jeoneun wondeogeolseureul jeil joahaeyo |
| B | There's not a singer I particularly like. | 특별히 좋아하는 가수는 없어요. |
| | | teukbyeolhi joahaneun gasuneun eopseoyo |
| | I want to get the singer's autograph. | 저는 그 가수의 사인을 받고 싶어요. |
| | | jeoneun geu gasu-ui saineul batgo sipeoyo |
| | Please give me your autograph. | 사인해 주세요. |
| | | sainhae juseyo |

| I want to join the fan club. | 팬클럽에 가입하고 싶어요.<br>paenkeulleobe gaipago sipeoyo |
| --- | --- |

## GAME

| I would like to see a <u>basketball</u> game. | <u>농구</u> 경기를 보고 싶은데요.<br><u>nonggu</u> gyeonggireul bogo sipeundeyo |
| --- | --- |
| Where's the <u>basketball</u> stadium? | <u>농구</u> 경기장이 어디에 있어요?<br><u>nonggu</u> gyeonggijang-i eodie isseoyo |
| When is there a <u>basketball</u> game? | 언제 <u>농구</u> 경기가 있어요?<br>eonje <u>nonggu</u> gyeonggiga isseoyo |

| basketball | 농구 nonggu |
| --- | --- |
| soccer | 축구 chukgu |
| baseball | 야구 yagu |
| tennis | 테니스 teniseu |
| taekwondo | 태권도 taekkwondo |

| Who is your favorite athlete? | 좋아하는 운동선수가 누구예요?<br>joahaneun undongseonsuga nuguyeyo |
| --- | --- |
| A Which team do you cheer for? | 어느 팀을 응원하세요?<br>eoneu timeul eungwonhaseyo |
| B I cheer for <u>FC Seoul</u>. | 저는 <u>FC Seoul</u> 팀을 응원해요.<br>jeoneun <u>epeusi seoul</u> timeul eungwonhaeyo |

## Famous Sports Teams in Korea

### Soccer

FC Seoul  FC 서울  epeusi seoul
Jeonbuk Hyundai  전북 현대  jeonbuk hyeondae
Suwon Samsung  수원 삼성  suwon samseong

### Baseball

SK  SK  eseukei
Samsung  삼성  samseong
Lotte  롯데  rotte

### Basketball

Seoul SK Knights  서울 SK 나이츠  seoul eseukei naicheu
Jeonju KCC Egis  전주 KCC 이지스  jeonju keisisi ijiseu
Changwon LG Sakers  창원 LG 세이커스  changwon elji seikeoseu

## NORAEBANG

A How many people are there in your group?

**몇 명이세요?**
myeot myeong-iseyo

B Five people all together.

**모두 다섯 명이에요.**
modu daseot myeong-ieyo

\* Refer to page 345 for numerals.
\* Refer to page 349 for countings.

281

| Do you have a large room? | 큰 방 있어요? |
| | keun bang isseoyo |

| Are there <u>foreign</u> songs? | <u>외국</u> 노래도 있어요? |
| | <u>oeguk</u> noraedo isseoyo |

| foreign | 외국 oeguk |
| English | 영어 yeong-eo |
| newest | 최신 choesin |

| How much is it per hour? | 한 시간에 얼마예요? |
| | han sigane eolmayeyo |

| Go to Room <u>3</u>. | <u>3</u>번 방으로 가세요. |
| | <u>sam</u>-beon bang-euro gaseyo |

\* Refer to page 345 for numerals.

| A How do I use a *noraebang* machine? | 노래방 기계는 어떻게 사용하는 거예요? |
| | noraebang gigyeneun eotteoke sayonghaneun geoyeyo |

| B You can operate it by remote control. | 이 리모컨을 쓰시면 돼요. |
| | i rimokeoneul sseusimyeon dwaeyo |

| Microphones are here. | 마이크는 여기에 있습니다. |
| | maikeuneun yeogie isseumnida |

## CLUB

| I'd like to go to a club. | 클럽에 가고 싶은데요. |
| | keulleobe gago sipeundeyo |

| Where's the famous club? | 유명한 클럽이 어디에 있어요?<br>yumyeonghan keulleobi eodie isseoyo |
| --- | --- |
| Do you know a famous club? | 유명한 클럽을 아세요?<br>yumyeonghan keulleobeul aseyo |

...................................................

| famous | 유명한 yumyeonghan |
| --- | --- |
| close | 가까운 gakkaun |
| good | 좋은 jo-eun |
| popular | 인기있는 ingiinneun |
| foreigner-friendly | 외국인들이 잘 가는 oegugindeuri jal ganeun |
| young people's | 젊은 사람들이 가는 jeolmeun saramdeuri ganeun |

...................................................

| A What time does it open? | 거기는 몇 시에 열어요?<br>geogineun myeot sie yeoreoyo |
| --- | --- |
| B You can get in the club from 7:00 p.m. | 그 클럽은 7시부터 들어갈 수 있어요.<br>geu keulleobeun ilgop-sibuteo deureogal su isseoyo<br>* Refer to page 356 for times. |
| A What time does it close? | 거기는 몇 시까지 해요?<br>geogineun myeot sikkaji haeyo |
| B It opens until 5:00 a.m. | 새벽 5시까지 해요.<br>saebyeok daseot-sikkaji haeyo |
| A What time is the most fun to go there? | 몇 시에 가야 제일 재미있어요?<br>myeot sie gaya jeil jaemiisseoyo |

**B** Around midnight is the best time to go there.

자정쯤 가야 제일 재미있어요.
jajeongjjeum gaya jeil jaemiisseoyo

**A** What is the cover charge?

입장료가 얼마예요?
ipjangnyoga eolmayeyo

**B** It's 10,000 won.

입장료는 10,000원이에요.
ipjangnyoneun man-wonieyo

\* Refer to page 95 for money.

The cover charge includes drinks.

입장료는 음료 포함 가격입니다.
ipjangnyoneun eumnyo poham gagyeogimnida

Minors are not admitted.

미성년자는 입장불가입니다.
miseongnyeonjaneun ipjangbulgaimnida

**A** What kind of dancing is popular these days in Korea?

요즘 한국에서 어떤 춤이 유행해요?
yojeum hangugeseo eotteon chumi yuhaenghaeyo

---

dancing
music

춤 chum
음악 eumak

---

**B** In Korea, the dancing trend is B-boy.

요즘 한국에서는 비보이 춤이 유행이에요.
yojeum hangugeseoneun biboi chumi yuhaeng-ieyo

| | |
|---|---|
| b-boy | 비보이 biboi |
| hip-hop | 힙합 hipap |
| poppin | 팝핀 papin |
| locking | 락킹 raking |
| salsa | 살사 salsa |
| valley | 벨리 belli |
| retro | 복고 bokgo |

## BARS

| | |
|---|---|
| I'd like to go out for a drink. | 술을 마시고 싶은데요.<br>sureul masigo sipeundeyo |
| Let's have a drink together. | 우리 같이 술 한 잔 해요.<br>uri gachi sul han jan haeyo |
| A What kind of spirits do you like? | 어떤 술을 좋아하세요?<br>eotteon sureul joahaseyo |
| B I like *soju*. | 저는 <u>소주</u>를 좋아해요.<br>jeoneun <u>soju</u>reul joahaeyo |

| | |
|---|---|
| *soju* | 소주 soju |
| *makgeoli* | 막걸리 makgeolli |
| *dongdongju* | 동동주 dongdongju |
| beer | 맥주 maekju |
| hard liquor | 양주 yangju |
| cocktail | 칵테일 kakteil |
| whiskey | 위스키 wiseuki |

**B** I enjoy drinking *makgeolli*.

저는 막걸리를 즐겨 마셔요.
jeoneun makgeollireul jeulgyeo masyeoyo

What goes well with *makgeolli*?

막걸리에 어울리는 안주가 뭐예요?
makgeollie eoullineun anjuga mwoyeyo

I cannot drink well.

저는 술을 잘 못 마셔요.
jeoneun sureul jal mot masyeoyo

Everytime I drink, my face turns red.

저는 술을 마시면 얼굴이 빨개져요.
jeoneun sureul masimyeon eolguri ppalgaejyeoyo

I get drunk easily.

저는 빨리 취해요.
jeoneun ppalli chwihaeyo

I'm a heavy drinker.

저는 술이 세요.
jeoneun suri seyo

Let's drink all night long!

밤새도록 마십시다!
bamsaedorok masipsida

**A** How much can you drink?

주량이 어떻게 되세요?
juryang-i eotteoke doeseyo

**B** I can drink a bottle of *soju*.

제 주량은 소주 한 병이에요.
je juryang-eun soju han byeong-ieyo

* Refer to page 349 for countings.

Here, take a drink.

자, 한 잔 하세요.
ja han jan haseyo

Let me pour you a drink.

제가 한 잔 따라 드릴게요.
jega han jan ttara deurilgeyo

| I brought my car, | 차를 가져 와서 술을 못 마셔요. |
| I can't drink. | chareul gajyeo waseo sureul mot |
| | masyeoyo |

| I brought my car | 차를 가져 와서 chareul gajyeo waseo |
| I have to drive | 운전을 해야 돼서 unjeoneul haeya |
| | dwaeseo |
| I'm in rough shape | 컨디션이 안 좋아서 keondisyeoni an |
| | joaseo |
| I'm on medication | 요즘 약을 먹고 있어서 yojeum yageul |
| | meokgo isseoseo |
| I have a stomachache | 배가 아파서 baega apaseo |
| I have a religious belief | 종교적인 이유로 jonggyojeogin iyuro |

| Cheers! | 건배! |
| | geonbae |

| Bottoms up! | 원샷! |
| | wonsyat |

| Here's to us! | 위하여! |
| | wihayeo |

| Is there any nice pub | 이 근처에 좋은 술집이 있어요? |
| around? | i geuncheo-e jo-eun suljibi isseoyo |

| nice | 좋은 jo-eun |
| quite | 조용한 joyonghan |
| traditional | 전통 jeontong |
| affordable | 가격이 저렴한 gagyeogi jeoryeomhan |
| live music | 라이브 음악을 하는 raibeu eumageul |
| | haneun |

| | |
|---|---|
| What would you like to <u>drink</u>? | <u>술은</u> 뭘로 하시겠어요? <br> <u>sureun</u> mwollo hasigesseoyo |

| | |
|---|---|
| to drink <br> for snack | 술은 sureun <br> 안주는 anjuneun |

| | |
|---|---|
| I would like <u>a bottle</u> of beer, here. | 여기 맥주 <u>한 병</u> 주세요. <br> yeogi maekju <u>han byeong</u> juseyo <br> * Refer to page 349 for countings. |
| What kind of beer do you have here? | 여기 맥주 종류는 뭐가 있어요? <br> yeogi maekju jongnyuneun mwoga isseoyo |
| Do you serve any food? | 식사가 될 만한 것 있어요? <br> siksaga doel manhan geot isseoyo |
| A What snack can I serve you? | 안주는 뭘 드릴까요? <br> anjuneun mwol deurilkkayo |
| B <u>Chips and nuts</u>, please. | <u>마른안주</u> 하나 주세요. <br> <u>mareunanju</u> hana juseyo |

| | |
|---|---|
| chips and nuts | 마른안주 mareunanju |
| dried squid | 마른 오징어 mareun ojing-eo |
| french fries | 감자튀김 gamjatwigim |
| fruit | 과일 gwail |
| chicken | 치킨 chikin |
| *golbaeng-i* | 골뱅이 golbaeng-i |
| tofu kimchi | 두부김치 dubugimchi |
| green onion pancake | 파전 pajeon |
| seafood pancake | 해물파전 haemulpajeon |

| | |
|---|---|
| Do you have <u>soda</u>? | <u>음료수</u> 있어요?<br><u>eumnyosu</u> isseoyo |

| | |
|---|---|
| soda | 음료수 eumnyosu |
| non-alcoholic beverage | 무알콜 음료 mualkol eumnyo |
| juice | 주스 juseu |
| water | 물 mul |

## Drinking Etiquette

*Judo* is the etiquette you are supposed to follow when you drink alcohol in Korea. Especially when you drink with people who are older than you are, you should follow *judo*. You pour for the older person first. As you pour, you should hold the bottle in one hand and support the bottom of the bottle with the other hand. Be careful so that the liquor does not spill or overflow. When someone who is older than you pours you a drink, you're supposed to hold your glass with two hands. When you drink it, turn your face to the side a little bit showing respect to the elders. Don't pour more liquor until the glass is completely empty.

## CASINO

| | |
|---|---|
| I want to go to a casino. | 카지노에 가고 싶은데요.<br>kajinoe gago sipeundeyo |

| Is there a casino in the hotel? | 호텔에 카지노가 있어요? |
| | hotere kajinoga isseoyo |

**A** Is a suit required in the casino?
카지노에서 정장을 입어야 해요?
kajinoeseo jeongjang-eul ibeoya haeyo

**B** You should get formally dressed at the casino.
그 카지노에서는 정장을 입으셔야 합니다.
geu kajinoeseoneun jeongjang-eul ibeusyeoya hamnida

**B** You may wear casual clothes.
편하게 입으셔도 됩니다.
pyeonhage ibeusyeodo doemnida

May I see your ID?
신분증 좀 보여 주십시오.
sinbunjeung jom boyeo jusipsio

This is my first time, what is a good game for a beginner?
제가 카지노에 처음 왔는데요, 초보자가 할 만한 게임 좀 소개해 주세요.
jega kajino-e cheo-eum wanneundeyo chobojaga hal manhan geim jom sogaehae juseyo

How do I play this?
이건 어떻게 하는 거예요?
igeon eotteoke haneun geoyeyo

I don't know the rules, could you tell me them?
제가 규칙을 잘 모르는데, 좀 가르쳐 주시겠어요?
jega gyuchigeul jal moreuneunde jom gareuchyeo jusigesseoyo

Where do I buy chips?
칩은 어디에서 사는 거예요?
chibeun eodieseo saneun geoyeyo

| 100 dollars in chips, please. | 100달러를 칩으로 주세요. |
| | baek-dalleoreul chibeuro juseyo |
| | * Refer to page 345 for numerals. |

| Please cash out my chips. | 정산해 주세요. |
| | jeongsanhae juseyo |

## SPORTS

## Golf

| I'd like to go golfing. | 골프를 치고 싶은데요. |
| | golpeureul chigo sipeundeyo |

| Where is the <u>nearest</u> golf course? | <u>가까운</u> 골프장이 어디에 있어요? |
| | <u>gakkaun</u> golpeujang-i eodie isseoyo |

| nearest | 가까운 gakkaun |
| most scenic | 경치가 좋은 gyeongchiga jo-eun |
| best arranged | 코스가 좋은 koseuga jo-eun |

| I'd like to make a reservation. | 예약을 하려고 하는데요. |
| | yeyageul haryeogo haneundeyo |

| Do you have an indoor driving range? | 실내 골프 연습장이 있어요? |
| | sillae golpeu yeonseupjang-i isseoyo |

| Desired date and time, please. | 원하시는 날짜와 시간을 말씀해 주세요. |
| | wonhasineun naljjawa siganeul malsseumhae juseyo |

**A** How many in your group?

일행이 몇 분이십니까?

ilhaeng-i myeot bunisimnikka

**B** It's <u>four</u> of us.

저희는 <u>네</u> 명이에요.

jeohuineun ne myeong-ieyo

<sup>*</sup> Refer to page 345 for numerals.

Can we tee off at <u>9:00 a.m.</u>?

<u>오전 9시</u>에 시작할 수 있어요?

ojeon ahop-sie sijakal su isseoyo

9:00 a.m.
2:00 p.m.
5:00 p.m.

오전 9시 ojeon ahop-si
오후 2시 ohu du-si
오후 5시 ohu daseot-si

<sup>*</sup> Refer to page 356 for times.

**A** How many caddies do you need?

캐디는 몇 명 필요하세요?

kaedineun myeot myeong piryohaseyo

**B** We need two caddies.

캐디는 두 명이 필요합니다.

kaedineun du myeong-i piryohamnida

**A** Are golf carts available?

골프카트를 사용할 수 있어요?

golpeukateureul sayonghal su isseoyo

**B** Yes, they are.

네, 사용하실 수 있습니다.

ne sayonghasil su isseumnida

## Ski & Snowboard

| Lift ticket for an adult. | 리프트 티켓 성인 한 명이요. |
| --- | --- |
| | ripeuteu tiket seongin han myeong-iyo |

| lift | 리프트 ripeuteu |
| --- | --- |
| lift and gondola | 리프트와 곤도라 ripeuteuwa gondora |
| equipment rental | 장비대여 jangbidaeyeo |

| adult | 성인 seongin |
| --- | --- |
| student | 학생 haksaeng |
| children | 어린이 eorini |

| A Can I rent skis? | 스키를 대여할 수 있어요? |
| --- | --- |
| | seukireul daeyeohal su isseoyo |

| skis | 스키를 seukireul |
| --- | --- |
| a snowboard | 스노보드를 seunobodeureul |
| ski clothing | 스키복을 seukibogeul |
| snowboard clothing | 스노보드복을 seunobodeubogeul |

| B Yes, you can rent it. | 네, 대여할 수 있습니다. |
| --- | --- |
| | ne daeyeohal su isseumnida |

| B No, you cannot rent it here. | 아니요, 여기서는 빌리실 수 없습니다. |
| --- | --- |
| | aniyo yeogiseoneun billisil su eopseumnida |

| Where can I buy <u>goggles</u>? | <u>고글은</u> 어디에서 살 수 있어요? |
| | <u>gogeureun</u> eodieseo sal su isseoyo |

| goggles | 고글은 gogeureun |
| gloves | 장갑은 janggabeun |
| a helmet | 헬멧은 helmeseun |
| knee and elbow pads | 보호대는 bohodaeneun |
| a hat | 모자는 mojaneun |

| Where are the <u>beginner</u> slopes? | <u>초급</u> 슬로프가 어디예요? |
| | <u>chogeup</u> seullopeuga eodiyeyo |

| beginner | 초급 chogeup |
| intermediate | 중급 junggeup |
| upper intermediate | 중상급 jungsanggeup |
| advanced | 상급 sanggeup |
| black diamond | 최상급 choesanggeup |

## Water Leisure

| I would like to ride on a <u>motor boat</u>. | <u>모터보트를</u> 타고 싶은데요. |
| | <u>moteoboteureul</u> tago sipeundeyo |

| I would like to learn to ride a <u>motor boat</u>. | <u>모터보트를</u> 배우고 싶은데요. |
| | <u>moteoboteureul</u> baeugo sipeundeyo |

| motor boat | 모터보트 moteoboteu |
| wake board | 웨이크보드 weikeubodeu |
| water ski | 수상스키 susangseuki |
| jet ski | 제트스키 jeteuseuki |
| banana boat | 바나나보트 bananaboteu |

A How many times have you ridden before?

전에 몇 번 타 보셨어요?
jeone myeot beon ta bosyeosseoyo

B It's my first time.

처음이에요.
cheo-eumieyo

B I've ridden it <u>three</u> times before.

<u>세</u> 번 타 봤어요.
<u>se</u> beon ta bwasseoyo

* Refer to page 345 for numerals.

A Do you have a license?

면허증이 있으세요?
myeonheojeung-i isseuseyo

B Yes, I have a license.

네, 면허증이 있어요.
ne myeonheojeung-i isseoyo

B No, I don't have a license.

아니요, 면허증이 없는데요.
aniyo myeonheojeung-i eomneundeyo

If you do not have a license, you will not be able to operate it by yourself.

면허증이 없으면 직접 운전을 하실 수 없습니다.
myeonheojeung-i eopseumyeon jikjeop unjeoneul hasil su eopseumnida

ENTERTAINMENT

## Scuba

A Do you have scuba certification?
스킨스쿠버 자격증이 있으세요?
seukinseukubeo jagyeokjeung-i isseuseyo

B Yes, I have scuba certification.
네, 자격증이 있어요.
ne jagyeokjeung-i isseoyo

A What is your rating?
등급이 뭐예요?
deunggeubi mwoyeyo

B My rating is open water.
제 등급은 오픈워터예요.
je deunggeubeun opeunwoteoyeyo

---

open water       오픈워터 opeunwoteo
advanced         어드밴스 eodeubaenseu
master           마스터 maseuteo
instructor       인스트럭터 inseuteureokteo

---

A How tall are you?
키가 몇이에요?
kiga myeochieyo

B I am 180 cm.
180센티미터예요.
baekpalsip-sentimiteoyeyo

---

180 cm       180센티미터 baekpalsip-sentimiteo
160 cm       160센티미터 baegyuksip-sentimiteo
175 cm       175센티미터 baekchilsibo-sentimiteo

---

* Refer to page 345 for numerals.

**A** How much do you weigh?

몸무게가 몇이에요?
mommugega myeochieyo

**B** I am 73 kg.

73킬로그램이에요.
chilsipsam-killogeuraemieyo

## Bowling

**A** How many in your group?

몇 분이세요?
myeot buniseyo

**B** There are four of us.

네 명이에요.
ne myeong-ieyo

**A** What size of shoes do you wear?

신발은 몇 신으세요?
sinbareun myeot sineuseyo

**B** I take a size <u>270</u> mm.

<u>270</u>밀리미터 신어요.
ibaekchilsip-millimiteo sineoyo

\* Refer to page 261 for shoe sizes.

You can choose your ball over there.

공은 저쪽에서 고르시면 됩니다.
gong-eun jeojjogeseo goreusimyeon doemnida

Go to lane <u>5</u>, please.

<u>5</u>번 레인으로 가세요.
o-beon leineuro gaseyo

\* Refer to page 345 for numerals.

## Swimming

Where's the <u>women's</u> locker room?

여자 탈의실은 어디에 있어요?
yeoja taruisireun eodie isseoyo

| | |
|---|---|
| women's locker room | 여자 탈의실은 yeoja taruisireun |
| men's locker room | 남자 탈의실은 namja taruisireun |
| swimming pool | 수영장은 suyeongjang-eun |
| sauna | 사우나는 saunaneun |
| surfing | 파도타기는 padotagineun |
| slide | 미끄럼틀은 mikkeureomteureun |
| amenities | 편의시설은 pyeonuisiseoreun |
| restaurants | 음식점은 eumsikjeomeun |

Where can I borrow
a <u>swimsuit</u>?

<u>수영복은</u> 어디에서 빌릴 수 있어요?
<u>suyeongbogeun</u> eodieseo billil su
isseoyo

Where can I buy
a <u>swimsuit</u>?

<u>수영복은</u> 어디에서 살 수 있어요?
<u>suyeongbogeun</u> eodieseo sal su
isseoyo

| | |
|---|---|
| swimsuit | 수영복은 suyeongbogeun |
| swimming cap | 수영모는 suyeongmoneun |
| life jacket | 구명 자켓은 gumyeong jakeseun |
| tube | 튜브는 tyubeuneun |
| beach towel | 비치타월은 bichitaworeun |
| gown | 가운은 gauneun |
| wrap skirt | 랩스커트는 raepseukeoteuneun |

Please be sure to wear
a <u>swimming cap</u> when
you enter the pool.

물에 들어갈 때는 <u>수영모를</u> 꼭 착용해
주십시오.
mure deureogal ttaeneun
<u>suyeongmoreul</u> kkok chagyonghae
jusipsio

| swimming cap | 수영모를 suyeongmoreul |
| life jacket | 구명 자켓을 gumyeong jakeseul |

**A** I'd like to use a <u>parasol</u>. How much is it?

파라솔을 이용하고 싶은데, 얼마죠?
<u>parasoreul</u> iyonghago sipeunde eolmajyo

| parasol | 파라솔을 parasoreul |
| sun bed | 썬베드를 sseonbedeureul |

**B** It's 20,000 won for 4 hours.

4시간에 20,000원입니다.
ne-sigane iman-wonimnida

## Fitness

**A** Are you a member of this fitness club?

이 헬스장 회원이세요?
i helseujang hoewoniseyo

**B** I'm not a member.

저는 회원이 아니에요.
jeoneun hoewoni anieyo

**A** Are you a guest of this hotel?

이 호텔 투숙객이세요?
i hotel tusukgaegiseyo

**B** Yes, I'm staying at this hotel.

네, 이 호텔에 머물고 있어요.
ne i hotere meomulgo isseoyo

**A** I would like to use the hotel gym. How much is it?

헬스장을 이용하고 싶은데요, 요금이 얼마예요?

helseujang-eul iyonghago sipeundeyo yogeumi eolmayeyo

**B** If you are a guest, it's free.

투숙객이시면 무료입니다.

tusukgaegisimyeon muryoimnida

**B** It's included in the room charge.

숙박료에 포함되어 있습니다.

sukbangnyoe pohamdoe-eo isseumnida

**B** It'll be added to your hotel bill.

호텔 숙박료에 가산될 겁니다.

hotel sukbangnyo-e gasandoel geomnida

Put it on my hotel bill, please.

호텔 숙박료에 포함시켜 주세요.

hotel sukbangnyo-e pohamsikyeo juseyo

**A** Where are (is) the <u>weight machines</u>?

<u>웨이트는</u> 어디에 있어요?

<u>weiteuneun</u> eodie isseoyo

**B** The <u>weight machines</u> are (is) over there.

<u>웨이트는</u> 저쪽에 있습니다.

<u>weiteuneun</u> jeojjoge isseumnida

---

| | | |
|---|---|---|
| weight machines | 웨이트는 | weiteuneun |
| treadmills | 런닝머신은 | reonningmeosineun |
| stationary bikes | 사이클은 | saikeureun |
| water purifier | 정수기는 | jeongsugineun |
| towels | 수건은 | sugeoneun |
| gym clothes | 헬스복은 | helseubogeun |
| shower room | 샤워실은 | syawosireun |

---

# HEALTH

## CHECKING-IN AT THE HOSPITAL

| | |
|---|---|
| Is there a <u>general hospital</u> around here? | 가까운 곳에 <u>종합병원이</u> 있나요?<br>gakkaun gose <u>jonghapbyeongwoni</u> innayo |

| | |
|---|---|
| general hospital | 종합병원이 jonghapbyeongwoni |
| surgeon | 외과가 oegwaga |
| internalist | 내과가 naegwaga |
| dentist | 치과가 chigwaga |
| ophthalmologist | 안과가 angwaga |
| dermatologist | 피부과가 pibugwaga |
| plastic surgeon | 성형외과가 seonghyeong-oegwaga |
| urologist | 비뇨기과가 binyogigwaga |

| | |
|---|---|
| I don't have an appointment, but I want to see a doctor. | 예약을 하지 않았는데, 진료를 받고 싶어서요.<br>yeyageul haji ananneunde jillyoreul batgo sipeoseoyo |
| This is my first time here. Do I need to fill out anything? | 여기 처음인데요. 뭐 작성할 거 있어요?<br>yeogi cheo-eumindeyo mwo jakseonghal geo isseoyo |
| Would you please fill out this form? | 이 양식 좀 작성해 주시겠어요?<br>i yangsik jom jakseonghae jusigesseoyo |

| Please state your <u>medical history</u> on this form. | 이 양식에 과거 병력에 대해 적어 주세요. |
| | i yangsige gwageo byeongnyeoge daehae jeogeo juseyo |

| medical history | 과거 병력 gwageo byeongnyeok |
| medications | 복용 약품 bogyong yakpum |
| current condition | 현재 상태 hyeonjae sangtae |

| I have insurance. | 보험에 가입이 되어 있어요. |
| | boheome gaibi doe-eo isseoyo |

| I don't have any insurance. | 보험에 가입이 안 되어 있어요. |
| | boheome gaibi an doe-eo isseoyo |

| How long do I have to wait? | 얼마나 기다려야 해요? |
| | eolmana gidaryeoya haeyo |

| You can go in now. | 지금 들어가세요. |
| | jigeum deureogaseyo |

| Please wait for a minute. | 조금만 기다려 주세요. |
| | jogeumman gidaryeo juseyo |

## TERMS FOR SYMTOMS

| What's bothering you? | 어디가 불편하세요? |
| | eodiga bulpyeonhaseyo |

| A Where does it hurt? | 어디가 아프세요? |
| | eodiga apeuseyo |

**B** I've got a pain right here.

여기가 아파요.
yeogiga apayo

**A** How long have you felt this way?

이런지 얼마나 됐죠?
ireonji eolmana dwaetjyo

**B** Since <u>last night</u>.

<u>어제 저녁부터요.</u>
<u>eoje jeonyeokbuteoyo</u>

. . . . . . . . . . . . . . . . . . . . . . . . . . . . . . . . . . .

| | |
|---|---|
| last night | 어제 저녁 eoje jeonyeok |
| this morning | 오늘 아침 oneul achim |

. . . . . . . . . . . . . . . . . . . . . . . . . . . . . . . . . . .

## Internal Medicine

My <u>stomach</u> hurts.

<u>배가</u> 아파요.
<u>baega</u> apayo

. . . . . . . . . . . . . . . . . . . . . . . . . . . . . . . . . . .

| | |
|---|---|
| stomach | 배가 baega |
| head | 머리가 meoriga |
| tooth | 이가 iga |

. . . . . . . . . . . . . . . . . . . . . . . . . . . . . . . . . . .

\* Refer to page 371 for body parts.

I think I have a cold.

감기에 걸린 것 같아요.
gamgie geollin geot gatayo

I have a <u>fever</u>.

<u>열이</u> 나요.
<u>yeori</u> nayo

. . . . . . . . . . . . . . . . . . . . . . . . . . . . . . . . . . .

| | |
|---|---|
| fever | 열이 yeori |
| runny nose | 콧물이 konmuri |
| headache | 두통이 dutong-i |

. . . . . . . . . . . . . . . . . . . . . . . . . . . . . . . . . . .

| | |
|---|---|
| I feel dizzy. | 어지러워요.<br>eojireowoyo |
| My chest feels heavy. | 숨 쉬기가 힘들어요.<br>sum swigiga himdeureoyo |
| I have <u>indigestion</u>. | <u>소화불량</u>인 것 같아요.<br><u>sohwabullyang</u>in geot gatayo |

- - - - - - - - - - - - - - - - - - - - - - - - - - - - - - - - - - - -

| | |
|---|---|
| indigestion | 소화불량 sohwabullyang |
| constipation | 변비 byeonbi |
| diarrhea | 설사 seolsa |

- - - - - - - - - - - - - - - - - - - - - - - - - - - - - - - - - - - -

| | |
|---|---|
| I think something was wrong with the food. | 음식을 잘못 먹은 것 같아요.<br>eumsigeul jalmot meogeun geot gatayo |
| I throw up. | 구토를 해요.<br>gutoreul haeyo |
| I'm nauseous. | 속이 메스꺼워요.<br>sogi meseukkeowoyo |
| I feel gassy. | 배에 가스가 찼어요.<br>bae-e gaseuga chasseoyo |
| I am feeling low. | 기운이 없어요.<br>giuni eopseoyo |
| I have no appetite. | 식욕이 없어요.<br>sigyogi eopseoyo |
| I have the chills. | 오한이 나요.<br>ohani nayo |

| I feel tired all the time. | 계속 피곤해요. |
| | gyesok pigonhaeyo |

| I'm stiff and sore all over. | 온 몸이 뻐근하고 쑤셔요. |
| | on momi ppeogeunhago ssusyeoyo |

| I can't stop <u>sneezing</u>. | <u>재채기가</u> 멈추지 않아요. |
| | <u>jaechaegiga</u> meomchuji anayo |

- - - - - - - - - - - - - - - - - - - - - - - - - - - - - -

| sneezing | 재채기가 jaechaegiga |
| going to the bathroom | 설사가 seolsaga |
| coughing | 기침이 gichimi |

- - - - - - - - - - - - - - - - - - - - - - - - - - - - - -

**A** When did the problem begin?

증상이 언제부터 시작됐어요?
jeungsang-i eonjebuteo sijakdwaesseoyo

**B** It's been hurting since <u>yesterday</u>.

<u>어제부터</u> 아팠어요.
<u>eojebuteo</u> apasseoyo

* Refer to page 356 for times.

**A** What did you have for dinner last night?

어제 저녁에 뭘 드셨어요?
eoje jeonyeoge mwol deusyeosseoyo

**B** I had <u>pork</u>.

<u>돼지고기를</u> 먹었어요.
<u>dwaejigogireul</u> meogeosseoyo

* Refer to page 233 for food.

## Surgery

| I hurt my <u>head</u>. | <u>머리를</u> 다쳤어요. |
| | <u>meorireul</u> dachyeosseoyo |

HEALTH

| | |
|---|---|
| head | 머리를 meorireul |
| leg | 다리를 darireul |
| hand | 손을 soneul |

* Refer to page 371 for body parts.

| | |
|---|---|
| I cut my finger. | 손가락을 베었어요.<br>songarageul be-eosseoyo |
| I've got a pus. | 고름이 생겼어요.<br>goreumi saenggyeosseoyo |
| I burned myself on a hot pan. | 뜨거운 팬에 데었어요.<br>tteugeoun paene deeosseoyo |
| The cut isn't healing well. | 베인 곳이 낫지 않아요.<br>bein gosi natji anayo |
| I stepped on a piece of broken glass. | 유리 조각을 밟았어요.<br>yuri jogageul balbasseoyo |
| I bled a lot. | 피가 많이 났어요.<br>piga mani nasseoyo |
| I sprained my ankle. | 발목을 삐었어요.<br>balmogeul ppieosseoyo |
| I think my <u>leg</u> is broken. | <u>다리가</u> 부러진 것 같아요.<br><u>dariga</u> bureojin geot gatayo |

| | |
|---|---|
| leg | 다리가 dariga |
| arm | 팔이 pari |
| ankle | 발목이 balmogi |

| I fell down some stairs. | 계단에서 넘어졌어요.<br>gyedaneseo neomeojyeosseoyo |
|---|---|

| some stairs | 계단 gyedan |
|---|---|
| on the street | 거리 geori |
| in the bathroom | 욕실 yoksil |

| A Can you move like this? | 이렇게 움직일 수 있어요?<br>ireoke umjigil su isseoyo |
|---|---|
| B Yes, I can. | 네, 할 수 있어요.<br>ne hal su isseoyo |
| B I can, but it hurts. | 할 수는 있는데 아파요.<br>hal suneun inneunde apayo |
| You will have to take an X-ray. | 엑스레이 촬영을 하겠습니다.<br>ekseurei chwaryeong-eul hagesseumnida |
| How did my X-ray turn out? | 엑스레이 촬영 결과가 어떻게 나왔어요?<br>ekseurei chwaryeong gyeolgwaga eotteoke nawasseoyo |
| Do I need to wear a cast? | 깁스를 해야 해요?<br>gipseureul haeya haeyo |
| Don't worry too much. It's nothing serious. | 너무 걱정하지 마세요. 큰 이상은 없습니다.<br>neomu geokjeonghaji maseyo keun isang-eun eopseumnida |

# Ophthalmology

My eyes hurt.

눈이 아파요.
nuni apayo

I have a sty in my eye.

눈에 다래끼가 났어요.
nune daraekkiga nasseoyo

I'm having discharge
in my eyes.

눈에 자꾸 눈곱이 껴요.
nune jakku nungobi kkyeoyo

My eyes are itchy.

눈이 간질간질해요.
nuni ganjilganjilhaeyo

My eyes are stinging.

눈이 따끔거려요.
nuni ttakkeumgeoryeoyo

My eyes are red.

눈이 충혈됐어요.
nuni chunghyeoldwaesseoyo

My eyes are blurry.

눈이 침침해요.
nuni chimchimhaeyo

My eyes keep tearing
up in the sun.

햇빛만 보면 자꾸 눈물이 나요.
haetbinman bomyeon jakku nunmuri
nayo

I've got something in
my eye and can't get
it out.

눈에 뭐가 들어갔는데 나오질 않아요.
nune mwoga deureoganneunde
naojil anayo

I want my eyes
checked.

시력검사를 하고 싶은데요.
siryeokgeomsareul hago sipeundeyo

| | |
|---|---|
| I'm thinking of getting LASIK surgery. | 라식수술을 받으려고요.<br>rasiksusureul badeuryeogoyo |
| My vision is blurry. | 흐릿하게 보여요.<br>heurithage boyeoyo |
| My vision is clear. | 잘 보여요.<br>jal boyeoyo |
| What's your vision? | 시력이 어떻게 되세요?<br>siryeogi eotteoke doeseyo |
| My vision is 1.0. | 제 시력은 1.0입니다.<br>je siryeogeun il-jeom-yeong imnida |

## Otolaryngology

ears

| | |
|---|---|
| I got water in my ear. | 귀에 물이 들어갔어요.<br>gwie muri deureogasseoyo |
| Pus is coming out of my ear. | 귀에서 고름이 나요.<br>gwieseo goreumi nayo |
| My ear is bleeding. | 귀에서 피가 나요.<br>gwieseo piga nayo |
| My ears are ringing. | 귓속이 울려요.<br>gwissogi ullyeoyo |
| I can't hear very well. | 소리가 잘 안 들려요.<br>soriga jal an deullyeoyo |

Something went in my ear.

귀에 뭐가 들어갔어요.
gwie mwoga deureogasseoyo

## nose

My nose is all stopped up.

코가 막혔어요.
koga makyeosseoyo

I have a runny nose.

콧물이 나요.
konmuri nayo

My nose is itchy.

코가 간질거려요.
koga ganjilgeoryeoyo

When I blow my nose, blood comes out.

코를 풀면 피가 나와요.
koreul pulmyeon piga nawayo

I get nosebleeds often.

자주 코피가 나요.
jaju kopiga nayo

My nosebleed won't stop.

코피가 멈추지 않아요.
kopiga meomchuji anayo

I'm having difficulty breathing.

숨 쉬는 게 힘들어요.
sum swineun ge himdeureoyo

## throat

It hurts when I swallow.

음식을 삼킬 때 목이 아파요.
eumsigeul samkil ttae mogi apayo

It hurts when I talk.

말할 때 목이 아파요.
malhal ttae mogi apayo

| | |
|---|---|
| I have a hoarse throat. | 목이 쉬었어요.<br>mogi swieosseoyo |
| I'm coughing up sputum. | 가래가 나와요.<br>garaega nawayo |
| I have a bad cough. | 기침이 심해요.<br>gichimi simhaeyo |
| I'm coughing up blood. | 기침할 때 피가 나와요.<br>gichimhal ttae piga nawayo |
| The back of my throat tickles. | 목 안쪽이 간질거려요.<br>mok anjjogi ganjilgeoryeoyo |
| I feel like there's something stuck in my throat. | 목에 뭔가 걸린 것 같아요.<br>moge mwonga geollin geot gatayo |
| I think my tonsils are swollen. | 편도선이 부은 것 같아요.<br>pyeondoseoni bueun geot gatayo |

## Dentist

| | |
|---|---|
| I have a really bad toothache. | 치통이 심해요.<br>chitong-i simhaeyo |
| My gums ache. | 잇몸이 아파요.<br>inmomi apayo |

| | |
|---|---|
| gums | 잇몸이 inmomi |
| molars | 어금니가 eogeumniga |
| jaws | 턱이 teogi |

| | |
|---|---|
| My tooth is loose. | 이가 흔들려요.<br>iga heundeullyeoyo |
| I've chipped a tooth. | 이가 부러졌어요.<br>iga bureojyeosseoyo |
| My gums are bleeding. | 잇몸에서 피가 나요.<br>inmomeseo piga nayo |
| I have swollen gums. | 잇몸이 부었어요.<br>inmomi bueosseoyo |
| I want to have my teeth whitened. | 치아미백을 하고 싶어요.<br>chiamibaegeul hago sipeoyo |
| Does it have to be pulled? | 이를 뽑아야 하나요?<br>ireul ppobaya hanayo |
| You need to get a filling. | 이를 때워야 해요.<br>ireul ttaewoya haeyo |
| I think I lost a filling. | 전에 때운 게 없어진 것 같아요.<br>jeone ttaeun ge eopseojin geot gatayo |
| You have a few cavities. | 충치가 좀 있네요.<br>chungchiga jom inneyo |
| You need to have your teeth cleaned. | 스케일링을 하셔야겠어요.<br>seukeilling-eul hasyeoyagesseoyo |
| You might need dentures. | 틀니가 필요할 것 같아요.<br>teulliga piryohal geot gatayo |
| Wide open your mouth. | 입을 크게 벌리세요.<br>ibeul keuge beolliseyo |

| You can gargle and spit. | 양치하고 뱉으세요. |
| | yangchihago baeteuseyo |

| I'll give you a shot to numb your gums. | 잇몸에 마취주사를 놓겠습니다. |
| | inmome machwijusareul nokesseumnida |

## Dermatology

| I've got a sunburn and it really hurts. | 피부가 햇볕에 타서 너무 아파요. |
| | pibuga haetbyeote taseo neomu apayo |

| My skin had been blistered by the sun. | 햇볕 때문에 물집이 생겼어요. |
| | haetbyeot ttaemune muljibi saenggyeosseoyo |

| It's so itchy I can't stand it. | 가려워서 못 참겠어요. |
| | garyeowoseo mot chamgesseoyo |

| I got stung by a bee. | 벌에 쏘였어요. |
| | beore ssoyeosseoyo |

| The bug bite is swollen. | 벌레 물린 곳이 부었어요. |
| | beolle mullin gosi bueosseoyo |

| I've got a blister on my hand. | 손에 물집이 생겼어요. |
| | sone muljibi saenggyeosseoyo |

| My acne is very severe. | 여드름이 심하게 났어요. |
| | yeodeureumi simhage nasseoyo |

| My skin is so dry, it's peeling. | 피부가 너무 건조해서 벗겨져요. |
| | pibuga neomu geonjohaeseo beotgyeojyeoyo |

| I am allergic to <u>fish</u>. | 생선 알레르기가 있어요. |
| | <u>saengseon</u> allereugiga isseoyo |

| fish | 생선 saengseon |
| pork | 돼지고기 dwaejigogi |
| chicken | 닭고기 dakgogi |
| metal | 금속 geumsok |
| cosmetic | 화장품 hwajangpum |
| perfume | 향수 hyangsu |
| sun | 햇볕 haetbyeot |

| My skin is very rough. | 제 피부가 아주 거칠어요. |
| | je pibuga aju geochireoyo |

| Apply this ointment to the insect bites. | 벌레 물린 데에 이 연고를 바르세요. |
| | beolle mullin de-e i yeongoreul bareuseyo |

| Can I have any information about <u>skin-peeling</u> procedure? | <u>박피</u> 시술에 대해 좀 알아보고 싶은데요. |
| | <u>bakpi</u> sisure daehae jom arabogo sipeundeyo |

| skin-peeling | 박피 bakpi |
| facelift | 주름살 제거 jureumsal jegeo |
| freckles removal | 주근깨 제거 jugeunkkae jegeo |
| spot removal | 점 제거 jeom jegeo |
| mole removal | 사마귀 제거 samagwi jegeo |
| Botox | 보톡스 botokseu |

**A** How much would it cost?

시술 비용이 얼마나 들까요?

sisul biyong-i eolmana deulkkayo

**B** It costs about 500,000 won.

<u>500,000</u>원 정도 합니다.

<u>osipman</u>-won jeongdo hamnida

*Refer to page 95 for money.

## MEDICAL CONDITION

I want to know what's wrong.

뭐가 문제인가요?

mwoga munjeingayo

What is the cause?

원인이 뭐예요?

wonini mwoyeyo

Will medicine take care of it?

약을 먹으면 괜찮아질까요?

yageul meogeumyeon gwaenchanajilkkayo

Will I need an operation?

수술을 해야 합니까?

susureul haeya hamnikka

Is it life-threatening?

생명이 위험할 정도예요?

saengmyeong-i wiheomhal jeongdoyeyo

What kind of rehab will I need?

어떤 재활 치료를 받아야 하죠?

eotteon jaehwal chiryoreul badaya hajyo

**A** How long will it take to recover completely?

완전히 회복하는데 얼마나 걸려요?

wanjeonhi hoebokaneunde eolmana geollyeoyo

**B** You will feel better
soon.

곧 나을 거예요.
got na-eul geoyeyo

You can get back to
work in a couple of
days.

며칠 후면 다시 일을 할 수 있을 거예요
myeochil humyeon dasi ireul hal su
isseul geoyeyo

**A** How long will I
have to stay in the
hospital?

병원에는 얼마나 있어야 해요?
byeongwoneneun eolmana isseoya
haeyo

**B** You should be here
for at least 2 days.

이틀 정도 입원해야 합니다.
iteul jeongdo ibwonhaeya hamnida

When can I <u>take
a shower</u> again?

언제 <u>샤워를</u> 다시 할 수 있어요?
eonje <u>syaworeul</u> dasi hal su isseoyo

shower
drink
exercise
work

샤워를 syaworeul
술을 sureul
운동을 undong-eul
일을 ireul

Make sure you get
enough <u>rest</u>.

충분히 <u>휴식을</u> 취하세요.
chungbunhi <u>hyusigeul</u> chwihaseyo

rest
sleep
nutrient

휴식을 hyusigeul
수면을 sumyeoneul
영양을 yeong-yang-eul

You need to keep it
dry.

물이 닿지 않게 하세요.
muri datji anke haseyo

## Pharmacy

I need to get this
prescription filled.

이 처방전대로 약 좀 지어주세요.
i cheobangjeondaero yak jom
jieojuseyo

I need some over-the-
counter medicine for
a cold.

처방전 없이 살 수 있는 감기약 주세요.
cheobangjeon eopsi sal su inneun
gamgiyak juseyo

Do you have
something for
<u>a headache</u>?

<u>두통</u>에 좋은 약 있어요?
<u>dutong</u>-e jo-eun yak isseoyo

- - - - - - - - - - - - - - - - - - - - - - - - - - - - - - - - - - -

| | |
|---|---|
| a headache | 두통 dutong |
| a toothache | 치통 chitong |
| indigestion | 소화불량 sohwabullyang |
| a stomachache | 배탈 baetal |
| diarrhea | 설사 seolsa |
| a cold | 감기 gamgi |
| a sinus cold | 코감기 kogamgi |
| a sore throat | 목감기 mokgamgi |
| a chest cold | 기침감기 gichimgamgi |
| phlegm | 가래 garae |

- - - - - - - - - - - - - - - - - - - - - - - - - - - - - - - - - - -

I have a sore throat.

목이 따가워요.
mogi ttagawoyo

Do you have any
<u>band-aid</u>?

<u>반창고</u> 있나요?
<u>banchanggo</u> innayo

| band-aid | 반창고 banchanggo |
|---|---|
| antiseptic | 소독약 sodognyak |
| gauze | 거즈 geojeu |
| bandage | 붕대 bungdae |
| antibiotic cream | 항생 연고 hangsaeng yeon-go |
| condom | 콘돔 kondom |
| birth control pill | 피임약 piimnyak |
| digestive medicine | 소화제 sohwaje |
| cold medicine | 감기약 gamgiyak |
| painkiller | 진통제 jintongje |
| fever reducer | 해열제 haeyeolje |

Are there any side
effects to this
medicine?

이 약에 부작용이 있나요?
i yage bujagyong-i innayo

I am allergic to aspirin.

저는 아스피린 알레르기가 있어요.
jeoneun aseupirin allereugiga
isseoyo

A Will this make me
drowsy?

이 약을 먹으면 졸린가요?
i yageul meogeumyeon jollingayo

B It could make you
drowsy.

이 약을 먹으면 졸릴 수 있어요.
i yageul meogeumyeon jollil su
isseoyo

A Do you have non-
drowsy medicine?

졸리지 않는 약이 있나요?
jolliji anneun yagi innayo

B Just a minute. Here
you are.

잠시만 기다리세요. 여기 있습니다.
jamsiman gidariseyo yeogi
isseumnida

**A** How often should I take this medicine?

이 약을 하루에 몇 번 복용해야 하나요?

i yageul harue myeot beon bogyonghaeya hanayo

**B** Take <u>one pill</u> at a time, <u>three times</u> a day.

한 번에 <u>한 알씩</u> 하루에 <u>세 번</u> 드세요.

han beone <u>han alssik</u> harue <u>se beon</u> deuseyo

\* Refer to page 345 for numerals.
\* Refer to page 349 for countings.

Take two pills <u>half an hour</u> after eating.

식후 <u>30분</u> 후에 두 알씩 드세요.

siku <u>samsip-bun</u> hue du alssik deuseyo

\* Refer to page 356 for times.

## Optician

I want to have my eyeglasses adjusted.

안경을 맞추고 싶은데요.

an-gyeong-eul machugo sipeundeyo

Please check my vision.

시력 좀 재 주세요.

siryeok jom jae juseyo

I want to have my vision checked again.

시력을 다시 재고 싶어요.

siryeogeul dasi jaego sipeoyo

Put in the same strength lenses as the ones in these glasses.

이 안경이랑 같은 도수로 맞춰 주세요.

i angyeong-irang gateun dosuro matchwo juseyo

I just want to buy frames.

안경테만 사고 싶어요.

angyeongteman sago sipeoyo

HEALTH

| I like these frames. | 이 테가 마음에 들어요.<br>i tega ma-eume deureoyo |
| Are there other colors besides this one? | 다른 색도 볼 수 있을까요?<br>dareun saekdo bol su isseulkkayo |
| Please show me other designs. | 다른 디자인도 좀 보고 싶어요.<br>dareun dijaindo jom bogo sipeoyo |
| Do you have something lighter? | 좀 더 가벼운 건 없나요?<br>jom deo gabyeoun geon eomnayo |
| I feel dizzy. The lenses are too strong. | 좀 어지러워요. 도수가 높은 것 같아요.<br>jom eojireowoyo dosuga nopeun geot gatayo |
| I can't see clearly. The lenses are too weak. | 잘 안 보여요. 도수가 낮은 것 같아요.<br>jal an boyeoyo dosuga najeun geot gatayo |
| I can see clearly. I'll take these ones. | 잘 보이네요. 이걸로 할게요.<br>jal boineyo. igeollo halgeyo |
| The frames for these glasses are too big. | 안경이 좀 큰 것 같아요.<br>angyeong-i jom keun geot gatayo |
| Please show me the one that model is wearing. | 저 모델이 쓴 것 좀 보여주세요.<br>jeo moderi sseun geot jom boyeojuseyo |
| I want to buy contact lenses. | 콘텍트 렌즈를 사고 싶은데요.<br>kontekteu renjeureul sago sipeundeyo |

| contact lenses | 콘텍트 렌즈를 kontekteu renjeureul |
| soft lenses | 소프트 렌즈를 sopeuteu renjeureul |
| hard lenses | 하드 렌즈를 hadeu renjeureul |
| one-day lenses | 일회용 렌즈를 ilhoeyong renjeureul |
| lense cleaner | 렌즈 세정액을 renjeu sejeong-aegeul |
| saline solution | 식염수를 sigyeomsureul |

| My eyes feel itchy. Can I try something else? | 눈에 이물감이 있어요. 다른 걸로 껴 봐도 될까요?<br>nune imulgami isseoyo dareun geollo kkyeo bwado doelkkayo |

## Traditional Korean Medicine Clinic

| I want to get a pack of restorative herbal medicine prescribed. | 보약을 짓고 싶어요.<br>boyageul jitgo sipeoyo |

| I want to have herbal medicine which is good for <u>losing weight</u>. | <u>다이어트</u>에 좋은 한약을 짓고 싶어요.<br><u>daieoteue</u> jo-eun hannyageul jitgo sipeoyo |

| losing weight | 다이어트 daieoteu |
| allergic coryza | 알레르기성 비염 allereugiseong biyeom |
| high blood pressure | 고혈압 gohyeorap |

| I want to get acupuncture. | 침을 맞고 싶어요. |
| | chimeul matgo sipeoyo |

| I want the cupping treatment. | 부항을 뜨고 싶어요. |
| | buhang-eul tteugo sipeoyo |

| My <u>lower back</u> hurts. | <u>허리가</u> 아파요. |
| | <u>heoriga</u> apayo |

| lower back | 허리가 heoriga |
| knee | 무릎이 mureupi |

* Refer to page 371 for body parts.

| I've got pins and needles in my legs. | 다리가 저려요. |
| | dariga jeoryeoyo |

| My <u>shoulder</u> aches. | <u>어깨가</u> 쑤셔요. |
| | <u>eokkaega</u> ssusyeoyo |

| shoulder | 어깨가 eokkaega |
| wrist | 손목이 sonmogi |

| I've never had acupuncture before. | 침은 맞아본 적이 없어요. |
| | chimeun majabon jeogi eopseoyo |

| Please try to make the needles not hurt. | 아프지 않게 놓아 주세요. |
| | apeuji anke noa juseyo |

| I don't want to get acupuncture; I just want to get a pack of restorative herbal medicine prescribed. | 침은 맞지 않고 한약만 먹고 싶어요.<br>chimeun matji anko hanyangman meokgo sipeoyo |
|---|---|
| I want to get acupuncture for <u>skin care</u>. | <u>피부 미용</u>에 좋은 침을 맞고 싶어요.<br><u>pibu miyong</u>-e jo-eun chimeul matgo sipeoyo |

| skin care | 피부 미용 pibu miyong |
|---|---|
| arthritis | 관절염 gwanjeolyeom |
| back pain | 허리 통증 heori tongjeung |

Thanks to improved Korean medical technology, many foreign patients are visiting Korea to receive health and medical treatment services. Now, many hospitals open international medical centers and offer foreign language services including English, Japanese, Chinese, Rissian, etc. Not only general hospitals but also private clinics like dermatologist and plastic surgeons also offer foreign language servies so foreign patients can get the proper treatment.

## ACUPRESSURE AND OTHER THERAPY

| I want to get a massage on my <u>feet</u>. | 발 마사지를 받고 싶어요.<br><u>bal</u> masajireul batgo sipeoyo |
|---|---|

\* Refer to page 371 for body parts.

| How much is it for an hour? | 한 시간에 얼마예요? |
| | han sigane eolmayeyo |

* Refer to page 356 for times.

| How long will this take? | 시간이 얼마나 걸려요? |
| | sigani eolmana geollyeoyo |

| Can I check my valuables with you? | 귀중품을 맡기고 싶은데요. |
| | gwijungpumeul matgigo sipeundeyo |

| Please don't be too hard on me. | 너무 강하게 하지 말아 주세요. |
| | neomu ganghage haji mara juseyo |

| I bruise easily. | 저는 멍이 잘 드는 체질이에요. |
| | jeoneun meong-i jal deuneun chejirieyo |

| Is there a shower? | 샤워실이 있어요? |
| | syawosiri isseoyo |

| I feel cold; turn up the heat, please. | 너무 추운데 온도 좀 올려 주세요. |
| | neomu chuunde ondo jom ollyeo juseyo |

| I feel hot; turn down the heat, please. | 너무 더운데 온도 좀 내려 주세요. |
| | neomu deounde ondo jom naeryeo juseyo |

# EMERGENCY

## WHEN FEELING SICK

Call an ambulance,
please.
구급차를 불러 주세요.
gugeupchareul bulleo juseyo

Please call a doctor.
의사를 불러 주세요.
uisareul bulleo juseyo

Is there a hospital
nearby?
근처에 병원이 있어요?
geuncheo-e byeongwoni isseoyo

How do I get to the
hospital?
병원에 어떻게 가요?
byeongwone eotteoke gayo

Please take me to the
hospital.
병원에 데려다 주세요.
byeongwone deryeoda juseyo

A What are your
symptoms?
증상이 어떠세요?
jeungsang-i eotteoseyo

B I have <u>an upset
stomach</u>.
<u>배가</u> 아파요.
<u>baega</u> apayo

a headache
a backache
머리가 meoriga
허리가 heoriga

* Refer to page 371 for body parts.

| | |
|---|---|
| I feel <u>dizzy</u>. | 현기증이 나요.<br>hyeongijeung-i nayo |

---

| | |
|---|---|
| dizzy | 현기증 hyeongijeung |
| chilly | 오한 ohan |

---

| | |
|---|---|
| I feel like throwing up. | 토할 것 같아요.<br>tohal geot gatayo |
| I have a fever and cough. | 열이 나고 기침이 나요.<br>yeori nago gichimi nayo |
| I'm having diarrhea. | 설사를 해요.<br>seolsareul haeyo |
| I sprained my ankle. | 발목이 삐었어요.<br>balmogi ppieosseoyo |
| I have a cramp in my foot. | 발에 쥐가 났어요.<br>bare jwiga nasseoyo |
| I feel itchy all over. | 온몸이 가려워요.<br>onmomi garyeowoyo |
| I'm allergic to <u>eggs</u>. | 저는 <u>계란</u> 알레르기가 있어요.<br>jeoneun <u>gyeran</u> allereugiga isseoyo |

---

| | |
|---|---|
| eggs | 계란 gyeran |
| honey | 꿀 kkul |
| peaches | 복숭아 boksung-a |
| MSG | 화학조미료 hwahakjomiryo |

| | |
|---|---|
| nuts | 땅콩 ttangkong |
| seafood | 해산물 haesanmul |
| prawns | 새우 sae-u |
| crabs | 게 ge |

| | |
|---|---|
| Will I need to be admitted to the hospital? | 입원해야 해요?<br>ibwonhaeya haeyo |
| How long do I need to rest? | 얼마나 안정을 취해야 해요?<br>eolmana anjeong-eul chwihaeya haeyo |
| How long will it take to recover? | 회복 되려면 얼마나 걸려요?<br>hoebok doeryeomyeon eolmana geollyeoyo |
| Can I keep on traveling? | 여행을 계속할 수 있을까요?<br>yeohaeng-eul gyesokal su isseulkkayo |
| I'll write a prescription for you. | 약을 처방해 드릴게요.<br>yageul cheobanghae deurilgeyo |

## FIRE

| | |
|---|---|
| Fire! | 불이 났어요!<br>buri nasseoyo |
| Where is the emergency exit? | 비상구가 어디에 있어요?<br>bisangguga eodie isseoyo |

| Use the stairway. | 계단을 이용하세요.<br>gyedaneul iyonghaseyo |
| Don't use the elevator. | 엘리베이터는 타지 마세요.<br>ellibeiteoneun taji maseyo |
| Help me! | 도와주세요!<br>dowajuseyo |
| Call 119, please. | 119에 전화해 주세요.<br>ililgu-e jeonhwahae juseyo |
| Please call an ambulance. | 구급차 좀 불러 주세요.<br>gugeupcha jom bulleo juseyo |
| Danger! Keep out! | 위험해요! 비키세요!<br>wiheomhaeyo bikiseyo |
| Look out! | 조심하세요!<br>josimhaseyo |
| A Is there anyone injured? | 다친 사람 있어요?<br>dachin saram isseoyo |
| B Someone is injured here. | 여기 다친 사람이 있어요.<br>yeogi dachin sarami isseoyo |

## CAR ACCIDENT

| It's an emergency! | 위급해요!<br>wigeupaeyo |

| I'm in a big rush. | 정말 급해요. |
| | jeongmal geupaeyo |

| I hurt my legs. | 다리를 다쳤어요. |
| | darireul dacheosseoyo |

| My friend is bleeding. | 제 친구가 피를 흘려요. |
| | je chinguga pireul heullyeoyo |

| Call the police, please. | 경찰을 불러 주세요. |
| | gyeongchareul bulleo juseyo |

- - - - - - - - - - - - - - - - - - - - - - - - - - - - - - - - - - - - - - - - -

| the police | 경찰을 gyeongchareul |
| 119 | 119를 ililgu-reul |
| ambulance | 구급차를 gugeupchareul |
| a doctor | 의사를 uisareul |

- - - - - - - - - - - - - - - - - - - - - - - - - - - - - - - - - - - - - - - - -

| I was in an accident. | 사고가 났어요. |
| | sagoga nasseoyo |

| I'd like to report a traffic accident. | 교통사고를 신고하려고 해요. |
| | gyotongsagoreul singoharyeogo haeyo |

| A Where are you now? | 지금 어디에 있어요? |
| | jigeum eodie isseoyo |

| B I am near Seoul Station. | 서울역 근처에 있어요. |
| | seoulyeok geuncheo-e isseoyo |

\* Refer to page 366 for areas.

| OK. We'll be there right away. | 알겠습니다. 지금 가겠습니다.<br>algesseumnida jigeum gagesseumnida |
| Is there a hospital around here? | 이 근처에 병원이 있어요?<br>i geuncheo-e byeongwoni isseoyo |
| Please take me to a hospital. | 병원에 데려다 주세요.<br>byeongwone deryeoda juseyo |
| Excuse me, but can I use your phone? | 죄송하지만 전화 좀 쓸 수 있을까요?<br>joesonghajiman jeonhwa jom sseul su isseulkkayo |

## THEFT OR LOSS

| I'm in a big rush. | 정말 급해요.<br>jeongmal geupaeyo |
| Someone stole my wallet. | 지갑을 도둑맞았어요.<br>jigabeul dodukmajasseoyo |
| I was robbed. | 강도를 당했어요.<br>gangdoreul danghaesseoyo |
| My wallet was taken by a pickpocket. | 지갑을 소매치기 당했어요.<br>jigabeul somaechigi danghaesseoyo |
| I lost my passport. | 여권을 잃어버렸어요.<br>yeogwoneul ireobeoryeosseoyo |

| passport | 여권을 yeogwoneul |
| cash | 현금을 hyeongeumeul |
| credit card | 신용 카드를 sinyong kadeureul |
| traveler's check | 여행자 수표를 yeohaengja supyoreul |
| backpack | 배낭을 baenangeul |
| digital camera | 디지털 카메라를 digiteol kamerareul |
| laptop | 노트북을 noteubugeul |

| Did you see my bag here? | 여기서 제 가방 못 보셨어요?<br>yeogiseo je gabang mot bosyeosseoyo |

| bag | 가방 gabang |
| wallet | 지갑 jigap |
| umbrella | 우산 usan |

| I don't know where I lost it. | 어디에서 잃어버렸는지 모르겠어요.<br>eodieseo ireobeoryeonneunji moreugesseoyo |

| Maybe I left it in the restaurant. | 아마도 식당에 놓고 온 것 같아요.<br>amado sikdang-e noko on geot gatayo |

| I can't find my baggage. | 제 짐이 보이지 않아요.<br>je jimi boiji anayo |

| I left my baggage in the taxi. | 택시에 짐을 두고 내렸어요.<br>taeksie jimeul dugo naeryeosseoyo |

| taxi | 택시 taeksi |
| bus | 버스 beoseu |
| subway | 지하철 jihacheol |
| train | 기차 gicha |

| Where's the Lost and Found? | 분실물센터가 어디예요?<br>bunsilmulsenteoga eodiyeyo |
| Call the police station, please. | 경찰서에 전화 좀 해 주세요.<br>gyeongchalseo-e jeonhwa jom hae juseyo |
| I'd like to report a theft. | 도난 신고를 하고 싶어요.<br>donan singoreul hago sipeoyo |
| I'd like to ask for a theft report. | 분실증명서를 발급해 주세요.<br>bunsiljeungmyeongseoreul balgeupae juseyo |
| I'm looking for my bag. | 잃어버린 가방을 찾고 있어요.<br>ireobeorin gabang-eul chatgo isseoyo |
| I want my passport reissued. | 여권을 재발급 받고 싶어요.<br>yeogwoneul jaebalgeup batgo sipeoyo |
| Reissue my ticket, please. | 티켓을 재발급해 주세요.<br>tikeseul jaebalgeupae juseyo |
| Could you reissue it right away? | 바로 재발급이 돼요?<br>baro jaebalgeubi dwaeyo |

| Can you cancel my credit card? | 신용카드를 정지해 주시겠어요?<br>sinyongkadeureul jeongjihae jusigesseoyo |
| --- | --- |
| I'd like to get my card reissued right now. | 카드를 바로 재발급 받고 싶어요.<br>kadeureul baro jaebalgeup batgo sipeoyo |
| A If we find it, where can we reach you? | 찾으면 어디로 연락드릴까요?<br>chajeumyeon eodiro yeollakdeurilkkayo |
| B Please contact this phone number. | 이 번호로 연락 주세요.<br>i beonhoro yeollak juseyo |

## WHEN LOST

| I'm lost. Please help me. | 길을 잃었어요. 도와주세요.<br>gireul ireosseoyo dowajuseyo |
| --- | --- |
| It's my first time here. | 저는 여기 처음 왔어요.<br>jeoneun yeogi cheo-eum wasseoyo |
| I'm in middle of nowhere. | 제가 어디에 있는지 모르겠어요.<br>jega eodie inneunji moreugesseoyo |
| Show me the way to the station, please. | 역까지 가는 길을 가르쳐 주세요.<br>yeokkkaji ganeun gireul gareuchyeo juseyo |
| Is it within walking distance? | 거기까지 걸어갈 수 있을까요?<br>geogikkaji georeogal su isseulkkayo |

| Where am I on this map? | 제가 이 지도 상에서 어디쯤에 있어요? |
| | jega i jido sang-eseo eodijjeume isseoyo |

| How can I get to the main street? | 큰 길로 나가려면 어느쪽으로 가야해요? |
| | keun gillo nagaryeomyeon eoneujjogeuro gaya haeyo |

| Where am I? | 여기가 어디예요? |
| | yeogiga eodiyeyo |

| Is this the right way? | 이 길이 맞아요? |
| | i giri majayo |

| Which way is <u>north</u>? | 어디가 <u>북쪽</u>이에요? |
| | eodiga <u>bukjjog</u>ieyo |

---

| north | 북쪽 bukjjok |
| south | 남쪽 namjjok |
| west | 서쪽 seojjok |
| east | 동쪽 dongjjok |

---

| Where is the nearest police office? | 가까운 경찰서가 어디죠? |
| | gakkaun gyeongchalseoga eodijyo |

| Do you know where the <u>US</u> Embassy is? | <u>미국</u> 대사관이 어디에 있어요? |
| | <u>miguk</u> daesagwani eodie isseoyo |

* Refer to page 362 for countries.

## Emergency Phone Numbers

Emergency phone numbers in Korea is a bit different than the ones in other countries. For fire and casualties, call 119. For car accidents, call 112, but if there is a casualty in a car accident, you can call 119 as well instead of 112.

## Robbery or Loss

According to what and where, you are supposed to report different places. If you lose your passport, you must visit your embassy. If it's your belongings, go to the police station. If you lose something at a subway station or at a bus terminal or in a taxi, visit the Lost and Found in person or check their websites.

# RETURNING

## CONFIRMING PLANE TICKETS

A I'd like to confirm
my reservation.

예약을 확인하고 싶은데요.
yeyageul hwaginhago sipeundeyo

B Would you tell me
your name and flight
number, please?

성함과 비행기편을 말씀해 주시겠어요?
seonghamgwa bihaenggipyeoneul
malsseumhae jusigesseoyo

A It's AC 065.

AC 065기예요.
eissi gongyugo-giyeyo

* Refer to page 345 for numerals.

B Your reservation is
confirmed.

예약이 확인되었습니다.
yeyagi hwagindoe-eosseumnida

B I can't find your
name on the list.

예약 명단에 없는데요.
yeyak myeongdane eomneundeyo

A When did you make
the reservation?

언제 예약하셨어요?
eonje yeyakasyeosseoyo

B I made the
reservation last
Wednesday.

지난주 수요일에 예약했어요.
jinanju suyoire yeyakaesseoyo

* Refer to page 356 for times.

I booked over the
Internet.

인터넷으로 예약했는데요.
inteoneseuro yeyakaenneundeyo

| Internet | 인터넷으로 inteoneseuro |
| phone | 전화로 jeonhwaro |

| What can I do now? | 어떻게 해야 해요? |
| | eotteoke haeya haeyo |

| A Do you want to book your ticket on the next flight? | 다음 비행기를 예약해 드릴까요? da-eum bihaenggireul yeyakae deurilkkayo |

| B Please book me on the next flight. | 다음 비행기로 예약해 주세요. da-eum bihaenggiro yeyakae juseyo |

| Please put me on the waiting list. | 대기자 명단에 넣어 주세요. daegija myeongdane neo-eo juseyo |

| We'll contact you if there is a vacancy. | 자리가 나면 연락드리겠습니다. jariga namyeon yeollakdeurigesseumnida |

| A Is there anything else you need? | 더 필요한 것 있으십니까? deo piryohan geot isseusimnikka |

| B No, that's all. | 아니요, 없어요. aniyo eopseoyo |

## CHAINGING FLIGHT SCHEDULE

| A I'd like to change my reservation with the date. | 예약 날짜를 변경하고 싶은데요. yeyak naljjareul byeon-gyeonghago sipeundeyo |

**B** When do you want to change it to?

어떻게 바꾸시겠어요?
eotteoke bakkusigesseoyo

**A** I'd like to change the date to <u>August 15th</u>. Is there anything available?

날짜를 <u>8월 15일</u>로 바꾸고 싶은데요. 가능해요?
naljjareul pal-wol sibo-illo bakkugo sipeundeyo ganeunghaeyo

\* Refer to page 353 for dates.

**B** There're no seats available at that time.

그 때는 좌석이 없습니다.
geu ttaeneun jwaseogi eopseumnida

What about the 16th?

16일은 어때요?
simyug-ireun eottaeyo

Yes, there is.

네, 있습니다.
ne isseumnida

Yes, it is possible.

네, 가능합니다.
ne ganeunghamnida

I would like to cancel my reservation.

예약을 취소하고 싶은데요.
yeyageul chwisohago sipeundeyo

**A** When is the next flight?

다음 비행기는 언제 있어요?
da-eum bihaenggineun eonje isseoyo

**B** The next flight is at <u>8:20 p.m.</u>

저녁 <u>8시 20분</u>에 있습니다.
jeonyeok yeodeol-si isip-bune isseumnida

\* Refer to page 356 for times.

## TO THE AIRPORT

**A** Where can I take the bus to the airport?

공항 가는 버스를 어디에서 탈 수 있어요?

gonghang ganeun beoseureul eodieseo tal su isseoyo

**B** There's a bus stop on the <u>left</u> at the front door.

정문 <u>왼쪽으로</u> 가시면 버스정류장이 있습니다.

jeongmun oenjjogeuro gasimyeon beoseujeongnyujang-i isseumnida

---

left

오른쪽 oenjjok

right

오른쪽 oreunjjok

* Refer to page 368 for directions.

**A** How long does it take from here to the airport?

여기에서 공항까지 얼마나 걸려요?

yeogieseo gonghangkkaji eolmana geollyeoyo

**B** It takes about <u>1 hour.</u>

<u>1시간</u> 정도 걸립니다.

<u>han-sigan</u> jeongdo geollimnida

---

1 hour

1시간 han-sigan

2 hours

2시간 du-sigan

* Refer to page 356 for times.

**A** What is the departure time?

출발 시간은 몇 시예요?

chulbal siganeun myeot siyeyo

**B** Schedules are here.

여기 시간표가 있습니다.

yeogi siganpyoga isseumnida

RETURNING

| A What time does the next bus depart? | 다음 버스는 몇 시에 출발해요?<br>da-eum beoseuneun myeot sie<br>chulbalhaeyo |
| --- | --- |
| B The next bus departs in <u>10 minutes</u>. | 다음 버스는 <u>10분</u> 후에 출발합니다.<br>da-eum beoseuneun <u>sip-bun</u> hue<br>chulbalhamnida<br>* Refer to page 356 for times. |
| I might miss my flight. | 비행기를 놓칠 것 같아요.<br>bihaenggireul nochil geot gatayo |
| Can I arrive at the airport by <u>1</u> o'clock? | <u>1</u>시까지 공항에 도착할 수 있을까요?<br>han-sikkaji gonghang-e dochakal su<br>isseulkkayo<br>* Refer to page 345 for numerals. |
| Yes, we have plenty of time. | 네, 시간이 충분해요.<br>ne sigani chungbunhaeyo |
| Please hurry. | 좀 서둘러 주세요.<br>jom seoduleo juseyo |

## RETURNING

| Where is international check-in? | 국제선 탑승 수속은 어디에서 해요?<br>gukjeseon tapseung susogeun<br>eodieseo haeyo |
| --- | --- |
| Where is the Korean Air counter? | 대한항공 카운터는 어디예요?<br>daehanhanggong kaunteoneun<br>eodiyeyo |

| When should I check in? | 탑승 수속은 언제 해요?<br>tapseung susogeun eonje haeyo |
| Can I check in now? | 지금 탑승 수속할 수 있어요?<br>jigeum tapseung susokal su isseoyo |
| Can I have your passport and ticket, please? | 여권과 항공권 좀 주시겠어요?<br>yeogwon-gwa hanggonggwon jom jusigesseoyo |
| <u>A window seat</u>, please. | <u>창가 자리</u>로 주세요.<br><u>changga jari</u>ro juseyo |

---

| a window seat | 창가 자리 changga jari |
| an aisle seat | 통로 자리 tongno jari |

---

| Do you have any luggage to check? | 부치는 짐이 있으세요?<br>buchineun jimi isseuseyo |
| **A** How many bags will you be checking? | 부치는 짐이 몇 개예요?<br>buchineun jimi myeot gaeyeyo |
| **B** I have <u>2</u> pieces of luggage. | 제 짐은 <u>2</u>개예요.<br>je jimeun <u>du</u>-gaeyeyo<br>* Refer to page 345 for numerals. |
| **B** I have no luggage to check. | 부칠 짐이 없어요.<br>buchil jimi eopseoyo |
| **A** Can I take this bag onboard with me? | 이 가방은 가지고 타도 돼요?<br>i gabang-eun gajigo tado dwaeyo |

**B** You may board with that bag.

그 가방은 가지고 타셔도 괜찮습니다.
geu gabang-eun gajigo tasyeodo
gwaenchansseumnida

Put your luggage here, please.

짐을 여기에 올려놓으세요.
jimeul yeogie ollyeonoeuseyo

Your baggage is over the weight limit.

손님의 짐은 무게가 초과됐습니다.
sonnimui jimeun mugega
chogwadwaesseumnida

Will you pay for the extra weight?

추가 요금을 내시겠습니까?
chuga yogeumeul
naesigesseumnikka

How much is the overweight luggage charge?

초과 금액이 얼마예요?
chogwa geumaegi eolmayeyo

**A** Which gate is it?

몇 번 게이트예요?
myeot beon geiteuyeyo

**B** Please go to Gate <u>10</u>.

<u>10</u>번 게이트로 가십시오.
sip-beon geiteuro gasipsio

* Refer to page 345 for numerals.

**A** Will the flight for <u>Hong Kong</u> depart on time?

<u>홍콩</u>행 항공편은 정각에 출발합니까?
hongkonghaeng hanggongpyeoneun
jeonggage chulbalhamnikka

**B** The flight for <u>Hong Kong</u> will depart on time.

<u>홍콩</u>행 항공편은 정각에 출발합니다.
hongkonghaeng hanggongpyeoneun
jeonggage chulbalhamnida

* Refer to page 362 for countries.

| The flight for NY has been canceled because of <u>fog</u>. | 뉴욕행 항공편이 <u>안개</u> 때문에 결항하였습니다. |
| | nyuyokaeng hanggongpyeoni angae ttaemune gyeolhanghayeosseumnida |

| fog | 안개 angae |
| heavy rain | 폭우 pogu |
| snow | 폭설 pokseol |

| The flight for NY has been delayed due to the <u>delayed arrival</u> of the aircraft from Hong Kong. | 뉴욕행 항공편이 홍콩발 비행기의 <u>연착으로</u> 출발이 지연되었습니다. |
| | nyuyokaeng hanggongpyeoni hongkongbal bihaenggiui yeonchageuro chulbari jiyeondoe-eosseumnida |

| delayed arrival | 연착으로 yeonchageuro |
| overbooking | 예약초과로 yeyakchogwaro |
| servicing the aircraft | 정비문제로 jeongbimunjero |

| A How long will the flight be delayed? | 비행기가 얼마나 연착될까요? |
| | bihaenggiga eolmana yeonchakdoelkkayo |

| B It will be delayed for an hour. | 한 시간 연착합니다. |
| | han sigan yeonchakamnida |

| When is the boarding time? | 탑승 시간은 언제예요? |
| | tapseung siganeun eonjeyeyo |

| I'm looking for Gate 7; which way do I have to go to? | 7번 게이트로 가려면 어느 쪽으로 가야 돼요? |
| | chil-beon geiteuro garyeomyeon eoneu jjogeuro gaya dwaeyo |

| Gate 7 | 7번 게이트로 chil-beon geiteuro |
| a restaurant | 식당으로 sikdang-euro |
| the bathroom | 화장실로 hwajangsillo |
| a coffee shop | 커피숍으로 keopisyobeuro |
| the duty-free shop | 면세점으로 myeonsejeomeuro |

| You can go this way. | 이쪽으로 가세요. |
| | ijjogeuro gaseyo |

| this way | 이쪽으로 ijjogeuro |
| that way | 저쪽으로 jeojjogeuro |
| to the right | 오른쪽으로 oreunjjogeuro |
| to the left | 왼쪽으로 oenjjogeuro |

| Has flight 062 started boarding already? | 062편의 탑승이 이미 시작되었나요? |
| | gongyugi-pyeonui tapseung-i imi sijakdoe-eonnayo |
| | * Refer to page 345 for numerals. |

| Please board the plane. | 탑승해 주십시오. |
| | tapseunghae jusipsio |

| May I see your passport and ticket? | 여권과 탑승권을 보여 주시겠어요? |
| | yeogwon-gwa tapseunggwoneul boyeo jusigesseoyo |

# Reference Section

## NUMERALS

| Arabic | Numeral | Cardinal Numeral | Ordinal Numeral |
|---|---|---|---|
| 0 | 영<br>yeong | | |
| 1 | 일<br>il | 하나<br>hana | 첫째/첫 번째<br>cheotjjae/<br>cheot beonjjae |
| 2 | 이<br>i | 둘<br>dul | 둘째/두 번째<br>duljjae/du beonjjae |
| 3 | 삼<br>sam | 셋<br>set | 셋째/세 번째<br>setjjae/se beonjjae |
| 4 | 사<br>sa | 넷<br>net | 넷째/네 번째<br>netjjae/ne beonjjae |
| 5 | 오<br>o | 다섯<br>daseot | 다섯째/다섯 번째<br>daseotjjae/<br>daseot beonjjae |
| 6 | 육<br>yuk | 여섯<br>yeoseot | 여섯째/여섯 번째<br>yeoseotjjae/<br>yeoseot beonjjae |
| 7 | 칠<br>chil | 일곱<br>ilgop | 일곱째/일곱 번째<br>ilgopjjae/ilgop beonjjae |

| Arabic | Numeral | Cardinal Numeral | Ordinal Numeral |
|--------|---------|------------------|-----------------|
| 8 | 팔<br>pal | 여덟<br>yeodeol | 여덟째/여덟 번째<br>yeodeoljjae/<br>yeodeol beonjjae |
| 9 | 구<br>gu | 아홉<br>ahop | 아홉째/아홉 번째<br>ahopjjae/ahop beonjjae |
| 10 | 십<br>sip | 열<br>yeol | 열째/열 번째<br>yeoljjae/yeol beonjjae |
| 11 | 십일<br>sibil | 열하나<br>yeol-hana | 열한 번째<br>yeolhan beonjjae |
| 12 | 십이<br>sibi | 열둘<br>yeol-dul | 열두 번째<br>yeoldu beonjjae |
| 13 | 십삼<br>sipsam | 열셋<br>yeol-set | 열세 번째<br>yeolse beonjjae |
| 14 | 십사<br>sipsa | 열넷<br>yeol-net | 열네 번째<br>yeolne beonjjae |
| 15 | 십오<br>sibo | 열다섯<br>yeol-daseot | 열다섯 번째<br>yeoldaseot beonjjae |
| 16 | 십육<br>sibyuk | 열여섯<br>yeol-yeoseot | 열여섯 번째<br>yeolyeoseot beonjjae |
| 17 | 십칠<br>sipchil | 열일곱<br>yeol-ilgop | 열일곱 번째<br>yeolilgop beonjjae |
| 18 | 십팔<br>sippal | 열여덟<br>yeol-yeodeol | 열여덟 번째<br>yeolyeodeol beonjjae |
| 19 | 십구<br>sipgu | 열아홉<br>yeol-ahop | 열아홉 번째<br>yeolahop beonjjae |

| Arabic | Numeral | Cardinal Numeral | Ordinal Numeral |
|--------|---------|------------------|-----------------|
| 20 | 이십<br>isip | 스물<br>seumul | 스무 번째<br>seumu beonjjae |
| 21 | 이십일<br>isibil | 스물하나<br>seumul-hana | 스물한 번째<br>seumulhan beonjjae |
| 22 | 이십이<br>isibi | 스물둘<br>seumul-dul | 스물두 번째<br>seumuldu beonjjae |
| 23 | 이십삼<br>isipsam | 스물셋<br>seumul-set | 스물세 번째<br>seumulse beonjjae |
| 30 | 삼십<br>samsip | 서른<br>seoreun | 서른 번째<br>seoreun beonjjae |
| 40 | 사십<br>sasip | 마흔<br>maheun | 마흔 번째<br>maheun beonjjae |
| 50 | 오십<br>osip | 쉰<br>swin | 쉰 번째<br>swin beonjjae |
| 60 | 육십<br>yuksip | 예순<br>yesun | 예순 번째<br>yesun beonjjae |
| 70 | 칠십<br>chilsip | 일흔<br>ilheun | 일흔 번째<br>ilheun beonjjae |
| 80 | 팔십<br>palsip | 여든<br>yeodeun | 여든 번째<br>yeodeun beonjjae |
| 90 | 구십<br>gusip | 아흔<br>aheun | 아흔 번째<br>aheun beonjjae |
| 100 | 백<br>baek | 백<br>baek | 백 번째<br>baek beonjjae |

For numbers over hundred, there is only way of counting.

| Arabic | Numeral | |
| --- | --- | --- |
| 200 | 이백 | ibeak |
| 300 | 삼백 | sambaek |
| 400 | 사백 | sabaek |
| 500 | 오백 | obaek |
| 600 | 육백 | yukbaek |
| 700 | 칠백 | chilbaek |
| 800 | 팔백 | palbaek |
| 900 | 구백 | gubaek |
| 1,000 | 천 | cheon |
| 2,000 | 이천 | icheon |
| 3,000 | 삼천 | samcheon |
| 4,000 | 사천 | sacheon |
| 5,000 | 오천 | ocheon |
| 6,000 | 육천 | yukcheon |
| 7,000 | 칠천 | chilcheon |
| 8,000 | 팔천 | palcheon |
| 9,000 | 구천 | gucheon |
| 10,000 | 만 | man |
| 20,000 | 이만 | iman |
| 50,000 | 오만 | oman |
| 100,000 | 십만 | simman |
| 1,000,000 | 백만 | baengman |

# COUNTING THINGS

| 1 (one) | 2 (two) | 3 (three) | 4 (four) |
|---------|---------|-----------|----------|

**people** 명 [myeong]

| 1명<br>han-myeong | 2명<br>du-myeong | 3명<br>se-myeong | 4명<br>ne-myeong |
|---|---|---|---|

**people** (one's superior) 분 [bun]

| 1분<br>han-bun | 2분<br>du-bun | 3분<br>se-bun | 4분<br>ne-bun |
|---|---|---|---|

**small objects** 개 [gae]

| 1개<br>han-gae | 2개<br>du-gae | 3개<br>se-gae | 4개<br>ne-gae |
|---|---|---|---|

**bound objects** (books, magazines, etc.)
권 [gown]

| 1권<br>han-gwon | 2권<br>du-gwon | 3권<br>se-gwon | 4권<br>ne-gwon |
|---|---|---|---|

**bowls** 그릇 [geureut]

| 1그릇<br>han-geureut | 2그릇<br>du-geureut | 3그릇<br>se-geureut | 4그릇<br>ne-geureut |
|---|---|---|---|

**bottles of drink** (beer, soda, etc.) 병 [byeong]

| 1병<br>han-byeong | 2병<br>du-byeong | 3병<br>se-byeong | 4병<br>ne-byeong |
|---|---|---|---|

**glasses of drink** (water, coffee, juice, etc.) 잔 [jan]

| 1잔<br>han-jan | 2잔<br>du-jan | 3잔<br>se-jan | 4잔<br>ne-jan |
|---|---|---|---|

**things to wear** (jackets, sweaters, shirts, etc.)
벌 [beol]

| 1벌<br>han-beol | 2벌<br>du-beol | 3벌<br>se-beol | 4벌<br>ne-beol |
|---|---|---|---|

**pairs of things to wear on feet or legs** (socks, shoes, slippers, etc.) 켤레 [kyeolle]

| 1켤레<br>han-kyeolle | 2켤레<br>du-kyeolle | 3켤레<br>se-kyeolle | 4켤레<br>ne-kyeolle |
|---|---|---|---|

**pairs of people or animals** 쌍 [ssang]

| 1쌍<br>han-ssang | 2쌍<br>du-ssang | 3쌍<br>se-ssang | 4쌍<br>ne-ssang |
|---|---|---|---|

**boxes, cases** 상자 [sangja]

| 1상자<br>han-sangja | 2상자<br>du-sangja | 3상자<br>se-sangja | 4상자<br>ne-sangja |
|---|---|---|---|

**thin, flat objects** (paper, bills, cloth, dishes, tickets, etc.) 장 [jang]

| 1장<br>han-jang | 2장<br>du-jang | 3장<br>se-jang | 4장<br>ne-jang |
|---|---|---|---|

**pencils, pens** 자루 [jaru]

| 1자루<br>han-jaru | 2자루<br>du-jaru | 3자루<br>se-jaru | 4자루<br>ne-jaru |
|---|---|---|---|

## vehicles, machines 대 [dae]

| 1대 | 2대 | 3대 | 4대 |
|---|---|---|---|
| han-dae | du-dae | se-dae | ne-dae |

## animals, insects, fish 마리 [mari]

| 1마리 | 2마리 | 3마리 | 4마리 |
|---|---|---|---|
| han-mari | du-mari | se-mari | ne-mari |

## houses 채 [chae]

| 1채 | 2채 | 3채 | 4채 |
|---|---|---|---|
| han-chae | du-chae | se-chae | ne-chae |

## flowers, bunches (grapes, bananas, etc.) 송이 [song-i]

| 1송이 | 2송이 | 3송이 | 4송이 |
|---|---|---|---|
| han-song-i | du-song-i | se-song-i | ne-song-i |

## slices, fragments, pieces 조각 [jogak]

| 1조각 | 2조각 | 3조각 | 4조각 |
|---|---|---|---|
| han-jogak | du-jogak | se-jogak | ne-jogak |

## floors of buildings 층 [cheung]

| 1층 | 2층 | 3층 | 4층 |
|---|---|---|---|
| il-cheung | i-cheung | sam-cheung | sa-cheung |

## portions, servings 인분 [inbun]

| 1인분 | 2인분 | 3인분 | 4인분 |
|---|---|---|---|
| il-inbun | i-inbun | sam-inbun | sa-inbun |

## COUNTING YEARS

| one year | 1년 | il-nyeon |
|---|---|---|
| two years | 2년 | i-nyeon |
| three years | 3년 | sam-nyeon |
| four years | 4년 | sa-nyeon |
| five years | 5년 | o-nyeon |
| six years | 6년 | yung-nyeon |
| seven years | 7년 | chil-nyeon |
| eight years | 8년 | pal-nyeon |
| nine years | 9년 | gu-nyeon |
| ten years | 10년 | sip-neyon |

## MONTHES OF THE YEAR

| January | 1월 | il-wol |
|---|---|---|
| February | 2월 | i-wol |
| March | 3월 | sam-wol |
| April | 4월 | sa-wol |
| May | 5월 | o-wol |
| June | 6월 | yu-wol |
| July | 7월 | chil-wol |
| August | 8월 | pal-wol |
| September | 9월 | gu-wol |
| October | 10월 | si-wol |
| November | 11월 | sibil-wol |
| December | 12월 | sibi-wol |

## DAYS OF THE MONTH

| | | | | | | |
|---|---|---|---|---|---|---|
| 1st | 1일 | il-il | 17th | 17일 | sipchil-il |
| 2nd | 2일 | i-il | 18th | 18일 | sippal-il |
| 3rd | 3일 | sam-il | 19th | 19일 | sipgu-il |
| 4th | 4일 | sa-il | 20th | 20일 | isip-il |
| 5th | 5일 | o-il | 21st | 21일 | isibil-il |
| 6th | 6일 | yuk-il | 22nd | 22일 | isibi-il |
| 7th | 7일 | chil-il | 23rd | 23일 | isipsam-il |
| 8th | 8일 | pal-il | 24th | 24일 | isipsa-il |
| 9th | 9일 | gu-il | 25th | 25일 | isibo-il |
| 10th | 10일 | sip-il | 26th | 26일 | isimnyuk-il |
| 11th | 11일 | sibil-il | 27th | 27일 | isipchil-il |
| 12th | 12일 | sibi-il | 28th | 28일 | isipal-il |
| 13th | 13일 | sipsam-il | 29th | 29일 | isipgu-il |
| 14th | 14일 | sipsa-il | 30th | 30일 | samsip-il |
| 15th | 15일 | sibo-il | 31st | 31일 | samsibil-il |
| 16th | 16일 | simnyuk-il | | | |

## COUNTING WEEKS

| | | |
|---|---|---|
| Sunday | 일요일 | iryoil |
| Monday | 월요일 | woryoil |
| Tuesday | 화요일 | hwayoil |
| Wednesday | 수요일 | suyoil |
| Thursday | 목요일 | mogyoil |
| Friday | 금요일 | geumyoil |
| Saturday | 토요일 | toyoil |

| | | | | | | |
|---|---|---|---|---|---|---|
| one week | 1주 | il-ju | six weeks | 6주 | yuk-ju |
| two weeks | 2주 | i-ju | seven weeks | 7주 | chil-ju |
| three weeks | 3주 | sam-ju | eight weeks | 8주 | pal-ju |
| four weeks | 4주 | sa-ju | nine weeks | 9주 | gu-ju |
| five weeks | 5주 | o-ju | ten weeks | 10주 | sip-ju |

## COUNTING DAYS

| | | | | | | |
|---|---|---|---|---|---|---|
| one day | 1일 | il-il | six days | 6일 | yuk-il |
| two days | 2일 | i-il | seven days | 7일 | chil-il |
| three days | 3일 | sam-il | eight days | 8일 | pal-il |
| four days | 4일 | sa-il | nine days | 9일 | gu-il |
| five days | 5일 | o-il | ten days | 10일 | sip-il |

A What's today's date?
**오늘이 며칠이에요?**
oneuri myeochirieyo

B It's May 1st.
**오늘은 <u>5월 1일</u>이에요.**
oneureun <u>o-wol il-il</u>ieyo

A What day is it today?
**오늘이 무슨 요일이에요?**
oneuri museun yoirieyo

B It's Friday.
**오늘은 <u>금요일</u>이에요.**
oneureun <u>geumyoil</u>ieyo

## TIME PHRASES

| | | |
|---|---|---|
| today | 오늘 | oneul |
| yesterday | 어제 | eoje |
| the day before yesterday | 그제 | geuje |
| tomorrow | 내일 | naeil |
| the day after tomorrow | 모레 | more |
| every day | 매일 | maeil |
| this week | 이번주 | ibeonju |
| last week | 지난주 | jinanju |
| next week | 다음주 | da-eumju |
| this year | 올해 | olhae |
| last year | 작년 | jangnyeon |
| next year | 내년 | naenyeon |
| for one week | 1주 동안 | il-ju dongan |
| for two weeks | 2주 동안 | i-ju dongan |
| in one day | 하루에 | harue |
| in two days | 이틀에 | iteure |
| three days ago | 3일 전 | sam-il jeon |
| four months ago | 4개월 전 | sa-gaewol jeon |
| five years ago | 5년 전 | o-nyeon jeon |
| six days later | 6일 후 | yuk-il hu |
| seven months later | 7개월 후 | chil-gaewol hu |
| eight years later | 8년 후 | pal-nyeon hu |
| morning | 아침 | achim |
| afternoon | 점심 | jeomsim |
| night | 저녁 | jeonyeok |

| this morning | 오늘 아침 | oneul achim |
| this afternoon | 오늘 점심 | oneul jeomsim |
| tonight | 오늘 밤 | oneul bam |
| tomorrow night | 내일 밤 | neail bam |
| in the morning | 아침에 | achime |
| in the afternoon | 오후에 | ohue |
| in the early evening | 초저녁에 | chojeonyeoge |
| in the evening | 저녁에 | jeonyeoge |
| in summer | 여름에 | yeoreume |
| in winter | 겨울에 | gyeoure |
| by Tuesday | 화요일까지 | hwayoilkkaji |
| by June | 6월까지 | yu-wolkkaji |
| by morning | 아침까지 | achimkkaji |

## TIMES

| dawn | 새벽 | saebyeok |
| morning | 오전 | ojeon |
| noon | 정오 | jeong-o |
| afternoon | 오후 | ohu |
| night | 밤 | bam |
| midnight | 자정 | jajeong |

## HOURS

| | | |
|---|---|---|
| 1 o'clock | 1시 | han-si |
| 2 o'clock | 2시 | du-si |
| 3 o'clock | 3시 | se-si |
| 4 o'clock | 4시 | ne-si |
| 5 o'clock | 5시 | daseot-si |
| 6 o'clock | 6시 | yeoseot-si |
| 7 o'clock | 7시 | ilgop-si |
| 8 o'clock | 8시 | yeodeol-si |
| 9 o'clock | 9시 | ahop-si |
| 10 o'clock | 10시 | yeol-si |
| 11 o'clock | 11시 | yeolhan-si |
| 12 o'clock | 12시 | yeoldu-si |

## MINUTES

| | | |
|---|---|---|
| 1 minute | 1분 | il-bun |
| 2 minutes | 2분 | i-bun |
| 3 minutes | 3분 | sam-bun |
| 4 minutes | 4분 | sa-bun |
| 5 minutes | 5분 | o-bun |
| 6 minutes | 6분 | yuk-bun |
| 7 minutes | 7분 | chil-bun |
| 8 minutes | 8분 | pal-bun |
| 9 minutes | 9분 | gu-bun |
| 10 minutes | 10분 | sip-bun |

| 11 minutes | 11분 | sibil-bun |
| 12 minutes | 12분 | sibi-bun |
| 13 minutes | 13분 | sipsam-bun |
| 14 minutes | 14분 | sipsa-bun |
| 15 minutes | 15분 | sibo-bun |
| 16 minutes | 16분 | simnyuk-bun |
| 17 minutes | 17분 | sipchil-bun |
| 18 minutes | 18분 | sippal-bun |
| 19 minutes | 19분 | sipgu-bun |
| 20 minutes | 20분 | isip-bun |
| 21 minutes | 21분 | isibil-bun |
| 22 minutes | 22분 | isibi-bun |
| 23 minutes | 23분 | isipsam-bun |
| 24 minutes | 24분 | isipsa-bun |
| 25 minutes | 25분 | isibo-bun |
| 26 minutes | 26분 | isimnyuk-bun |
| 27 minutes | 27분 | isipchil-bun |
| 28 minutes | 28분 | isippal-bun |
| 29 minutes | 29분 | isipgu-bun |
| 30 minutes | 30분 | samsip-bun |
| 31 minutes | 31분 | samsibil-bun |
| 32 minutes | 32분 | samsibi-bun |
| 33 minutes | 33분 | samsipsam-bun |
| 34 minutes | 34분 | samsipsa-bun |
| 35 minutes | 35분 | samsibo-bun |
| 36 minutes | 36분 | samsimnyuk-bun |

| 37 minutes | 37분 | samsipchil-bun |
| 38 minutes | 38분 | samsippal-bun |
| 39 minutes | 39분 | samsipgu-bun |
| 40 minutes | 40분 | sasip-bun |
| 41 minutes | 41분 | sasibil-bun |
| 42 minutes | 42분 | sasibi-bun |
| 43 minutes | 43분 | sasipsam-bun |
| 44 minutes | 44분 | sasipsa-bun |
| 45 minutes | 45분 | sasibo-bun |
| 46 minutes | 46분 | sasimnyuk-bun |
| 47 minutes | 47분 | sasipchil-bun |
| 48 minutes | 48분 | sasippal-bun |
| 49 minutes | 49분 | sasipgu-bun |
| 50 minutes | 50분 | osip-bun |
| 51 minutes | 51분 | osibil-bun |
| 52 minutes | 52분 | osibi-bun |
| 53 minutes | 53분 | osipsam-bun |
| 54 minutes | 54분 | osipsa-bun |
| 55 minutes | 55분 | osibo-bun |
| 56 minutes | 56분 | osimnyuk-bun |
| 57 minutes | 57분 | osipchil-bun |
| 58 minutes | 58분 | osippal-bun |
| 59 minutes | 59분 | osipgu-bun |
| half | 반 | ban |

A What time is it?

지금 몇 시예요?

jigeum myeotsiyeyo

B It's <u>5</u> o'clock.

<u>5</u>시예요.

<u>daseot</u>-siyeyo

| 5:05 | 5시 5분 | daseot-si o-bun |
|------|--------|-----------------|
| 5:10 | 5시 10분 | daseot-si sip-bun |
| 5:15 | 5시 15분 | daseot-si sibo-bun |
| 5:20 | 5시 20분 | daseot-si isip-bun |
| 5:25 | 5시 25분 | daseot-si isibo-bun |
| 5:30 | 5시 30분 | daseot-si samsip-bun |
| 5:35 | 5시 35분 | daseot-si samsibo-bun |
| 5:40 | 5시 40분 | daseot-si sasip-bun |
| 5:45<br>(a quarter to six) | 5시 45분<br>(6시 15분 전) | daseot-si sasibo-bun<br>(yeoseot-si sibo-bun jeon) |
| 5:50<br>(ten to six) | 5시 50분<br>(6시 10분 전) | daseot-si osip-bun<br>(yeoseot-si sip-bun jeon) |
| 5:55<br>(five to six) | 5시 55분<br>(6시 5분 전) | daseot-si osibo-bun<br>(yeoseot-si o-bun jeon) |
| 5:57<br>(three to six) | 5시 57분<br>(6시 3분 전) | daseot-si osipchil-bun<br>(yeoseot-si sam-bun jeon) |

For time schedules, as in railway and airline timetables, numbers 1 to 59 are used for minutes, not "a quarter to" or "ten to" the hour.

- My train leaves at 1:48 p.m.
  제 기차는 오후 1시 48분에 출발해요.
  je gichaneun ohu han si sasippal bune chulbalhaeyo

- My plane arrives at 10:53 a.m.
  제 비행기는 오전 10시 53분에 도착해요.
  je bihaenggineun ojeon yeol-si osipsam-bune dochakaeyo

Transportation timetables are based on the 24-hour clock. Airline and train schedules are expressed in terms of a point within a 24-hour sequence.

## FOUR SEASONS

| spring | 봄 | bom |
| summer | 여름 | yeoreum |
| fall | 가을 | ga-eul |
| winter | 겨울 | gyeoul |

## PUBLIC HOLIDAYS

| New Year's Day (January 1) | 신정 | sinjeong |
| Lunar New Year's Day (1st of the 1st lunar month) | 설날 | seollal |
| Independence Movement Day (March 1) | 삼일절 | samiljeol |
| Buddha's Birthday (8th of the 4th lunar month) | 석가탄신일 | seokgatansinil |

| Children's Day (May 5) | 어린이 날 | eorini nal |
| Memorial Day (June 6) | 현충일 | hyeonchung-il |
| Liberation Day (August 15) | 광복절 | gwangbokjeol |
| Korean Thanksgiving Day (15th of the 8th lunar month) | 추석 | chuseok |
| National Foundation Day (October 3) | 개천절 | gaecheonjeol |
| Christmas (December 25) | 성탄절 | seongtanjeol |

## COUNTRIES

| Argentina | 아르헨티나 | areuhentina |
| Australia | 호주 | hoju |
| Austria | 오스트리아 | osteuria |
| Bangladesh | 방글라데시 | bangladesi |
| Belgium | 벨기에 | belgie |
| Brazil | 브라질 | brajil |
| Cambodia | 캄보디아 | kambodia |
| Canada | 캐나다 | kaenada |
| Chile | 칠레 | chille |
| China | 중국 | jung-guk |
| Czech Republic | 체코 | cheko |
| Denmark | 덴마크 | denmakeu |
| Ecuador | 에콰도르 | ekwadoreu |
| Egypt | 이집트 | ijipteu |

| Finland | 핀란드 | pilland |
| France | 프랑스 | peurangseu |
| Germany | 독일 | dogil |
| Ghana | 가나 | gana |
| Greece | 그리스 | geuriseu |
| Hong Kong | 홍콩 | hongkong |
| India | 인도 | indo |
| Indonesia | 인도네시아 | indonesia |
| Iran | 이란 | iran |
| Ireland | 아일랜드 | aillaendeu |
| Israel | 이스라엘 | iseura-el |
| Italy | 이탈리아 | itallia |
| Japan | 일본 | ilbon |
| Jordan | 요르단 | yoreudan |
| Kazakhstan | 카자흐스탄 | kajaheuseutan |
| Kenya | 케냐 | kenya |
| Korea | 한국 | hanguk |
| Kuwait | 쿠웨이트 | kuweiteu |
| Kyrgyzstan | 키르기스스탄 | kireugiseuseutan |
| Lebanon | 레바논 | rebanon |
| Lithuania | 리투아니아 | rituania |
| Malayisa | 말레이시아 | malleisia |
| Mexico | 멕시코 | meksiko |
| Mongolia | 몽골 | mong-gol |
| Myanmar | 미얀마 | miyanma |
| Netherlands | 네덜란드 | nedeollandeu |

| New Zealand | 뉴질랜드 | nyujilaend |
| Nigeria | 나이지리아 | naijiria |
| Norway | 노르웨이 | noreuwei |
| Pakistan | 파키스탄 | pakiseutan |
| Peru | 페루 | peru |
| Philippines | 필리핀 | pillipin |
| Poland | 폴란드 | pollandeu |
| Portugal | 포르투갈 | poreutugal |
| Russia | 러시아 | reosia |
| Saudi Arabia | 사우디아라비아 | saudiarabia |
| Singapore | 싱가포르 | sing-gaporeu |
| South Africa | 남아프리카 공화국 | namapeurika gonghwaguk |
| Spain | 스페인 | seupein |
| Sweden | 스웨덴 | seuweden |
| Switzerland | 스위스 | seuwiseu |
| Taiwan | 대만 | daeman |
| Thailand | 태국 | taeguk |
| Turkey | 터키 | teoki |
| United Kingdom | 영국 | yeong-guk |
| United States | 미국 | miguk |
| Uruguay | 우루과이 | urugwai |
| Uzbekistan | 우즈베키스탄 | ujeubekiseutan |
| Venezuela | 베네수엘라 | benesuella |
| Vietnam | 베트남 | beteunam |

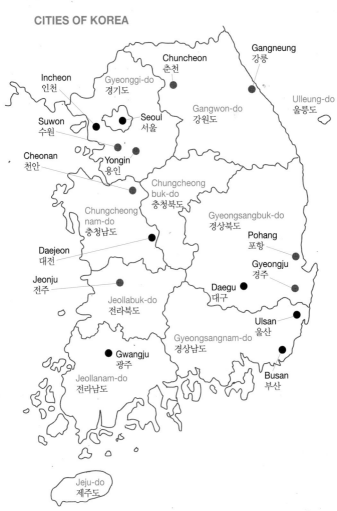

# CITIES OF KOREA

Chuncheon
춘천

Gangneung
강릉

Incheon
인천

Gyeonggi-do
경기도

Ulleung-do
울릉도

Gangwon-do
강원도

Suwon
수원

Seoul
서울

Cheonan
천안

Yongin
용인

Chungcheong
buk-do
충청북도

Chungcheong
nam-do
충청남도

Gyeongsangbuk-do
경상북도

Pohang
포항

Daejeon
대전

Gyeongju
경주

Jeonju
전주

Daegu
대구

Jeollabuk-do
전라북도

Ulsan
울산

Gwangju
광주

Gyeongsangnam-do
경상남도

Jeollanam-do
전라남도

Busan
부산

Jeju-do
제주도

## AREAS IN SEOUL

| | | |
|---|---|---|
| Myeong-dong | 명동 | myeongdong |
| Hongdae | 홍대 | hongdae |
| Sinchon | 신촌 | sinchon |
| Apgujeong | 압구정 | apgujeong |
| Itaewon | 이태원 | itaewon |
| Gwanghwamun | 광화문 | gwanghwamun |
| Gyeongbokgung | 경복궁 | gyeongbokgung |
| Insa-dong | 인사동 | insadong |
| Samcheong-dong | 삼청동 | samcheongdong |
| Cheonggyecheon | 청계천 | cheonggyecheon |
| City Hall | 시청 | sicheong |
| Namsan | 남산 | namsan |
| Seodaemun | 서대문 | seodaemun |
| Dongdaemun | 동대문 | dongdaemun |
| Namdaemun | 남대문 | namdaemun |
| Express Bus Terminal | 고속터미널 | gosokteomineol |

## SUBWAY STATIONS

| | | |
|---|---|---|
| Incheon Int'l Airport Station | 인천국제공항역 | incheon-gukjegonghang-yeok |
| Gimpo Airport Station | 김포공항역 | gimpo-gonghang-yeok |
| Hongik Univ. Station | 홍대입구역 | hongdaeipgu-yeok |
| Sindorim Station | 신도림역 | sindorim-yeok |
| Yeouido Station | 여의도역 | yeouido-yeok |

| | | |
|---|---|---|
| Gyeongbokgung Station | 경복궁역 | gyeongbokgung-yeok |
| Anguk Station | 안국역 | angung-yeok |
| Jonggak Station | 종각역 | jonggak-yeok |
| Jongno-3ga Station | 종로3가역 | jongnosamga-yeok |
| City Hall Station | 시청역 | sicheong-yeok |
| Seoul Station | 서울역 | seoul-yeok |
| Daehangno Station | 대학로역 | daehangno-yeok |
| Myeong-dong Station | 명동역 | myeongdong-yeok |
| Hoegi Station | 회기역 | hoegi-yeok |
| Itaewon Station | 이태원역 | itaewon-yeok |
| Yongsan Station | 용산역 | yongsan-yeok |
| Dongdaemun Station | 동대문역 | dongdaemun-yeok |
| Cheongryangri Station | 청량리역 | cheongnyangni-yeok |
| Wangsimni Station | 왕십리역 | wangsimni-yeok |
| Apgujeong Station | 압구정역 | apgujeong-yeok |
| Gangbyeon Station | 강변역 | gangbyeon-yeok |
| Jamsil Station | 잠실역 | jamsil-yeok |
| Express Bus Terminal Station | 고속터미널역 | gosokteominal-yeok |
| Gangnam Station | 강남역 | gangnam-yeok |
| Yangjae Station | 양재역 | yangjae-yeok |

* Visit http://www.seoulmetro.co.kr/eng/ for subway map and other
  information in English.

## DIRECTIONS

| | | |
|---|---|---|
| left | 왼쪽 | oenjjok |
| right | 오른쪽 | oreunjjok |
| this way | 이쪽 | ijjok |
| that way | 저쪽 | jeojjok |
| up | 위 | wi |
| down | 아래 | arae |
| front | 앞 | ap |
| back | 뒤 | dwi |
| side | 옆 | yeop |
| straight | 똑바로/직진 | ttokbaro/jikjin |
| right turn | 우회전 | uhoejeon |
| left turn | 좌회전 | jwahoejeon |
| east | 동쪽 | dongjjok |
| west | 서쪽 | seojjok |
| south | 남쪽 | namjjok |
| north | 북쪽 | bukjjok |

## COLORS

| | | |
|---|---|---|
| red | 빨간색 | ppalgansaek |
| orange | 주황색 | juhwangsaek |
| yellow | 노란색 | noransaek |
| green | 초록색/녹색 | choroksaek/noksaek |
| blue | 파란색 | paransaek |
| navy | 남색 | namsaek |

368

| purple | 보라색 | borasaek |
| white | 하얀색/흰색 | hayansaek/huinsaek |
| black | 까만색/검정색 | kkamansaek/geomjeongsaek |
| pink | 핑크색 | pingkeusaek |
| sky blue | 하늘색 | haneulsaek |
| brown | 갈색 | galsaek |
| grey | 회색 | hoesaek |

## SHAPES

| circle | 원 | won |
| oval | 타원형 | tawonhyeong |
| triangle | 삼각형 | samgakyeong |
| square | 사각형 | sagakyeong |
| quadrangle | 정사각형 | jeongsagakyeong |
| pentagon | 오각형 | ogakyeong |
| hexagon | 육각형 | yuggakyeong |
| polygon | 다각형 | dagakyeong |
| rhombus | 마름모 | mareummo |
| checkered | 체크무늬 | chekeumunui |
| striped | 줄무늬 | julmunui |
| polka dots | 물방울무늬 | mulbangulmunui |
| floral pattern | 꽃무늬 | kkonmunui |

## FAMILY

| | | |
|---|---|---|
| grandfather | 할아버지 | harabeoji |
| grandmother | 할머니 | halmeoni |
| maternal grandfather | 외할아버지 | oeharabeoji |
| maternal grandmother | 외할머니 | oehalmeoni |
| father | 아버지 | abeoji |
| mother | 어머니 | eomeoni |
| husband | 남편 | nampyeon |
| wife | 아내 | anae |
| brother | 형제 | hyeongje |
| sister | 자매 | jamae |
| elder brother (for man) | 형 | hyeong |
| elder brother (for woman) | 오빠 | oppa |
| elder sister (for man) | 누나 | nuna |
| elder sister (for woman) | 언니 | eonni |
| younger brother | 남동생 | namdongsaeng |
| younger sister | 여동생 | yeodongsaeng |
| son | 아들 | adeul |
| daughter | 딸 | ttal |
| husband's father | 시아버지 | siabeoji |
| husband's mother | 시어머니 | sieomeoni |
| wife's father | 장인 | jang-in |
| wife's mother | 장모 | jangmo |
| son-in-law | 사위 | sawi |
| daughter-in-law | 며느리 | myeoneuri |
| grandson | 손자 | sonja |

| granddaughter | 손녀 | sonnyeo |
| uncle (father's brother) | 삼촌 | samchon |
| aunt (father's sister) | 고모 | gomo |
| uncle (mother's brother) | 외삼촌 | oesamchon |
| aunt (mother's sister) | 이모 | imo |
| nephew | 조카 | joka |
| cousin | 사촌 | sachon |

## BODY PARTS

| body | 몸 | mom |
| head | 머리 | meori |
| eyebrow | 눈썹 | nunsseop |
| eye | 눈 | nun |
| nose | 코 | ko |
| ear | 귀 | gwi |
| mouth | 입 | ip |
| neck/throat | 목 | mok |
| stomach/abdomen | 배 | bae |
| navel | 배꼽 | baekkop |
| lower abdomen | 아랫배 | araetbae |
| waist | 허리 | heori |
| back | 등 | deung |
| elbow | 팔꿈치 | palkkumchi |
| wrist | 손목 | sonmok |
| finger | 손가락 | son-garak |

| hand | 손 | son |
| leg | 다리 | dari |
| knee | 무릎 | mureup |
| backside | 엉덩이 | eongdeong-i |
| thigh | 허벅지 | heobeokji |
| ankle | 발목 | balmok |
| foot | 발 | bal |
| toe | 발가락 | balgarak |

# Vocabulary

## A

| | | |
|---|---|---|
| abdomen | 복부 | bokbu |
| accept | 받아 주다 | bada juda |
| accessible | 이용 가능한 | iyong ganeunghan |
| accident | 사고 | sago |
| acne | 여드름 | yeodeureum |
| action | 행동 | haengdong |
| activity | 활동 | hwaldong |
| actor | 남자 배우 | namja bae-u |
| actress | 여자 배우 | yeoja bae-u |
| acupuncture | 침 | chim |
| admission | 입장료/관람료 | ipjangnyo/gwallamnyo |
| adult | 성인 | seong-in |
| advanced | 상급 | sanggeup |
| affordable | (가격이) 알맞은 | (gagyeogi) almajeun |
| after-sales service | 에이에스 | eieseu |
| air-conditioner | 에어컨 | e-eokeon |
| aircraft | 항공기 | hanggong-gi |
| airplane | 비행기 | bihaeng-gi |
| airport bus | 공항버스 | gonghangbeoseu |
| airport limousine | 공항 리무진 | gonghang rimujin |
| airport railroad | 공항철도 | gonghangcheoldo |
| airsickness | 비행기 멀미 | bihaenggi meolmi |
| aisle | 통로 | tongno |
| aisle side | 통로 쪽 | tong-ro jjok |
| alarm | 알람 | allam |
| album | 앨범 | aelbeom |
| alcohol | 술 | sul |
| alone | 혼자 | honja |
| amenities | 편의시설 | pyeonuisiseol |

| | | |
|---|---|---|
| ancient palace | 고궁 | gogung |
| angry | 화난 | hwanan |
| ankle | 발목 | balmok |
| announcement | 안내 방송 | annae bangsong |
| another | 또 하나 | tto hana |
| antibiotic cream | 항생 연고 | hangsaeng yeon-go |
| antique | 골동품 | goldongpum |
| antiseptic | 소독약 | sodongnyak |
| apologize | 사과하다 | sagwahada |
| apology | 사과 | sagwa |
| apple | 사과 | sagwa |
| apply | 적용(신청)하다 | jeogyong(sincheong)hada |
| appointment | 예약/약속 | yeyak/yaksok |
| arm | 팔 | pal |
| arrive | 도착하다 | dochakada |
| arrow | 화살표 | hwasalpyo |
| art | 예술/미술 | yesul/misul |
| ashamed | 부끄러운 | bukkeureoun |
| aspirin | 아스피린 | aseupirin |
| associated card | 제휴카드 | jehyukadeu |
| at most | 최대한 | choedaehan |
| athlete | 운동선수 | undongseonsu |
| atmosphere | 분위기 | bunwigi |
| autograph | 사인 | sain |
| available | 이용할 수 있는 | iyonghal su inneun |

## B

| | | |
|---|---|---|
| baby | 아기 | agi |
| back (body) | 등 | deung |
| back (location) | 뒤 | dwi |
| back tooth | 어금니 | eogeumni |
| baggage | 짐/수하물 | jim/suhamul |
| baggage claim area | 수하물 찾는 곳 | suhamul channeun got |

| | | |
|---|---|---|
| baggage claim tag | 수화물표 | suhwamulpyo |
| baggage/luggage | 수화물 | suhwamul |
| balcony | 발코니 | balkoni |
| ball | 공 | gong |
| ballet company | 발레단 | balledan |
| ball-point pen | 볼펜 | bolpen |
| banana | 바나나 | banana |
| bandage | 붕대 | bungdae |
| band-aids | 반창고 | banchanggo |
| baseball | 야구 | yagu |
| basketball | 농구 | nonggu |
| bathroom | 욕실/화장실 | yoksil/hwajangsil |
| beautiful | 예쁜 | yeppeun |
| beef | 쇠고기 | soegogi |
| beer | 맥주 | maekju |
| begin | 시작하다 | sijakada |
| beginner | 초급 | chogeup |
| behavior | 행동 | haengdong |
| believe | 믿다 | mitda |
| belongings | 소지품 | sojipum |
| best | 제일 좋은 | jeil jo-eun |
| best way | 가장 좋은 방법 | gajang jo-eun bangbeop |
| beverage | 음료수 | eumnyosu |
| big | 큰 | keun |
| bill | 계산서 | gyesanseo |
| birth control pill | 피임약 | piimnyak |
| birthday | 생일 | saeng-il |
| black | 까만(검정)색 | kkaman(geomjeong) saek |
| black tea | 홍차 | hongcha |
| blanket | 담요 | damnyo |
| blister | 물집 | muljip |
| blood | 피 | pi |
| blue | 파란색 | paransaek |

| blurry | 침침하다 | chimchimhada |
| blushing | 얼굴이 빨개진 | eolguri ppalgaejin |
| board | 탑승하다 | tapseunghada |
| book/reserve | 예약하다 | yeyakada |
| bookstore | 서점 | seojeom |
| borrow | 빌리다 | billida |
| bother | 귀찮게 하다 | gwichanke hada |
| bottle | 병 | byeong |
| bracelet | 팔찌 | paljji |
| breakfast | 아침 식사 | achim siksa |
| breathe | 숨쉬다 | sumswida |
| bring | 갖다 주다 | gatda juda |
| broadcasting station | 방송국 | bangsongguk |
| broken | 고장난 | gojangnan |
| brown | 갈색 | galsaek |
| brush | 붓 | but |
| bug | 벌레 | beolle |
| burn | 데이다 | deida |
| burp | 트림 | teurim |
| bus stop | 버스 정류장 | beoseu jeongnyujang |
| bus ticket | 차표/버스표 | chapyo/beoseupyo |
| business | 사업 | sa-eop |
| buy | 사다 | sada |

## C

| calendar | 달력 | dallyeok |
| call | 전화 걸다 | jeonhwa geolda |
| cancel | 취소하다 | chwisohada |
| candy | 사탕 | satang |
| capacity | 용량 | yongnyang |
| car | 차 | cha |
| car wash | 세차 | secha |
| carelessness | 부주의 | bujuui |

| | | |
|---|---|---|
| carry-on | 기내 수화물 | ginae suhwamul |
| cash | 현금 | hyeon-geum |
| casual | 평상시의 | pyeongsangsiui |
| cavity | 충치 | chungchi |
| cell phone | 휴대폰 | hyudaepon |
| certification | 증명서 | jeungmyeongseo |
| change | 바꾸다 | bakkuda |
| change | 잔돈/거스름돈 | jandon/geoseureumdon |
| charge | 충전하다 | chungjeonhada |
| cheap | 싼 | ssan |
| check | 점검하다 | jeomgeomhada |
| check-in | 수속하다 | susokada |
| cheek | 볼 | bol |
| cheer | 응원하다 | eungwonhada |
| chest | 가슴 | gaseum |
| chicken | 닭고기/치킨 | dakkogi/chikin |
| children | 어린이 | eorini |
| chill | 오한 | ohan |
| chilly | 추운 | chuun |
| choose | 선택하다 | seontaekada |
| chopstick | 젓가락 | jeotgarak |
| cigarette | 담배 | dambae |
| city | 도시/시내 | dosi/sinae |
| cleaner | 세정액 | sejeong-aek |
| clock | 시계 | sigye |
| close | 가까운 | gakkaun |
| close | 닫다 | datda |
| clothes | 옷 | ot |
| cold | 차가운/시원한 | chagaun/siwonhan |
| cold medicine | 감기약 | gamgiyak |
| cold/flu | 감기 | gamgi |
| color | 색깔 | saekkal |
| comfortable | 편한 | pyeonhan |

| comics | 만화 | manhwa |
| commemorative | 기념하는 | ginyeomhaneun |
| commission | 수수료 | susuryo |
| compact car | 소형차 | sohyeongcha |
| compartment | 짐칸 | jimkan |
| composer | 작곡가 | jakgokga |
| concern | 염려 | yeomnyeo |
| concert | 연주회/공연 | yeonjuhoe/gong-yeon |
| condition | 상태 | sangtae |
| conductor | 지휘자 | jihwija |
| confirm | 확인하다 | hwaginhada |
| connection | 연결 | yeongyeol |
| constipation | 변비 | byeonbi |
| contact | 연락하다 | yeollakada |
| contents | 내용물 | naeyongmul |
| control device | 제어 장치 | je-eo jangchi |
| convenience store | 편의점 | pyeonuijeom |
| cook | 요리하다 | yorihada |
| corner | 모퉁이 | motung-i |
| cosmetic | 화장품 | hwajangpum |
| cost | 비용이 들다 | biyong-i deulda |
| cough | 기침 | gichim |
| co-worker | 동료 | dongnyo |
| crab | 게 | ge |
| craft | 공예 | gong-ye |
| credit card | 신용카드 | sinyongkadeu |
| cross | 건너다 | geonneoda |
| culture | 문화 | munhwa |
| cultured pearls | 양식 진주 | yangsik jinju |
| cupping treatment | 부항 | buhang |
| currency | 통화 | tonghwa |
| current condition | 현재 상태 | hyeonjae sangtae |
| currently/now | 지금 | jigeum |

| customer parking | 고객용 주차장 | gogaegyong juchajang |
| customs | 세관 | segwan |
| customs declaration form | 세관 신고서 | segwan singoseo |
| cut | 깎다/베이다 | kkakda/beida |

## D

| daily necessity | 생필품 | saengpilpum |
| dairy products | 유제품 | yujepum |
| dance | 춤 | chum |
| dash into | 부딪히다 | budichida |
| date | 날짜 | naljja |
| day trip | 당일 여행 | dang-il yeohaeng |
| decide | 결심하다 | gyeolsimhada |
| declare | 신고하다 | sin-gohada |
| defective | 결함이 있는 | gyeolhami inneun |
| dentures | 틀니 | teulli |
| depart | 출발하다 | chulbalhada |
| department store | 백화점 | baekwajeom |
| departure | 출국 | chulguk |
| deposit | 보증금/예약금 | bojeunggeum/yeyakgeum |
| detour | 우회로 | uhoero |
| diaper | 기저귀 | gijeogwi |
| diarrhea | 설사 | seolsa |
| dictionary | 사전 | sajeon |
| different | 다른 | dareun |
| digestive medicine | 소화제 | sohwaje |
| dining car | 식당차 | sikdangcha |
| dinner | 저녁 식사 | jeonyeok siksa |
| direction | 방향 | banghyang |
| director | 감독 | gamdok |
| disappoint | 실망시키다 | silmangsikida |
| discount | 할인 | harin |

| discount coupon | 할인 쿠폰 | harin kupon |
| display | 전시하다 | jeonsihada |
| disposable contact lenses | 일회용 렌즈 | ilhwoeyong renjeu |
| dizzy | 어지러운 | eojireoun |
| document | 서류 | seoryu |
| downtown | 시내 | sinae |
| draw | 그리다 | geurida |
| dress | 원피스 | wonpiseu |
| dress shirt | 와이셔츠 | waisyeocheu |
| dress shoes | 정장 구두 | jeongjang gudu |
| dried | 마른 | mareun |
| drink | 마시다 | masida |
| drink | 음료수 | eumnyosu |
| drive | 운전하다 | unjeonhada |
| driver's license | 운전면허증 | unjeonmyeonheojeung |
| driving experience | 운전 경력 | unjeon gyeongnyeok |
| drowsy | 졸리다 | jollida |
| dry | 건조한 | geonjohan |
| duty | 의무/관세 | uimu/gwanse |
| duty-free | 면세품 | myeonsepum |
| duty-free store | 면세점 | myeonsejeom |

## E

| earring | 귀걸이 | gwigeori |
| easily | 쉽게 | swipge |
| economy car | 일반 승용차 | ilban seungyongcha |
| education | 교육 | gyoyuk |
| egg | 계란 | gyeran |
| electronic | 전자 | jeonja |
| embassy | 대사관 | daesagwan |
| emergency | 비상 | bisang |
| emergency exit | 비상구 | bisanggu |

| empty | 빈 | bin |
| English | 영어 | yeong-eo |
| enjoy | 즐기다 | jeulgida |
| entrance fee | 입장료 | ipjangnyo |
| entrance ramp | 고속도로 진입로 | gosokdoro jinimno |
| envelope | 봉투 | bongtu |
| envy | 부러워하다 | bureowohada |
| equipment | 장비 | jangbi |
| eraser | 지우개 | jiugae |
| estimate | 견적 | gyeonjeok |
| everything | 모두 | modu |
| excellent | 훌륭한 | hullyunghan |
| exchange | 교환/교환하다 | gyohwan/gyohwanhada |
| exchange rate | 환율 | hwanyul |
| exercise | 운동/운동하다 | undong/undonghada |
| exhibition | 전시회 | jeonsihoe |
| expense | 비용 | biyong |
| expiration | 만료 | mallyo |
| explain | 설명하다 | seolmyeonghada |
| export | 수출품 | suchulpum |
| express bus | 고속버스 | gosokbeoseu |
| expressway rest service area | 휴게소 | hyugeso |
| extra | 추가 | chuga |
| eye | 눈 | nun |
| eye patch | 안대 | andae |
| eyebrow | 눈썹 | nunsseop |
| eyesight test | 시력검사 | siryeokgeomsa |

# F

| family | 가족 | gajok |
| famous | 유명한 | yumyeonghan |
| fantasy | 환상/공상 | hwansang/gongsang |

| far | 멀리 | meolli |
| fare | 요금 | yogeum |
| fart | 방귀 | banggwi |
| fast | 빨리 | ppalli |
| fasten | 매다 | maeda |
| fat | 지방 | jibang |
| fault | 과실 | gwasil |
| favor | 부탁 | butak |
| favorite | 좋아하는 | joahaneun |
| feel | 느끼다 | neukkida |
| feeling low | 기운없다 | giuneopda |
| fever | 열 | yeol |
| fever reducer | 해열제 | haeyeolje |
| fill out | 작성(기재)하다 | jakseong(gijae)hada |
| fill up | 가득 채우다 | gadeuk chaeuda |
| film/movie | 영화 | yeonghwa |
| find | 찾다 | chatda |
| finger | 손가락 | son-garak |
| first | 처음/첫 | cheo-eum/cheot |
| first aid | 응급 치료 | eunggeup chiryo |
| first train(bus) | 첫차 | cheotcha |
| fish | 생선 | saengseon |
| fit | 맞다 | matda |
| fitness center(gym) | 헬스장 | helseujang |
| fitting room | 탈의실 | taruisil |
| flat shoes | 단화 | danhwa |
| flat tire | 공기 빠진 타이어 | gonggi ppajin taieo |
| flight | 비행기 | bihaenggi |
| floor | 바닥 | badak |
| flower shop | 꽃집 | kkotjib |
| fly | 날다 | nalda |
| fog | 안개 | an-gae |
| follow | 따라가다 | ttaragada |

| food court | 식당가 | sikdangga |
| football | 축구 | chukgu |
| for a moment | 잠깐 | jamkkan |
| forehead | 이마 | ima |
| foreign | 외국의 | oegukui |
| foreigner | 외국인 | oegugin |
| form | 양식/서식 | yangsik/seosik |
| forward | 앞으로 | apeuro |
| fragile | 깨지기 쉬운 | kkaejigi swiun |
| freckles removing | 주근깨 제거 | jugeunkkae jegeo |
| free | 무료 | muryo |
| free parking | 무료 주차 | muryo jucha |
| free time | 자유 시간 | jayu sigan |
| french fries | 감자튀김 | gamjatwigim |
| fresh | 신선하다 | sinseonhada |
| friend | 친구 | chin-gu |
| front | 앞 | ap |
| fruit | 과일 | gwail |
| fun | 재미있는 | jaemiinneun |
| furniture | 가구 | gagu |

## G

| gallery | 화랑 | hwarang |
| game | 경기 | gyeonggi |
| gargle | 양치 | yangchi |
| garnet | 석류석 | seongnyuseok |
| gas pump | 주유기 | juyugi |
| gate/door | 문 | mun |
| general anesthetics | 전신 마취 | jeonsin machwi |
| generation | 세대 | sedae |
| genre | 장르 | jangneu |
| get by | 지나가다 | jinagada |

| get off | 내리다 | naerida |
| getting sunburn | 햇빛에 타다 | haetbite tada |
| gift | 선물 | seonmul |
| girl | 소녀 | sonyeo |
| giveaway | 사은품 | sa-eunpum |
| glad | 기쁜 | gippeun |
| glass craft | 유리공예 | yurigong-ye |
| glasses frame | 안경테 | angyeongte |
| gloves | 장갑 | janggab |
| go straight | 직진하다 | jikjinhada |
| goggles | 고글 | gogeul |
| gold | 금 | geum |
| good | 좋은 | jo-eun |
| gorgeous | 아주 멋진 | aju meotjin |
| green tea | 녹차 | nokcha |
| group discount | 단체 할인 | danche harin |
| guards | 보호대 | bohodae |
| guidebook | 관광(여행)<br>안내서 | gwan-gwang(yeohaeng)<br>annaeseo |
| gums | 잇몸 | inmom |

## H

| hand | 손 | son |
| hard liquor | 양주 | yangju |
| hat | 모자 | moja |
| have | 가지다/있다 | gajida/itda |
| have a runny nose | 콧물이 나다 | konmuri nada |
| head | 머리 | meori |
| headache | 두통 | dutong |
| heavily | 심하게 | simhage |
| heavy | 무거운 | mugeoun |
| heel | 굽 | gub |
| height | 키 | ki |

| English | Korean | Romanization |
|---|---|---|
| help | 돕다 | dopda |
| herbal medicine | 보약/한약 | boyak/hanyak |
| here | 여기에 | yeogie |
| high | 높은 | nopeun |
| highest | 최상급 | choesanggeup |
| hold | 잡다/들다 | japda/deulda |
| home appliances | 가전제품 | gajeonjepum |
| honey | 꿀 | kkul |
| horror | 공포 | gongpo |
| hospital | 병원 | byeongwon |
| hot | 뜨거운 | tteugeoun |
| hour(time) | 시간 | sigan |
| hurry | 서두르다 | seodureuda |
| hurt | 다친/아프다 | dachin/apeuda |
| husband | 남편 | nampyeon |

## I

| English | Korean | Romanization |
|---|---|---|
| immediately | 즉시 | jeuksi |
| immigration | 출입국 | churipguk |
| immigration cards | 입국 카드 | ipguk kadeu |
| in advance | 사전에/선불로 | sajeone/seonbullo |
| include | 포함하다 | pohamhada |
| inclusive | 포함된 | pohamdoen |
| indigestion | 소화불량 | sohwabullyang |
| indoor | 실내 | sillae |
| inexpensive | 싼 | ssan |
| information desk | 안내소 | annaeso |
| insole | 깔창 | kkalchang |
| installation | 설치 | seolchi |
| instruction | 설명 | seolmyeong |
| insurance | 보험 | boheom |
| insurance company | 보험 회사 | boheom hoesa |

| insurance policy | 보험 | boheom |
| insurance premium | 보험료 | boheomnyo |
| interesting | 흥미(재미)있는 | heungmi(jaemi)inneun |
| intermediate | 중급 | junggeup |
| international | 국제적인 | gukjejeogin |
| international driving license | 국제 면허증 | gukje myeonheojeung |
| interpretation | 통역 | tongyeok |
| interpreter/ translator | 통역사 | tongyeoksa |
| intersection | 교차로 | gyocharo |
| itchy | 가려운 | garyeoun |
| item | 물품 | mulpum |
| itinerary | 여행 일정 | yeohaeng iljeong |

## J

| jade | 옥/비취 | ok/bichwi |
| jaw | 턱 | teok |
| jeans | 청바지 | cheongbaji |
| jeweler | 보석가게 | boseokgage |

## K

| key ring | 열쇠고리 | yeolsoegori |
| kick | 차다 | chada |
| kind | 친절한 | chinjeolhan |
| kindness | 친절 | chinjeol |
| Korean | 한국어 | han-gugeo |

## L

| lane | 도로/길 | doro/gil |
| large bill | 고액 지폐 | goaek jipye |
| last train(bus) | 막차 | makcha |
| late | 늦은/늦게 | neujeun/neutge |

| later | 나중에 | najung-e |
| latest | 최근의 | choegeunui |
| lavatory | 화장실 | hwajangsil |
| leading actor/<br>actress | 주연 배우 | juyeon bae-u |
| leak | 새다 | saeda |
| leather | 가죽 | gajuk |
| leave | 남기다/떠나다/<br>출발하다 | namgida/tteonada/<br>chulbalhada |
| leg | 다리 | dari |
| lend | 빌려주다 | billyeojuda |
| lesson | 수업/강습 | sueop/gangseup |
| level/floor | 층 | cheung |
| license | 면허증 | myeonheojeung |
| life jacket | 구명조끼 | gumyeongjokki |
| lift | 승강기 | seungganggi |
| like | 좋아하다 | joahada |
| line | 줄/노선 | jul/noseon |
| liner | 여객선 | yeogaekseon |
| list | 목록 | mongnok |
| living goods | 생활 용품 | saenghwal yongpum |
| local product store | 토산품 가게 | tosanpum gage |
| location | 장소 | jangso |
| locker | 물품 보관함 | mulpum bogwanham |
| long | 길다 | gilda |
| look around | 둘러 보다 | dulleo boda |
| look for | 찾다 | chatda |
| loose | 헐렁한 | heolleonghan |
| lost and found | 분실물 보관소 | bunsilmul bogwanso |
| lounge | 휴게실 | hyugesil |
| low | 낮은 | najeun |
| lower back | 허리 | heori |
| luggage | 짐 | jim |

| | | |
|---|---|---|
| lunch | 점심 식사 | jeomsim siksa |
| lunch box | 도시락 | dosirak |
| luxury car | 고급 승용차 | gogeup seungyongcha |

## M

| | | |
|---|---|---|
| magazine | 잡지 | japji |
| main street | 중심가 | jungsimga |
| make | 만들다 | mandeulda |
| man | 남자 | namja |
| market | 시장 | sijang |
| match | 어울리다 | eoullida |
| meal | 식사 | siksa |
| meaning | 의미 | uimi |
| meat | 고기/육류 | gogi/yungnyu |
| medical history | 병력 | byeongnyeok |
| medication | 약 | yak |
| member | 회원/구성원 | hoewon/guseongwon |
| men's wear | 신사복 | sinsabok |
| metal | 금속 | geumsok |
| metal craft | 금속공예 | geumsokgong-ye |
| mild | 순한 | sunhan |
| milk | 우유 | uyu |
| mine | 나의 것 | naui geot |
| minors | 미성년자 | miseongnyeonja |
| mirror | 거울 | geoul |
| miss | 놓치다 | nochida |
| mistake | 실수 | silsu |
| moisture | 수분 | subun |
| moment | 잠깐/잠시 | jamkkan/jamsi |
| money | 돈 | don |
| money exchange | 환전 | hwanjeon |
| museum | 박물관 | bangmulgwan |

| museum of art | 미술관 | misulgwan |
| music | 음악 | eumak |

## N

| narrow | 좁다 | jopda |
| nauseated | 메스껍다 | meseukkeopda |
| nearby | 근처(에) | geuncheo(e) |
| nearest | 가장 가까운 | gajang gakkaun |
| necklace | 목걸이 | mokgeori |
| need | 필요하다 | piryohada |
| new | 새/새로운 | sae/saeroun |
| news | 소식 | sosik |
| newspaper | 신문 | sinmun |
| newsstand | 신문 가판대 | sinmun gapandae |
| next stop | 다음 정류장 | da-eum jeongnyujang |
| no-parking area | 주차 금지 구역 | jucha geumji guyeok |
| normal | 보통의 | botong-ui |
| nosebleed | 코피 | kopi |
| notebook | 공책 | gongchaek |
| nothing to declare | 신고할 게 없다 | singohal ge eopda |
| novel | 소설 | soseol |
| now | 지금 | jigeum |
| nowadays | 요즘 | yojeum |
| nursery | 놀이방 | noribang |
| nutrition | 영양 | yeongyang |

## O

| offend | 기분 상하게 하다 | gibun sanghage hada |
| off-season | 비수기 | bisugi |
| oil painting | 유화 | yuhwa |
| oily | 기름기 많은 | gireumgi maneun |
| ointment | 연고 | yeon-go |
| on foot | 걸어서 | georeoseo |

| | | |
|---|---|---|
| on the way | 도중 | dojung |
| one way ticket | 편도 승차권 | pyeondo seungchagwon |
| open | 열다 | yeolda |
| operate | 조작하다 | jojakada |
| operation | 수술 | susul |
| orchestra | 교향악단/<br>관현악단 | gyohyang-akdan/<br>gwanhyeonakdan |
| order | 지시(주문)하다 | jisi(jumun)hada |
| organic | 유기농 | yuginong |
| Oriental painting | 동양화 | dongyanghwa |
| overbooked | 예약초과 | yeyakchogwa |
| overheat | 과열 | gwayeol |

## P

| | | |
|---|---|---|
| pain | 고통 | gotong |
| painkiller | 진통제 | jintongje |
| pants | 바지 | baji |
| parcel | 소포 | sopo |
| parcel service | 택배 | taekbae |
| park | 공원 | gong-won |
| parking fee | 주차 요금 | jucha yogeum |
| parking lot | 주차장 | juchajang |
| parking space | 주차할 공간 | juchahal gonggan |
| passport | 여권 | yeogwon |
| pay | 내다/지불하다 | naeda/jibulhada |
| peach | 복숭아 | boksunga |
| peak season | 성수기 | seongsugi |
| peanut | 땅콩 | ttangkong |
| pearl | 진주 | jinju |
| pencil | 연필 | yeonpil |
| people | 사람들 | saramdeul |
| performance | 공연 | gong-yeon |
| perfume | 향수 | hyangsu |

| personal belongings | 소지품 | sojipum |
| personal check | 개인 수표 | gaein supyo |
| pharmacy | 약국 | yakkuk |
| phone | 전화 | jeonhwa |
| photo/picture | 사진 | sajin |
| photo studio | 사진관 | sajin-gwan |
| photogenic | 사진이 잘 받는 | sajini jal banneun |
| pill/tablet | 알약 | alyak |
| place | 곳/장소 | got/jangso |
| platform | 승강장 | seunggangjang |
| plating | 도금 | dogeum |
| platinum | 백금 | baekgeum |
| player | 선수 | seonsu |
| police station | 경찰서 | gyeongchalseo |
| political | 정치적인 | jeongchijeogin |
| pool | 수영장 | suyeongjang |
| pop music | 팝송 | papsong |
| popular | 인기 있는 | in-gi inneun |
| pork | 돼지고기 | dwaejigogi |
| possible | 가능한 | ganeunghan |
| postcards | 우편엽서 | upyeonyeopseo |
| prawn | 새우 | saeu |
| prepaid | 선불된 | seonbuldoen |
| prepare | 준비하다 | junbihada |
| prescription | 처방전 | cheobangjeon |
| present | 선물 | seonmul |
| preview/trailer | 예고편 | yegopyeon |
| price | 값/가격 | gap/gagyeok |
| print/engraving | 판화 | panhwa |
| problem | 문제 | munje |
| product | 상품/제품 | sangpum/jepum |
| prohibited | 금지된 | geumjidoen |

| prohibited articles/items | 반입금지품 | banipgeumjipum |
| pronounce | 발음하다 | bareumhada |
| pull | 끌다/당기다 | kkeulda/danggida |
| pull over | 한쪽으로 차를 대다 | hanjjogeuro chareul daeda |
| purchase | 구입/구매 | guip/gumae |
| pure gold | 순금 | sungeum |
| purpose | 목적 | mokjeok |
| pus | 고름 | goreum |
| put | 놓다/넣다 | nota/neota |

## Q

| question | 질문 | jilmun |
| quick | 빠른 | ppareun |
| quiet | 조용히 | joyonghi |

## R

| rain | 비 | bi |
| rating | 등급 | deunggeup |
| rattle | 덜컹 거리다 | deolkeong georida |
| read | 읽다 | ikda |
| reading light | 독서등 | dokseodeung |
| rear | 뒤 | dwi |
| receipt | 영수증 | yeongsujeung |
| recently | 최근에 | choegeune |
| recharge | 충전 | chungjeon |
| rechargeable | 재충전되는 | jaechungjeondoeneun |
| recommend | 추천하다 | chucheonhada |
| recover | 회복하다 | hoebokada |
| red | 빨간/빨강색 | ppalgan/ppalgangsaek |
| refund | 환불/환불하다 | hwanbul/hwanbulhada |
| refund charge | 환불 수수료 | hwanbul susuryo |

| | | |
|---|---|---|
| register | 등록(신고)하다 | deungnok(sin-go)hada |
| rehap | 재활 | jaehwal |
| relatives | 친척 | chincheok |
| release | 발매(출시)하다 | balmae(chulsi)hada |
| religion | 종교 | jonggyo |
| religious | 종교의 | jonggyoui |
| remit | 송금하다 | songgeumhada |
| remote | 원격의 | wongyeogui |
| renew | 연장하다 | yeonjanghada |
| rent | 빌리다/대여하다 | billida/daeyeohada |
| rental | 사용료/임대료 | sayongnyo/imdaeryo |
| repair | 고치다 | gochida |
| repair cost | 수리비 | suribi |
| replace | 교체하다 | gyochehada |
| report | 신고하다 | singohada |
| reserve | 예약하다 | yeyakada |
| rest | 휴식 | hyusik |
| retro | 복고 | bokgo |
| return | 돌아가다/돌려주다 | doragada/dollyeojuda |
| rice | 밥 | bap |
| rich | 풍부하다 | pungbuhada |
| ride | 타다 | tada |
| ring | 반지 | banji |
| rough map | 약도 | yakdo |
| round-trip ticket | 왕복 승차권 | wangbok seungchagwon |
| rule | 규칙 | gyuchik |
| ruler | 자 | ja |

## S

| | | |
|---|---|---|
| sale | 판매 | panmae |
| salty | 짠 | jjan |
| sanitary bag | 위생 봉투 | wisaeng bongtu |

| | | |
|---|---|---|
| saving | 적립/저축 | eongnip/jeochuk |
| scar | 흉터 | hyungteo |
| scarf | 스카프/목도리 | seukapeu/mokdori |
| scary | 무서운 | museoun |
| scene | 현장 | hyeonjang |
| school | 학교 | hakgyo |
| science fiction | 공상과학 | gongsanggwahak |
| scissors | 가위 | gawi |
| scratch | 자국 | jaguk |
| sculpture | 조각/조소 | jogak/joso |
| seafood | 해물 | haemul |
| seat | 자리/좌석 | jari/jwaseok |
| seat belt | 안전벨트 | anjeonbelteu |
| sell | 팔다 | palda |
| send | 보내다 | bonaeda |
| separate | 따로 떨어진 | ttaro tteoleojin |
| several | 몇몇의 | myeonmyeochui |
| shape | 모양 | moyang |
| shelter | 보호소 | bohoso |
| shoes | 신발 | sinbal |
| short | 짧다 | jjalda |
| shorts | 반바지 | banbaji |
| shoulder | 어깨 | eokkae |
| show | 보여주다 | boyeojuda |
| shower room | 샤워실 | syawosil |
| sick | 아프다 | apeuda |
| side dish | 반찬 | banchan |
| side effect | 부작용 | bujagyong |
| sightseeing | 관광 | gwan-gwang |
| sign | 표지판 | pyojipan |
| silver | 은 | eun |
| singer | 가수 | gasu |
| single | 단 하나의 | dan hanaui |

| | | |
|---|---|---|
| skin | 피부 | pibu |
| skin care | 피부 미용 | pibu miyong |
| skirt | 치마 | chima |
| sleep | 잠 자다 | jam jada |
| slide | 미끄럼틀 | mikkeureomteul |
| slope | 경사지 | gyeongsaji |
| slow | 느린 | neurin |
| slowly | 천천히 | cheoncheoni |
| small | 작은 | jageun |
| small bills | 소액 지폐 | soaek jipye |
| smoking | 흡연 | heubyeon |
| snack | 간식/안주 | gansik/anju |
| sneakers | 운동화 | undonghwa |
| sneeze | 재채기 | jaechaegi |
| snow | 눈 | nun |
| social | 사회적인 | sahoejeogin |
| socks | 양말 | yangmal |
| soda | 탄산음료 | tansaneumnyo |
| soft drinks | 음료수 | eumnyosu |
| sold out | 다 팔린/매진된 | da palin/maejindoen |
| some | 조금 | jogeum |
| sorry | 미안한 | mianhan |
| souvenir | 기념품 | ginyeompum |
| specific | 구체적인 | guchejeogin |
| speeding | 과속 | gwasok |
| spicy | 매콤한 | maekomhan |
| spoon | 숟가락 | sutgarak |
| sputum | 가래 | garae |
| squid | 오징어 | ojing-eo |
| stadium | 경기장 | gyeonggijang |
| stained | 얼룩이 묻은 | eollugi mudeun |
| stairs | 계단 | gyedan |
| stall | 엔진 정지 | enjin jeongji |

| | | |
|---|---|---|
| start | 시작(출발)하다 | sijak(chulbal)hada |
| station/stop | 정류장 | jeongnyujang |
| stationery | 문방구 | munbanggu |
| stay | 머무르다 | meomureuda |
| stitch | 실밥 | silbab |
| stomach | 배/위 | bae/wi |
| stomachache | 복통 | boktong |
| strap | 줄 | jul |
| strawberry | 딸기 | ttalgi |
| street | 거리/도로 | geori/doro |
| stretch | 늘이다 | neurida |
| strong | 강한/독한 | ganghan/dokan |
| student | 학생 | haksaeng |
| study | 공부 | gongbu |
| stuff | 물건 | mulgeon |
| sty | 눈다래끼 | nundaraekki |
| subtitle | 자막 | jamak |
| subway map | 지하철 노선도 | jihacheol noseondo |
| subway station | 지하철역 | jihacheolyeok |
| suddenly | 갑자기 | gapjagi |
| sugar | 설탕 | seoltang |
| suit | 정장 | jeongjang |
| sunscreen | 선크림 | seonkeurim |
| supermarket | 마트 | mateu |
| supplement | 추가물 | chugamul |
| surfing | 파도타기 | padotagi |
| surprise | 놀라게 하다 | nollage hada |
| sweet | 달다 | dalda |
| swimming cap | 수영모 | suyeongmo |
| swimsuit | 수영복 | suyeongbok |
| syrup | 시럽 | sireop |

# T

| tag | 꼬리표 | kkoripyo |
|---|---|---|
| take | 받다 | batda |
| tall | 키가 큰 | kiga keun |
| tangerine | 귤 | gyul |
| taxi stand | 택시 타는 곳 | taeksi taneun got |
| teach | 가르치다 | gareuchida |
| telephone | 전화 | jeonhwa |
| temple | 절/사원 | jeol/sawon |
| test | 시험/검사 | siheom/geomsa |
| textile crafts | 섬유공예 | seomyugong-ye |
| theater | 극장 | geukjang |
| there | 거기에 | geogie |
| think | 생각하다 | saenggakada |
| throw up | 토하다 | tohada |
| ticket | 표 | pyo |
| ticket booth | 매표소 | maepyoso |
| ticket machine | 표 판매기 | pyo panmaegi |
| ticket plan | 요금표 | yogeumpyo |
| time | 시간 | sigan |
| tire pressure | 타이어 공기압 | taieo gonggiap |
| tissue | 휴지 | hyuji |
| title | 제목 | jemok |
| toast | 건배 | geonbae |
| tofu | 두부 | dubu |
| together | 함께 | hamkke |
| toll-free call | 수신자부담 전화 | susinjabudam jeonhwa |
| toner | 스킨 | seukin |
| tongue | 혀 | hyeo |
| tonsil | 편도선 | pyeondoseon |
| tooth | 이/치아 | i/chia |
| toothache | 치통 | chitong |
| touching | 감동적인 | gamdongjeogin |

| | | |
|---|---|---|
| tourist bus | 관광 버스 | gwan-gwang beoseu |
| tourist information center | 여행(관광) 안내소 | yeohaeng(gwan-gwang) annaeso |
| tourist map | 관광지도 | gwan-gwangjido |
| towaway zone | 견인지역 | gyeoninjiyeok |
| towel | 수건 | sugeon |
| tradition | 전통 | jeontong |
| traditional | 전통적인 | jeontongjeogin |
| traffic signal | 교통신호 | gyotongsinho |
| train | 기차 | gicha |
| train ticket | 기차표 | gichapyo |
| transfer | 환승/갈아타다 | hwanseung/garatada |
| transit pass | 통행증 | tonghaengjeung |
| translator | 통역사 | tongyeoksa |
| transportation card | 교통카드 | gyotongkadeu |
| travel | 여행/여행하다 | yeohaeng/yeohaenghada |
| traveler's check | 여행자 수표 | yeohaengja supyo |
| treadmill | 런닝머신 | reonningmeosin |
| treatment | 치료 | chiryo |
| trouble | 문제/곤란 | munje/gollan |
| turning left | 좌회전 | jwahoejeon |
| turning right | 우회전 | uhoejeon |

## U

| | | |
|---|---|---|
| uncomfortable | 불편한 | bulpyeonhan |
| underpants | 팬티 | paenti |
| understand | 이해하다 | ihaehada |
| underwear | 속옷 | sogot |
| upper intermediate | 중상급 | jungsanggeup |
| upright | 똑바로 | ttokbaro |
| urgent | 긴급한 | gingeupan |
| use | 쓰다/사용하다 | sseuda/sayonghada |

## V

| | | |
|---|---|---|
| vacation | 휴가 | hyuga |
| valet parking | 대리 주차 | daeri jucha |
| valuables | 귀중품 | gwijungpum |
| van | 승합차 | seunghapcha |
| vegetable | 채소 | chaeso |
| video | 동영상 | dong-yeongsang |
| view/sight | 시야 | siya |
| visit | 방문하다 | bangmunhada |
| visual design | 시각디자인 | sigakdijain |
| volleyball | 배구 | baegu |

## W

| | | |
|---|---|---|
| wait | 기다리다 | gidarida |
| wake | 깨우다 | kkaeuda |
| walk | 걷다 | geotda |
| wall | 벽 | byeok |
| want | 원하다 | wonhada |
| war | 전쟁 | jeonjaeng |
| warranty | 품질보증서 | pumjil bojeungseo |
| watch | 시계 | sigye |
| water | 물 | mul |
| water purifier | 정수기 | jeongsugi |
| water skiing | 수상스키 | susangseuki |
| watercolor | 수채화 | suchaehwa |
| wear | 입다 | ipda |
| wear a cast | 깁스하다 | gipseu hada |
| weather | 날씨 | nalssi |
| weight | 체중/몸무게 | chejung/mommuge |
| white | 하얀/흰색 | hayan/huinsaek |
| whole body | 전신 | jeonsin |
| wide | 넓다 | neoldda |
| wife | 아내 | anae |

| window | 창문 | changmun |
| window side | 창문 쪽 | changmun jjok |
| wireless | 무선의 | museonui |
| withdraw | 인출하다 | inchulhada |
| witness | 목격자 | mokgyeokja |
| woman | 여자 | yeoja |
| wood craft | 목공예 | mokgong-ye |
| word | 단어 | daneo |
| work | 일/일하다 | il/ilhada |
| wrap | 포장하다 | pojanghada |
| wrinkle | 주름 | jureum |
| wrist | 손목 | sonmok |
| writer | 작가 | jakga |
| wrong | 잘못된 | jalmotdoen |

## XYZ

| X-ray | 엑스레이 | exseurei |
| yellow | 노란/노랑색 | noran/norangsag |
| yet | 아직 | ajik |
| young | 젊은 | jeolmeun |
| youth hostel | 유스호스텔 | yuseuhoseutel |
| zip code | 우편번호 | upyeonbeonho |
| zoo | 동물원 | dongmurwon |

# Hangeul Writing Models

Perpendicular strokes are written from top to bottom; horizontals from left to right. (Read these charts left and down.)

| | | | | | | | | | | | | | | |
|---|---|---|---|---|---|---|---|---|---|---|---|---|---|---|
| **ㄱ**[g] | ㄱ | | **ㅌ**[t] | ㅡ ㄷ ㅌ | | **아**[a] | ㅇ 아 아 | | **애**[yae] | ㅇ 아 아 / 야 애 | | | | |
| **ㄴ**[n] | ㄴ | | **ㅍ**[p] | ㅡ ㅠ ㅠ / ㅍ | | **야**[ya] | ㅇ 아 야 / 야 | | **에**[e] | ㅇ 아 어 / 에 | | | | |
| **ㄷ**[d] | ㅡ ㄷ | | **ㅎ**[h] | ㅡ ㅎ ㅎ | | **어**[eo] | ㅇ 어 어 | | **예**[ye] | ㅇ 어 여 / 여 예 | | | | |
| **ㄹ**[r] | ㄱ ㄹ ㄹ | | **ㄲ**[kk] | ㄱ ㄲ | | **여**[yeo] | ㅇ 어 여 / 여 | | **외**[oe] | ㅇ 오 오 / 외 | | | | |
| **ㅁ**[m] | ㅣ ㅁ ㅁ | | **ㄸ**[tt] | ㄷ ㄸ / ㄸ | | **오**[o] | ㅇ 오 오 | | **위**[wi] | ㅇ 우 우 / 위 | | | | |
| **ㅂ**[b] | ㅣ ㅔ ㅂ / ㅂ | | **ㅃ**[pp] | ㅣ ㅔ ㅐ / ㅂ ㅃ ㅃ / ㅃ ㅃ | | **요**[yo] | ㅇ ㅇ ㅛ / 요 | | **의**[ui] | ㅇ 으 의 | | | | |
| **ㅅ**[s] | ノ ㅅ | | **ㅆ**[ss] | ノ ㅅ ㅆ / ㅆ | | **우**[u] | ㅇ 으 우 | | **와**[wa] | ㅇ 오 오 / 외 와 | | | | |
| **ㅇ**[ng] | ㅇ | | **ㅉ**[jj] | ㄱ ㅈ ㄲ / ㅉ | | **유**[yu] | ㅇ 으 우 / 유 | | **워**[wo] | ㅇ 으 우 / 우 워 | | | | |
| **ㅈ**[j] | ㄱ ㅈ | | | | | **으**[eu] | ㅇ 으 | | **왜**[wae] | ㅇ 오 오 / 외 와 왜 | | | | |
| **ㅊ**[ch] | ㅡ ㅊ ㅊ | | | | | **이**[i] | ㅇ 이 | | **웨**[we] | ㅇ 으 우 / 우 워 웨 | | | | |
| **ㅋ**[k] | ㄱ ㅋ | | | | | **애**[ae] | ㅇ 이 아 / 애 | | | | | | | |

# Syllable Writing Models

| Syllable | Model | Syllable | Model | Syllable | Model | Syllable | Model |
|---|---|---|---|---|---|---|---|
| 가 [ga] | ㄱ 가 | 고 [go] | ㄱ 고 | 극 [geuk] | ㄱ 그 / 극 | 값 [gap] | ㄱ 가 / 값 |
| 나 [na] | ㄴ 나 | 노 [no] | ㄴ 노 | 남 [nam] | ㄴ 나 / 남 | 넋 [neok] | ㄴ 너 / 넋 |
| 다 [da] | ㄷ 다 | 도 [do] | ㄷ 도 | 덮 [deop] | ㄷ 더 / 덮 | 닭 [dak] | ㄷ 다 / 닭 |
| 라 [ra] | ㄹ 라 | 로 [ro] | ㄹ 로 | 록 [rok] | ㄹ 로 / 록 | | |
| 마 [ma] | ㅁ 마 | 모 [mo] | ㅁ 모 | 몸 [mom] | ㅁ 모 / 몸 | 많 [man] | ㅁ 마 / 많 |
| 바 [ba] | ㅂ 바 | 보 [bo] | ㅂ 보 | 봄 [bom] | ㅂ 보 / 봄 | 밟 [bap] | ㅂ 바 / 밟 |
| 사 [sa] | ㅅ 사 | 소 [so] | ㅅ 소 | 실 [sil] | ㅅ 시 / 실 | 삶 [sam] | ㅅ 사 / 삶 |
| 아 [a] | ㅇ 아 | 오 [o] | ㅇ 오 | 앞 [ap] | ㅇ 아 / 앞 | 앓 [al] | ㅇ 아 / 앓 |
| 자 [ja] | ㅈ 자 | 조 [jo] | ㅈ 조 | 집 [jip] | ㅈ 지 / 집 | 젊 [jeom] | ㅈ 저 / 젊 |
| 차 [cha] | ㅊ 차 | 초 [cho] | ㅊ 초 | 춤 [chum] | ㅊ 추 / 춤 | | |
| 카 [ka] | ㅋ 카 | 코 [ko] | ㅋ 코 | 콩 [kong] | ㅋ 코 / 콩 | | |
| 타 [ta] | ㅌ 타 | 토 [to] | ㅌ 토 | 통 [tong] | ㅌ 토 / 통 | | |
| 파 [pa] | ㅍ 파 | 포 [po] | ㅍ 포 | 필 [pil] | ㅍ 피 / 필 | | |
| 하 [ha] | ㅎ 하 | 호 [ho] | ㅎ 호 | 홍 [hong] | ㅎ 호 / 홍 | 훑 [hul] | ㅎ 후 / 훑 |

\* Pronunciation is altered when two consonants appear together.